Deforestation
and
Socio-Economic Environment

About the Author

Dr. Jasleen Kewlani is working as Assistant Professor of Sociology at Rajiv Gandhi National University of Law, Patiala, Punjab. She is also holding the charge of Programme Incharge and Coordinator of IGNOU's School of Law's Programme Study Centre at RGNUL, Patiala. Dr. Kewlani has also been an executive member of the North-West Sociological Association. In the year 2003, the USA Human Rights Campaign awarded her scholarship for two years. She has also been honorary advisor to the Northern Frontiers of B.S.F. for national debate competitions.

In the working experience of more than seven years, Dr. Kewlani has been associated with the editing of journals and books. There is an edited (co-edited by Professor Dr. M.S. Gill) in her credit entitled, Environmental Conscience: Socio-Legal and Judicial Paradigm (2009). She has presented about thirty-five research papers in various national and international seminars, conferences and workshops. She has also authored about twenty-five research papers which have been published in reputed national as well as international reference journals and reference books too. Her areas of expertise are Environmental and Rural Sociology, Women Studies and Research Methodology.

Deforestation and Socio-Economic Environment

Jasleen Kewlani
Assistant Professor of Sociology
Rajiv Gandhi National University
of Law, Patiala

CONCEPT PUBLISHING COMPANY PVT LTD.,
NEW DELHI-110059

ISBN-13 : 978-81-8069-826-2

First Published 2012

Published and Printed by

Concept Since 1974

Concept Publishing Company Pvt. Ltd.
A/15-16, Commercial Block, Mohan Garden
New Delhi-110059 (India)
T: 25351460, 25351794, *F*: 091-11-25357109
E: publishing@conceptpub.com, W: www.conceptpub.com
Editorial Office: H-13, Bali Nagar, New Delhi-110 015, India.

Cataloging in Publication Data--*Courtesy:* D.K. Agencies (P) Ltd. <docinfo@dkagencies.com>

Kewlani, Jasleen.
Deforestation and socio-economic environment / Jasleen Kewlani.
p. cm.
Includes bibliographical references (p.) and index.
ISBN 9788180698262

1. Deforestation—India—Gurdaspur (District) 2. Deforestation—Social aspects—India—Gurdaspur (District) 3. Deforestation—Economic aspects—India—Gurdaspur (District) 4. Economic development—Environmental aspects—India--Gurdaspur (District) 5. Agriculture—Environmental aspects—India—Gurdaspur (District) 6. Gurdaspur (India : District).—Rural conditions. I. Title.

DDC 634.9560954552 23

Dedicated to
My Parents
and
Brother

Preface

The aims set for economic development and material progress have almost made the human race blind for ecological concern. The available natural resources are being used in the present times with no thought and apologies for the future. This clearly reflects a non-sustainable pattern of growth. Economic development is attained by modes of urbanization, industrialization deforestation, technological advancements and the like. The effects of these processes are not singular rather encapsulate the whole gambit of survival into their prey. The unhesitant cutting of the green cover has affected socio-cultural as well as economic rubrics of human life. While propagating the claims of 'group welfare and growth', the individual concerns are being conveniently compromised, thereby eroding the very base of an overall development. A forest is a magnificent natural wealth for the regions where it is available. Universally saying, the livelihood of the people of such regions gets almost dependent on their natural resource for multiple purposes. People consider forests as a potential source of fuel wood, fodder for animals, herbal medicines, income through commercial utilization, employment and many other advantages. Forests maintain the fertility of the soil thereby supporting the agricultural production of the region too. The temperature maintenance is another function attributed to forests which further is bliss for human health. It can be said that forests create a 'system' of survival in the regions falling in their geographical proximity. In such a scenario, 'deforestation' is not merely a threat, rather a 'disaster' in its own way. Deforestation disrupts the very basic groundings of human life which further derails the human existence of the affected region. This book is focused on a similar scenario found in the Kandi area of Punjab State. The communities and the villages of this area have experienced the transition from a thickly green phase to the phase of rampant deforestation.

While having a discourse on 'deforestation' in a specific region, few questions knock the track of the undertaken research. What are the reasons behind deforestation in the area? What are the impacts of deforestation on economic and the social life of the people of the area? What is the nature of the land-use pattern after the green cover has been eroded? What is the role being played by the communities in context of environmental management? What is the role of State and Non-Government Organization in Afforestation programmes and rehabilitation of the affected people? The book explores all such questions and provides a detailed explanation of the phenomenal alterations which have occurred in the region after deforestation. The book is a product of an empirical research work undertaken in five villages of Kandi area of Punjab falling under Dhar Block of Tehsil Pathankot, namely Gho, Kot Teeka Samanu (known as 'Samanu' in the present study), Tarhari Basa (known as 'Basa' in the present study), Uparla Thara and Dunera. Multiple aspects of the survival of the communities of these five villages have been researched and linkage between the environment and other chores of survival has been established. In all, the study reflects the adoption of a multi-dimensional approach for the study of community and village life in pertinence to deforestation.

The Organization of the Book

The book opens the discourse by emphasizing on the concept and types of Environmental Risk and then it makes a move to Ecological Perspectives reflecting the ecological mind frames of different times. Chapter one of the book elaborates the difference between 'Deep Ecological Perspective' and 'Shallow Ecological Perspective' also known as 'Reformist Ecological Perspective.' The discussion in these two perspectives revolves around the core context of the 'basic social paradigm'. In the times when environmental degradation remained in tolerant limits, Reformist Ecological Perspective could sustain the dais. But Deep Ecological Perspective took over the lead when the ecological hubris of man required to be redefined and the 'basic social paradigm' needed alterations with the ongoing environmental worsening. Theories propounded by Arne Naes, Eckersely, Carlos Castaneda, Orustein, Guha, Bil Devall have been referred to. 'Ecofeminism' follows the course of the flow of knowledge, whereby the perspectives fertilized by Boserup and Cranney Brende have been made into component of the discussion. Ecofeminism and its notions get empirically endorsed in the later part of chapter five under the sub-theme of 'Women and Environment.' The study finds an authentication through the 'System Theory' and its application. If System Theory is complied with, the developmental process can be a balanced one. To attain a sustained pattern of growth there is a need to incorporate the connotations of this theory into the developmental paradigm. The theories framed by the components of System Theory-Merchant, Kuhn, Einstein, Heisenberg and Capra strongly correspond to the empirical findings and facts elaborated in the book.

After exploring the theoretical perspectives on Ecology to the depth and establishing their research relevance the reader takes the theme of deforestation as a crucial concern of the time. To provide contextual and situational clarity chapter three inclusive of the profiles of the villages forward a broad base for understanding the environmental scenario of the region, which of course give the very first approximation about the study. The detailed analysis of social, economic, cultural, political and environmental profile of the villages anticipates the consequences of deforestation on the communities of the area. The profile of respondents has been incorporated under chapter four which elaborates the nature of the sample under various heads like sex, age, caste, occupation, income, marital status, family type, along with correlation drawn out of some of these factors.

Deforestation has affected multiple aspects of life of the communities of the region but the impacts are not alike in all the five villages under study. There are some astonishing facts which demarcate villages under study from each other, leaving a research gap for multiple future studies. Three villages namely Gho, Samanu and Basa have matching conditions with small differences in economic standings. On the other hand, the villages Dunera and Uparla Thara possess completely different scenarios respectively. Dunera been adopted by an International NGO and Uparla Thara being in the closest vicinity and frame of the developmental project named 'Ranjit Sagar Dam' hold distinct environmental and socio-economic status which further has largely influenced the dwelling communities to a large extent. These differences in the villages under study are a matter for the administration to ponder over. All villages have not been equally affected by defoıestation. The impacts are positive in some and adverse in other instances.

The situation in Uparla Thara has ameliorated after deforestation since the purpose behind cutting green cover was construction of the Ranjit Sagar Dam. This developmental project has raised the standard of living of the people of Uparla Thara in multiple ways, which has been explained in chapter five. The village Dunera has not experienced environmental degradation, which is totally attributed to the role being played by the NGOs functioning in the vicinity thereby encouraging community participation. In case of the villages Gho, Samanu and Basa, the conditions have worsened with deforestation. It has affected almost all angles of survival; and the same can be explored well through this book. Chapter Five titled "Deforestation and its Impacts" forms the broadest base of empirical analysis whereby multiple domains have been incorporated. The chapter is inclusive of discussions on impact of deforestation on availability of trees/plants, effects of the changing availability of flora; factors behind deforestation; effects of deforestation on extinction of species, availability of water, agricultural productivity, employment scenario and women life. This chapter finds a complete reflection of 'System Theory' on the community and village life in context of impacts of deforestation.

The book concludes the discussion in chapter six whereby the role of Panchayats, Mahila Mandals and NGOs functioning in the region has been analyzed. Multiple suggestions forwarded by the respondents constitute the core part of this chapter. People have greater realization of the need of community participation but for that they find themselves economically inadequate due to shortage of funds. This shifts the focus on a greater expectation from NGOs, governmental bodies and forest departments. This phenomenon is deeply featured with the need of a corporate effort, which implies joint hands of the ordinary masses with the administration and public oriented organizations. The book in all explores the issue of deforestation with multi-dimensional grip and a socio-cognitive approach. This will sensitize the people to understand the impacts of deforestation categorically, which may help to create a platform for further improvement in the area under study.

Dr. Jasleen Kewlani

Acknowledgements

I am highly indebted to the institution, Rajiv Gandhi National University of Law, Patiala, for giving me an apt atmosphere to carry on my research along with fulfilling the professional obligations.

I commend and revere to the guidance of my teacher Dr. M.S. Gill, Professor of Sociology at Guru Nanak Dev University and his better half Mrs. Ravinder Kaur for making this research work completed. Without the support and guidance of this couple, the task could not have achieved fruition.

I forward a sincere thanks with heart felt regards for Concept Publishing Company, Pvt. Ltd. New Delhi for having been invested a faith in my academic potential. I am equally thankful to my friends and students who have been a strong support for me while undertaking any such research oriented academic activity.

I owe very deep gratitude to Mrs. & Mr. A.B. Gupta from Pathankot who have rendered an intense support for making this project complete and have been with me as a support in all important tasks related to this research work right from the initiation of the work till its fruitful completion.

My younger brother, Brajesh Kewlani, an endless moral strength for me has always been an inspiration behind my achievements and success. 'Thanks' is a small word for his endless moral investment and faith in me. My pet Tyson though has no words to say, but I realize his prayers made for me with every success I achieve in life. I am heartily thankful to this wordless being who possesses extreme of humanism even not being a human with power to speak.

Lastly I refer back to rather beginning of my life, my parents who are in fact the periphery of my survival. Claiming to be the luckiest daughters of the universe, I thank them for being with me in each decision and supporting me by all means in all the efforts I make to develop myself as a human being student, academician, researcher and also as an author.

I dedicate this task of literary engineering to my father Mr. Surinder Kewlani and my mother Mrs. Satinder Kewlani.

Dr. Jasleen Kewlani
(Assistant Professor of Sociology)
Rajiv Gandhi National University of Law, Patiala

Contents

List of Tables

List of Figures

1 Introduction

In contemporary era of globalization, the cardinal aim of all the nations is to attain consistent growth and development. In traditional approach, 'Development' as a concept was interpreted in mere economic terms, but the dynamism entailed in the social structure and the global forces influencing the paradigm have resulted into changing conceptualization of development. 'Sustainability' has become a crucial criterion for development in present times. 'Sustainability' as an approach to development implies an encapsulation of all chores of survival. Sustainable development cannot be achieved until and unless a well regulated and an efficaciously preserved environment is facilitated, and ecological issues are rendered due significance. Human society cannot progress in a sustained pattern until and unless the natural environment is preserved. Environmental Degradation is the serious most hindrance in the way of attainment of the goal of 'Sustainability'. Mankind in the race of proceeding and developing on economic grounds has conveniently compromised the environmental onus; creating a non-sustained pattern of growth. When the concept of Environmental Degradation is being referred to, it transcends the natural geographical limits and becomes universalized in terms of effects and dimensions.

The present environmental threat is not national rather an international one, constituting a devastating Global Environmental Risk (Kasperson, 2003). This risk is a means and also an 'end' in itself. 'End' of the developmental projects for economic upliftment and a 'means' of further improvement. But the dimensions of this risk get even intensified in context of a small geographical area which is dependent upon the environment and its units for a satisfactory survival. Change is a part of dynamism of human life and ever developing world is bound to experience some changes in the environmental structures. The Environmental Change is of two types, (i) Systematic Environmental Change, (ii) Cumulative Environmental Change. In case of the systematic environmental change, change at any locale can affect the characteristics of the environment anywhere else, or even the global system itself (Turner *et al.*, 1994). On the other hand, the cumulative environmental change may well eclipse systematic changes in both long-term and the short-term consequences. This type of change refers to accumulation of regional and localized changes that further get distributed widely throughout the world after a while causing irreparable damages to the local zones of demography which are thickly populated but scarcely resourced. Environmental changes and their relative intensity pose distinctive challenges to the creation of an adequate knowledge base concerning both the environmental perturbations and the vulnerability of human and ecological system, to the establishment causal linkages in the structures of the risk. This environmental risk further shapes the societal responses and shakes the responsibility of the global state to respond effectively.

To have deep rooted study or analysis of the environmental issues, it is crucial to understand what *'ecology'* implies because ecology and environment are diaphanously entangled parts of any environmental study. Environment means physical, chemical, biological conditions surrounding the living organism, which influence them externally and internally. Ecology has been defined by Botanical scientists, zoologists and urban sociologists as scientific study of relationship between man and his environment. In 1866, human zoologists gave first definition of ecology as, "the body of knowledge concerning the economy of nature—the investigation of the total relations of the animal to its inorganic and organic environment" (Dhaliwal *et al.*, 1998). In 1859, St. Hilaire Isoclore Geoffory, a French zoologist, proposed a term 'ethnology' for "the study of the relations of organism within the family and society in the aggregate and in the community" (Saxena, 1999). Ecology has further got divided into branches. These branches are social ecology and human ecology, referring to social and human development respectively.

Similarly, a British Naturalist, St. George Jackson Mivart, used the term 'hexicology', which he defined in 1894 as "denoted to the study of relations between the organisms and their environment as regards the nature of the locality...". The term 'Ecology' was coined by combining two Greek words, viz., 'Oikos' (means 'house' or a 'dwelling place') and 'logos' (means 'the study of') to denote the relationship between organisms and their environment. Although, there is some controversy about the original coining of the term but there is consensus that German biologist, Erust Haeckel first gave substance to this term. He used this term first in 1886 but defined for the first time in 1870 as follows, "By ecology we mean the body of knowledge concerning the economy of nature—the investigation of the total relations with those animals and plants with which it comes directly and indirectly into contact". Today, ecology is a systematic and well-developed science. Study of ecology and an in-depth research over ecological issues is important because it is not only environment which influences the man rather man also influences the environment in subtle ways (Karkara, 2007). The two components of nature—organisms and their environment—are not only complex and dynamic but also interdependent. Ecology is relatively a new science, dealing with various principles, which govern such relationships between organisms and their environment (Saxena, 2006).

The increasing realization of the vitality of environment and its issues, has led to emergence of 'environmentalism', "which means ideologies and practices which inform and flow from a concern with environment" (Pepper, 1986, p. 13). In context of contemporary environment crisis, environmental science takes a prenatal position, since it deals with the application of knowledge gained with the help of ecology for managing environment, along with its various offshoots. Environment can be natural as well as man-made. Natural environment consists of air, water, soil, land, forests, wildlife, etc., and man-made environment which includes housing, technology, transportation, settlement, utilities, etc. There exists a link between these two forms of environment, which further forwards multiple consequences.

The environmental studies are very much related with Botany, Zoology, Chemistry, Pedology, Geography, Climatology, Oceanography, Geomorphology, Sociology, Political Science, Economics, Management, etc. Since environment and man are the primary concerns of environmental studies, all the subjects related with these aspects have a relationship. Environment is a 'Controller' of life and living styles of human beings (Saxena, 2006). Environmental studies are the need of the hour because with an in-depth understanding of environment; firstly various facets and problems of survival are interpreted in authentic terms; and secondly, a strategic planning can be made. To have complete analysis of environment and ecology there is a need to refer to various ecological perspectives, which have been given by prominent environmentalists, sociologists and geologists. These ecological perspectives forward sundry approaches which have been used till date for rendering ecological analysis or environmental studies.

Ecological Perspectives

While analyzing ecological issues, two perspectives came forward. Those are (1) "Reformist Ecological perspective" and (2) "Deep Ecological perspective". Reformist ecological perspective is also known by the name of "Shallow Ecological Perspective". The difference between these two perspectives, did not lie in the 'ends' but in the 'means' which were adopted to achieve those ends. Though target of both of these ecological perspectives is environmental protection, but the ideology and means to manage or reconcile environmental destruction are distinct. The reformist ecology targets to reform and control the worst which has gone with the environmental entities of nature, i.e., air, water, land, etc. It refers to several social movements, which were a product of man's quest to improve the degenerating environmental quality. Environment has always been considered an important part of one's life, hence, the goal of all such movements initiated by reformist ecologists, was to change society for 'better living'. Along with the motive of changing environment's scene, criteria for survival remained intact. According to Reformists, any alternate process must not attack the premise of the "dominant social paradigm", which expresses the mental image of social reality that guides expectation in society. This dominant social paradigm, according to reformist ecologists consists of basic values, culture and heritage of masses, which is deep rooted in their social survival entangled with their relative environmental circumstances and ecological surroundings. Hence, they believe that environment must improve but it should not be accompanied with any alteration in basic dominant socio-cultural paradigm of individuals (Merchant, 1996).

On the other hand, "Deep Ecological Perspective" forwards an altered mode of discussion, posing an absolutely contrary notion to that of the Reformist Ecological Perspective. The norms and tendencies of the Deep Ecology Movements are not derived calculatively from ecology or induction, rather from the knowledge and attributes gained by the researchers working in ecological domain. The contents and their understanding require an ability to construct a conserver society. When Reformist Ecology failed to protect environment and ecology from further deterioration, Deep Ecological Perspective began functionally crucial. Naes (1989) was the founder of this school of ecological thought who thinks that 'Environmental Crisis' is the 'Crises of Consciousnes'. Arne Naes has been an environmentalist who stressed on "Ecological Egalitarianism' as a reflexive component of Deep Ecological perspective. Ecological Egalitarianism implied that all individuals have equal rights to live and blossom in an intuitively clear and obvious value axiom. This assertion supported that Deep Ecology is forcefully normative in nature. It is ecophilosophical not mere ecological. In addition to this view, Naes talk of Principles of 'Diversity' and 'Symbiosis'. According to him 'diversity' enhances the potentialities of survival and the chores of new modes of life; and 'Symbiosis' tends to reduce the multiplicity of kinds of forms of life and create integration within the communities of the same species. This helps to maintain equilibrium which smoothens the survival of individuals. In fact Deep Ecology and its supporters support the fight against economic, cultural, military invasion and domination which leads to degradation of environmental quality.

His thought was strengthened by Eckersley (1995), who added dimension of social justice and human emancipation along with a change in the way of thinking about the natural world. These ideas were further strengthened by Carlos Castaneda. Carlos Castaneda (1971) says that it is a challenging task for modern man to acquire and develop understanding of Deep Ecology because it requires a major perceptual shift of man's nature. Further, Deep Ecology gained popularity in Native Americans during 1960-1970s. These Native Americans had 'separate realities' which were entangled to their lifestyle and closely linked with environment around them. In fact Castaneda aimed at understanding how did these tribes of Native Americans cope with the changes occurring due to technological innovations and advancements in their natural environment. According to him, the modern western man cannot understand these 'separate realities', which owe their origin to the basic norms of the tribes. In reaction to Castaneda's views about Deep Ecological Perspective, Robert Orustein (1996) forwarded his views that the Western trained and even those who are a 'seeker' are by their culture almost unprepared to understand the esoteric traditions constituting the separate realities. This counter response shows that Castaneda's work on Deep Ecology had been critically appraised due to his undermining of the modern man's perceptual ability to interpret the importance of environment.

Another imminent component of Deep Ecology is Rama Chandra Guha (1996) who stated that Deep Ecology shows man's arrogance and his ecological hubris, which puts environment at the top of apex of life choices. This perspective according to Guha depicts a transition from anthropocentric to a biocentric approach of man. Anthropocentric approach is a 'human centred approach and bio-centric approach interprets human as only one of the elements in the ecosystems but does not attribute indispensability to his existence. In simple terms, anthropocentric approach gives importance to human as an element of study but bio-centric approach gives cardinal emphasis to ecology and environment. According to Guha any form of intervention in nature and its paradigm should be guided primarily by the need to preserve biotic integrity rather than by the needs of humans: Guha upheld a statement that Deep Ecology encourages political militancy not negotiations and advances philosophical arguments not aesthetic notions. This statement in fact makes the comparison between reformist and Deep Ecological perspectives more ocular. In simple terms, Deep Ecological Perspective is fundamentally normative in nature, providing importance to ethics determining the attitude of individuals. According to Pojman (2000), if environment is to be protected, a deep rooted, normative as well as an attitudinal approach is to be adopted, which ought to be objective in nature.

A prominent sociologist named Bill Devall (1996) further elaborated the contents of Deep Ecological Perspective making its notions more ocular and accepted by the masses. According to him, usable instruments of Deep Ecological Perspectives are local autonomy, decentralization of power, steady scale economy and a radically changed social structure. The word 'radical' was specifically stressed by Devall. He provided alternate terminology for 'Deep Ecology'. He used some terms like 'Radical Sociology' and 'Revolutionary Ecology'. He upheld that Deep Ecology Perspective was a reaction to the successes and excesses of the implementation of the dominant social paradigm and its assumptions. This 'dominant social paradigm' reflects mental image of social reality that guides the expectation in a society. The Reformist Ecology did not intend to alter the dominant social Paradigm which was attacked by normative strategy of Deep Ecology later. The 'Dominant Social Paradigm' comprises of the social fabrics including kinship and family structure; naturalistic tendencies of a society; and modes of adapting to the recently occurring social changes. Deep Ecological Perspective aims at improving environmental quality and checking further degradation of environment by attacking the fundamental nature of this paradigm, because it needs a shift of normative aspect of human attitude. When environmental degradation has reached a drastic extent, an abrupt and a strong action is needed to manage it. Keeping this assertion in view, Deep Ecology becomes the most functional tool to formulate the required management strategy. In all, a stress is laid to understand those cultural, religious and social values that related man to his environment and made a social binding on the individual to protect the environment. The major emphasis will is on empowerment, social justice, class differentiation and struggle against resource depletion and environmental pollution. When Deep Ecology encompasses various aspects of various lives; it facilitates an open platform to explore the holistic approach, which strengthens the objectives of the present studies and the like.

Other than the above discussed ecological perspectives, another theory has been very prominent in environmental studies, i.e., "System Theory". Moving towards the importance of a holistic approach to analysis; 'System Theory' is of a great relevance for environmental studies. The conception of development has changed and the new concept of development as a process incorporates various fields of life together. Living organisms cover a wide range of phenomenon including individual organisms, social systems and ecosystems. Hence, Systems theory becomes vital. "System theory renders a common framework and language for biology, psychology, medicine, economics, ecology and many other sciences; a framework in which the so urgently needed ecological perspective is explicitly manifest" (Merchant, 1996). System theory assumes that all the aspects of life together formulate a system, which is to be regularized in order to attain an "all over development". This theory implies (i) shift from part to the whole, (ii) shift from structure to the process of maintenance, (iii) shift from objective to epistemic science; which aims at clearly defining the ecological concepts, (iv) shift from "building" to "network" as a metaphor of knowledge, and (v) shift from truth to approximate description, which reinforces human dominance as an 'observer' who identifies various objects of nature and describes them. An imminent supporter and contributor of the theory Heisenberg (1971), wrote a book titled *Physics and Philosophy* and his book titled *Der Teil Und Ganze* written in 1970, states that nature is also exposed to questions. Capra (1985) while taking an interview of Geoffrey Chew, reproduced Chew's views in one of his intellectual productions and explains Chew's idea that understanding of nature needs to be undertaken entirely through self-consistency, because environment as a subject cannot be reduced to any fundamental entities. There are no fundamental equations or fundamental symmetries in environmental understanding. Environment as a physical reality is seen as a dynamic web of interrelated events related to socio-cultural systems as well. Therefore, these interrelated events need a cognitive understanding for an absolute interpretation of the social world.

Thomas Kuhn (1970) also finds System Theory of great importance and states in his theory of Scientific Revolution that changes of Paradigms occur in discontinuous, revolutionary breaks, called 'paradigm shifts'. Keeping this alternation in view, it can be said that the modern world recognizes, paradigm shift in physics as an integral part of a much larger cultural transformation. Einstein Albert (1949) has also presumed a similar view to Kuhn that no fundamental theoretical foundation exists in physics and rich its understanding. Hence, an amalgamated approach is needed which is catered by System Theory. The motive of explaining "system theory" and its components is not to add one more theoretical perspective, but to reaffirm that all the aspects of life are interwoven and constitute a system in all. The developmental process being undertaken in developing and the underdeveloped nations is consciously or unconsciously evading the concept of sustainability. If System Theory is complied with; the developmental process can become a balanced one. If the target of Human Social Development is to be achieved, there is a need to incorporate the connotations of this theory into the developmental paradigm. It shall bring about the widely desired welfare of the human race.

In all, it cannot be denied that the Ecological Perspectives give completion to any environment related study. The applicability of these Thought Perspectives formulates a strong base for understanding the environmental orientations of the masses of various eras of human survival; further making it efficacious for the researcher to compare the situations of the present with that of the past.

Along with this, another purpose is to explore multiple factors which lead to alterations in the environmental conscience of the masses.

Deforestation and Environmental Degradation : A Review

Environmental Degradation is a global issue at present, because 'environment' is such a context which cannot be restricted to geographical boundaries. Amidst universalization of the issue of environmental degradation, its acute state in India cannot be ignored. India's environmental problems are gaining global significance because of the rapid and offensive speed of urbanization and lack of infrastructure. Increasing urbanization, industrialization, deforestation and transportations as the other cousins of economic development put tremendous pressure on natural resources and, therefore, there is a pressing need to strike a balance between developmental planning and urgency to safeguard the environment (Ghosh, 2007). As asserted by Speth (2004), through an environmental analysis, there are ten drivers of Environmental Deterioration. Those are: (1) population, (2) affluence, (3) technology, (4) poverty, (5) market failure, (6) policy and political failure, (7) the scale and rate of economic growth, (8) the nature of our economic system, (9) our culture and its values, and (10) the forces loosed upon the world by the globalization of the economy. All these forces lead to misuse and over-exploitation of the natural resources, which is a danger to preservation of the environment. These forces do not function in a similar way and intensity in all the regions, rather, each zone of environmental degradation is dominated by specific reasons behind it. One of the objectives of the present study is to explore the causes behind deforestation the Kandi region of Punjab.

The emphatic discourse of economic growth and industrialization dominant in the 1950s lost its vigour when it became obvious that large parts of the population would not profit under the existing development strategy (Linkenbech, 2007). With a priority given to industrialization the agricultural sector had been significantly neglected. Neither land reform, nor structural adjustments and technological investments in favour of the rural population had taken place (Parekh, 1995). Firstly by stressing more upon the industrialization; air pollution, water pollution and deforestation become prominent invitees and; secondly, when agrarian frontiers made available for catering to the industrial needs. All this directly result into rural life deterioration. Excess and an unbalanced bias for economic development through industrialization, development of science and technology; construction of dams for generating power for the industries; ever increasing population; expanding residential areas and cities; mushrooming of Special Economic Zone (SEZs) for regional and national economic growth, etc., have altogether posed remarkable threat to India's environment, further creating innumerable adversities for the indigenous masses and even the species surviving in the national boundaries.

A specific component of India's environment is that urbanization associated with growth of industries and trade contributes efficiently and magnificently in environmental pollution and toxication of groundwater and soil. Industrial chemicals released by iron and steel production units contribute to nearly 70 per cent of the effluent released; on the contrary 20 per cent of their chemicals are used for the industrial output. The unregulated disposal of pollution occurs through drains joining into rivers, streams and reservoirs. This is because the industrial estate lacks waste water treatment systems, leading to all over pollution of water and contamination of the drinking water also

(U.S.-A.E.P., 1996). In the race of being 'globalised' the basic paradigmatic management is being forgotten, on which a large part of Indian survival relies.

'Globalization' as a concept refers to the compression of the world and the intensification of the consciousness of the world as a whole (Robertson, 1992; Reddy, 2008). When consciousness of the world gets intensified, it gives bounce to the quest for development; which encapsulates multiple angles of survival including that of the environment also. The process of Development under globalization implies hyper-consumption of energy and natural resources, leading to environmental degradation. This kind of imbalanced development further results into emergence of many social inequalities and issues. In such an adverse situation, it is only ten per cent of the world's population which is consuming the bulk of non-replenishable natural resources for satiating the avarice of the developed world at the cost of ninety per cent of the world population. This reflects a threatening phenomenon in which the present generation of the world is not only damaging nature and its environment against the interests of contemporary relatively less developed populations but also against the interests of their own future generation (Agarwal, 2007). 'How can the interests of both the generations be protected', needs a deep thought.

Environment can be managed if all the entities of environment are managed simultaneously, which refers to a planned and systematic approach for protection of land, air, water, forests, etc. All the environmental entities hold a vital position, but forests are the most productive and protective part of environment and ecology. Change in forest cover and its structure certainly effects air, water and other allied elements that is why forests are considered an important concern of environmental protection. Forests act as 'carbon sink', which absorbs a large quantity of carbon and produces oxygen for the sake of humanity.

The forest resources are valuable as an integral part of the ecosystem, from the commercial point of view, and as providers of shelter to wildlife. Today, forests provide raw materials for over 5,000 products with about 23 million dollars. They support industry which employs 1.3 million people. In such a context, deforestation is a devastating 'man-made disaster' against his own peaceful and healthy existence (Saxena, 2006). If deforestation occurs, it makes the air easily prone to pollution leading to disastrous effects on mankind (Aggarwal, 2002). 'Flood control is another function performed by forest.Loss incurred due to deforestation is simple irreparable. Forests influence climate by controlling the wind speed and its direction. They effect soil composition and its structure. Considering such a vitality of forests, the study aims at discussing deforestation as the most aggravating and contemporary problem of the present times.

Asserting the chemical potential of forests, it is upheld that all the processes like precipitation, evaporation, accelerated erosion of soil, etc., are effected by deforestation because forests directly or indirectly control them (Negi, 1994). The importance of forests doubles in context of communities living around and dependent upon them. Poor, rural and tribal societies are those dependent communities, which depend upon forests for fuel wood, fodder and even for earning their livelihood. They are deprived of this blessing with deforestation as fuel scarcity in certain areas has become intensively acute. It perhaps becomes a hindrance for a smooth survival in case the masses are deprived of the forests. This scarcity further has serious economic repercussions too. How far has the economic condition of the residents of Kandi area been affected due to deforestation; is also incorporated in the following chapters.

In the past, all the tribes and communities earning livelihood from natural resources had in fact developed a tradition of resource use that kept a balance between human needs and environmental imperatives, but unfortunately this tradition has been eroded now; specially through intervention in form of alien intrusions, aimed at satisfying over-consumption in the rich countries of environmental worth (Sheth, 1997). It is not only forests, but other natural resources also that have been depleted in the process of intrusion and intervention. The constructive dependence of the past has changed its form to destructive dependence of present but still the dependence cannot be denied. This shift of human concern directly threatens the forests; and indirectly cautions other aspects of survivalhood of the forthcoming dangers.

Development and women's life have always been into an ocular relationship. Development leads to innumerable consequences on the survival of women, and the women's working pattern further influence development. Boserup in 1970 produced a work titled,

"Women's role in economic development", and held that women are an imminent part of gendered division of labour, participating in economic development. This book was considered as a catalyst for the growth of a body of literature on Women's role in development. In addition to Boserup's theory, Brenda Cranney (2001) stressed upon one aspect of social reproduction, which is sexual or social division of labour in home and in farm work. Sexual division of labour refers to a division created by cultural and social norms and not by biological difference. On the other hand, Cranney Brenda aimed at analyzing women's contribution to production and social reproduction, which is necessary to determine what labour women perform for the family and how and why specific tasks are allocated. Both in primitive and in more developed communities, traditional division of labour in both farms and families, is usually considered natural, being sexually determined.

An encapsulation of research findings shows that all societies develop a sexual division of labour that varies across countries, cultures and history, thereby implying that there is nothing natural or biological in such division (Beneria and Roldan 1987; Kelkar and Nathan 1991; Rogers 1981; Jayapalan, 2002; Rubin 1975).

The persons of a specific community may feel that in other communities, there exist different ways of determining division of labour (dividing the work burden among sexes), which even they state as 'natural' basis of division of labour (Boserup, 1970). Anyhow, women's work does not happen in a vacuum. It is influenced by capitalistic development, which in turn influences the dynamics of family life. Linking all these thoughts and facts with the main theme of the research, it is evident that environmental degradation affects females, their livelihood and their household chores up to a large extent. Specifically feminist context, deforestation affects the availability of the forest products like fuelwood, food, etc. and also the time required to collect these products. This very phenomenon increases the workload for women and decreases household nutrition (Venkateshwaran, 1995).

The study carried out by Brenda, in mountain region of Himachal Pradesh proves that deforestation doubles the women's workload. The women of this area identify water and the forests as two single most important factors in their daily work and life that consumes most of their time. They still consider water supply as a secondary issue to forests as in falls, winters and early springs, their water needs are met but the forests affect every aspect of their life everyday. Women collect two types of wood; for fodder and for fuel consumption. Fodder consists of branches of specific trees that produce leaves suitable for animals to eat. Fodder is usually collected twice a day as the leaves need to be fresh for the cows to eat. The branches are once thrown in the cowsheds and after the leaves are eaten, the twigs are used for fuel wood in *chullah* (Cranney Brenda, 2001).

A study conducted by Cranney Brenda states that women go and collect these products from forests and when deforestation occurs women's burden of work gets intensified in terms of time and energy. A common complaint of women of Himachal Pradesh has been that they had to travel from 1 to 10 kilometres to collect wood. The weight of the load varies from 10 to 40 kilos which is inappropriate connotation with each woman's stamina and potential. Eventually if not immediately, the incident has alarming effects on women's general health latently. Not only health, but also education, which is the strongest wheel of future development of women, also suffers. Girl child is withdrawn from her school and is imposed upon to share the household burden of the mothers because after deforestation they spend about 8-10 hours a day on walking to the forests and coming back after collection of the forest products required for household maintenance.

Another content to be considered in context of women's relation with development and her importance in growth paradigm is 'Ecofeminism'. Contributions have been made by 'Liberal', 'Socialist' and 'Radical' Ecofeminists. Liberal ecofeminists aim at redistributive policy changes and do not at all recommend a full-fledged restructuring of the whole setups. On the other hand, socialist feminists want equal representation of women in government and non-governmental organisation (Berman, 1993). Another ecofeminist perspective is 'Radical Ecofeminism' which asserts that women have a spiritual and biological link to the non-human world and of course are closer to nature posing a 'divinity factor', as compared to other gender.

Analysing the intellectual push given by the Ecofeminist Perspective, it becomes a crucial obligation to interpret its influence on the present environmental scenario. Many studies linked to the environment have shown that women and environment are observed in a complementing scenario to each other. For this reason, this perspective has always found a significant space in environmental discussions. The present study also aims at exploring the distinct relationship between women and environment and explaining the impacts of deforestation on the life on women of Kandi area.

According to a study made in Wayanad district of Kerala, Kerala High Court has directed the Collector of the district to prevent extraction of timber from plantations in the region (Vyas, 2001). Not only this, villagers of Kerala also consider 'forest job' as a status symbol while fixing up a marriage; Elder's major point of satisfaction is a forest job of either of the spouses. In addition to it, forests are the source of employment to the rural people; provide skilled, semi-skilled and unskilled labour in forest based industries. Small scale forest based industry provides principle employment to rural labour force by accommodating 20-30 per cent of rural unemployed persons, in many developing nations. Hence, it can be well identified and realized that the life of dependent tribals and villagers is ruined in all ways, if excess deforestation continues. Another aim of the research emerges here. It is to assess the effects of deforestation, on professional aspect of the people of the concerned region and to understand the consequences of deforestation on employment generation in the region.

The concomitant relation between economic development and environment cannot be ruled out. In modern era, environmental decline and economic contractions cannot be delinked, specially in case of those societies which have developed deep roots in their soil, which provides life protecting medicine and diction, demons and totems to construct a religion of their own (Chauhan, 1998; Iyer, 1996; Aggarwal, 2002; Vaidyanathan, 2006; Liverman, 2003, Shiva 1991; Smith, 1997; Singh, 2003; Punalikar, 2000; Brown *et al.*, 2002). No effort pertinent to economic development can be sustained eternal enough under the current system of massive destruction and wanton exploitation of scarce natural resources, including both renewable and non-renewable ones. Many activities oriented to economic growth have been a manifest cause of deforestation and even latent one at some instances.

The process of development can be fruitful only if all the available natural and human resources are wisely and thriftily used, rigorously concerned, rapidly regenerated, thoroughly renovated, wherever possibly without upsetting the currently prevailing ecological balance within a geographical region. The reason is that general approach adopted for development is not featured with a balance maintaining content (Gupta, 2007). Developmental paradigm has produced disenchanting results, which were earlier unforeseen due to unidimensional strategy. Due to this consequence, the third world nations have begun regarding development as enemy number one of mankind and have looked upon 'non-development' as the only way out. But, the developing nation cannot do away with the process of development despite talking of treading the path of non-development as these countries have to catch the developed nations and states. Development in many instances becomes deterrent to the environmental frontiers and its preservation (Mohanty, 1998).

Development forwards a Marxian trend by increasing the gap between the poor and the rich people and communities which further becomes a source of aggravation of the issues. Hass (1990) and Hjorth (1994) forwarded a distinct notion emphasizing on another realm of though for the fraternity thinking on tracks of environmental upgradation. According to them, there prevails a lack of co-operation between the lesser and more developed regions of the world. The reason of this lack of cooperation is the feasibility to adhere to a suitable defense mechanism in case of any losses occurs due to degradation of the environment. Rich people can afford artificial means of comfortable survival; whereas the poor cannot afford those. This view given by Hass and Hjorth is applicable to small as well as to the large geographical entities.

The notion further got strengthened when Pezzoli (1998) illustrated that although in Mexico both rich and the poor segments are exposed to ambient air and water pollution equally; but the richer can afford air-conditioning, bottled water, rural retreats, good nutrition and health care, but the poor people suffer the most. The notion further got encapsulated in the study conducted by Ezcurra (1999). The situation referred to by these two environmentalists, pose a threat to sustainability and many other human concerns too, since economic development is enhancing the capacity to compromise the environmental frontiers.

It emerges as an academic obligation to refer to 'Sustainable Development' in detail. The term 'Sustainable Development' was coined at the Cocoyoc Declaration on Environment and Development in 1970. It is such a form of development, which was advocated for, in many events like Stockholm Declaration (1972); Brundland Commission Report (1987) and recently in the Copenhagen Accord (2009) and too many more. Sustainability is a crucial criterion for development as the future cannot be scarified to make the present contended. It is that development which meets the needs of the present generation, without compromising the ability of future generations to meet their own needs. To bring about a sustained society, the developmental process needs to be economically viable and environment friendly (Vyas, 1996). Evanescent or short term benefits often turn to failures in long term. To attain eternal advantages, exploitation of resources, direction for investments, orientation of technological development and institutional changes must be consistent with the requirements of the present and future both. A symbiotic relationship between consumer human race and producer natural system needs to be recognized, which implies a compatibility between economy and ecology. This compatibility is missing in case of the developmental planning undertaken by Indian governance (Khanna, 2000). In the regions, where deforestation is being undertaken rampantly, the further use of the land by the government for developmental purpose also becomes another chore of thought.

In this lieu, construction of dams and industrial development foot a large part in process of deforestation and other forms of environmental degradation. Major objectives of construction of dams include providing a boost to irrigation, control of floods and replenishing the depleting groundwater or aquifers. Other than these objectives; a latent objective of dams is to produce a sufficient bulk of electricity, to regulate and feed the industrial requirements for an efficient production. The aim of developing or developed societies is to rise per unit productivity, which is considered to be a great indicator of economic development. In this process of targeting economic upliftment, the environment suffers, (Aggarwal, 1996).

Construction of dams is directly or indirectly a cause of deforestation as development of industry (an aim of construction of dams), further aggravates the problem of deforestation. Commercial exploitation has come out to be the most unfortunate setback to the forests, leading to their mass destruction and causing irreparable damages to the mankind. Deforestation is done to establish industry and also transportation to access these economic establishments, which further reinforces a decline in the green cover of the nation. Forests are used and destroyed to achieve all these economic motives. The work being conducted in sub-mountainous region of Pathankot Tehsil, aims at analyzing that how far developmental process contributes to deforestation and what are the other causes, which intensified this environmental crisis?

Incessant industrialization leads to pollution and resource depletion which leads to multiplier adversities in environmental context. This is not only that the nature places limits on societal development, societal development too affects the nature. Rather, the effects of societal development on nature rebound on human societies again as advocated by Martell (1994). Understanding the relationship between the nature and the communities residing in an environment-dependent area forwards crucial dimensions of analysis. This relationship is of course not a matter of stability, rather a subject to dynamism and change. The present study also intends to explore the factors behind such a change.

In case of India in general, it has been able to achieve substantial progress since the year of independence but the benefits incurred from this progress are not in a positive connotation with ecology, as many of these benefits have consequently led to environmental degradation. For example, India achieved food security by means of input intensive agriculture but the adversities emerging out of this strategy address to certain effects like degraded soil, lowering of water tables, poor water management, and many other alarming impact, with the use of pesticides and fertilizers (Lee, 1985; Vanclav, 1933). What effects has agricultural development and expansion had on green cover and its structure of the area and also the *vice versa,* will also be one of the objectives of this research. Not only agriculturists, but timber companies and other developers also deface the forest land of the nation. Timber merchants and other industrialists draw material and energy from environment, which leads to a severe deficit of natural resources (Bhattacharya, 2000; Rathore, 1996). This decline in the quantity and the quality of the natural resources further intensifies the crises related to soil erosion; declining soil fertility; availability of water for drinking and other purposes; availability of herbal medicines, etc. The present study also incorporates all such issues.

New inventions and discoveries, the development of science and technology, along with modernization have all been considered the causes of environmental decline. Technological development in form of establishing new industries; harm the forest land by attacking the earlier land-use pattern. Modern society has blessed humans with many developed and enhanced dimensions. But according to great historians like Toynbee, Daisuka and Ikede, the contemporary culture and civilization produce various evils also. War and environmental pollution are two major threats to humanity. On the other hand, geological structure gets devastated along with severe climatic changes.

It is rightly said that scientific and technological development taking place in the world leads to noticeable environmental damages (Sinha, 1977; Singh, 1992). Additional destruction of forests has accompanied the search for petroleum resources in the region and an influx of impoverished refugees from Central America and migrants from other parts of Mexico seeking farmland. These issues sound largely similar to Indian context whereby deforestation, climatic changes have forwarded largely resembling problems. This form of degradation of environment has immense climatic consequences, which may lead to change in cropping pattern and agricultural productivity. Crops as compared to forests, reflects more sunlight; this increases the cooling of the land. In such a context, it becomes crucial to analyze the differences between the temperatures in predominantly forested area and in connected croplands and understand how it affects the agricultural productivity of the region. Reduction in the forest cover, followed by the climatic changes, affects the cropping pattern to a large extent. In some regions the cropping pattern get drastically altered, further mushrooming multiple troubles for the agrarian communities. Further, the scarcity of water for irrigation purpose makes the situation even worst. A similar change has occurred in the Kandi region too; which has also been encompassed in the contexts referred further. Lack of water in the region makes the conditions even more serious.

Factors like agricultural land-cover modification, ecosystem degradation, technological change, invasive species, etc., constitute some of the non-climatic factors which further have a large influence on the climatic variables, specially reflected through solar radiations and evaporation. These alterations further affect the rainfall pattern further creating a vicious circle of adversities encompassing decline in the soil fertility of the region, decreased agricultural production, finally leading to immense degradation of the economic standards of the villages and the communities (Parry, 2007). Cutting of forests has affected the temperature, thereby bringing about evident changes in the climate of the region. Simultaneously, the climatic changes further influence the vegetation/cropping pattern and the fauna as well. Is such a vicious circle of factors existing on the bases of a negative mutuality of reflectivity, also being experienced in the area under the study? The consequences have been empirically endorsed with the help of the discourses undertaken in the study.

In context of adverse effects of environmental degradation, many other impacts have been enumerated by various researchers. Forests claim protection for themselves and for the sake of mankind. Where deforestation has led to declining availability of natural resources, the loss of biodiversity cannot be ruled out (Gupta, 2000). Deforestation has resulted in extinction of 15-20 per cent of species. According to data estimated, about 0.2 to 0.3 per cent of all species in forests are lost every year and there is a loss of one species everyday. This extinction of various species of plants and animal species will increase drastically if deforestation is not checked (Salgare and Iyer, 1993). The variety of species are an imminent source of knowledge and entertainment for human race and also a source of revenue for the nation, hence, the implication of extinction of species needs to be explored well in the environmental studies.

United Nations Environmental Project (UNEP) undertook a project, which elaborated a fact that the global warming is a highly contravened issue and is the most stimulating cause of Asian Haze. UNEP blamed developing Asian nations for the brown haze being formed on Indian Ocean and is stated to be alarming for the global atmospheres. According to its report, the first brown haze was an effect of Indonesia forest fires of 1999. According to the results delivered by this project, forest fires, bio-mass burning and other pollutants in Asia are threatening the earth's environment. (Singh, 2000; Kellynich, 1995; Peter, 1999; Kayastha, 1992). It makes it clear that development stands in a combat with the environment in the present times.

Many changes have occurred in Indian society, which further lead to reformulation of innumerable social structures. In the continuous process of alternations, development and its conception have taken a turn. A sociologist-cum-environmentalist 'Tolba' gave a definition of Development in 1978 and said that development (1) presupposes new direction for growth, (ii) should have implications for all the countries, i.e., rich as well as poor, and (iii) it must incorporate environment dimensions also. But paradoxically, with increasing development the issue of environmental degradation has further aggravated (Aggrawal and Dubey, 2002). In India also, earlier the economic analysis used to be purely economic in nature and environmental assessment was never a part of this evaluation scheme. Perhaps, it could be termed as "International Fallacy". But accounting for the available natural resources, incorporating environmental criteria has become crucial (Kulshreshtra, 2000; Singh 2000; Ghazala, 2001). In recent years noticeable deforestation has occurred in sub-mountainous zone of Punjab. The reasons have been euphemistically quoted by the government. The government states that economic growth is a credential for human growth and development, which virtually leads to excessive deforestation to establish more and more industries and to construct more dams to cater to the power needs of the industries. This phenomenon forwards an assertion that economic development and approaches rendered to it, lead to degradation of environmental domain in context of both, its quality as well as its quantity. Environmental frontiers need a protection and maintenance priority in the course of the economic development so that the communities are not jeopardized. This statement orients itself to the aim of sustainability'.

To bring about sustainability (which implies using a natural resource for the sake of present generation along with protecting the ability of future generations to use the same resource, for their own motive of development) participation of common people NGOs and Civic forums, etc., is an important tool (Rao, 2001; Hazra, 2001; Hanningam, 1997; Rajagopalan, 2005). At this stage of discussion Joint Forest Management (JFM) holds an imminent place. Joint management of forests is a management through united efforts of government and public and it can well maintain and protect the environmental units (Moosvi Ali, 2000). Any judicious analysis being made in context of environmental issues cannot ignore the importance of participation of common masses in the improvement paradigm. Human beings themselves become the causation factor of environmental degradation leading to their own victimization in forthcoming times. Solutions emerge and even succeed at mass level only. Sustainable development is possible if common people develop a sense of environmental democracy under an objective rule of conduct posing a neutral concern for economy as well as for environment too.

This discussion reflects the people's interest and faith in the civil society perhaps. Two villages in Gadchiroli district of Maharashtra, namely, Menda Lekha and Marda, have become the first in the country to win community rights over forests under the *Scheduled Tribes and other Forest Dwellers (Recognition of Forest Rights) Act, 2006* (Pallavi, 2009). In the same discourse forwarded on community ownership over forests, Devaji Tofa, the community leader of village 'Mendha Lekha' says, "the Gram Sabha has been managing the village, forests resources till now but, this is through tacit arrangement with the forests department. For this reason, we have not been able to take long term decisions" (Pallavi, 2009). According to Devaji Tofa, the village after getting ownership over the forests in its vicinity will be able to take decisions on water harvesting structures like check dams in the forests, managing collection of minor forest produce like bamboo, and plan sustainable income generation forest-based projects. Giving the rights to the community over the natural resources available in the region where the community dwells does not only provide a notional reflection to the 'ecological democracy'; rather also inspires the community develop a stronger sense of belongingness and responsibility for those resources. These feelings make communities efficient to utilize the available natural resources in a nature and in an accountable manner; accountable for the present as well as for the future generations, paving a contributive way for a sustainable future. The governance needs to focus upon the natural surroundings, which is perhaps the most authentic ecological rationale for good governance.

People must generate an attitude which undertakes just one notion that nature has blessed us with potential resources which are 'ours'; and are to be 'regulated by us' and even 'protected for the coming generations' (Aggarwal, 2002). People must be given more powers if they are expected to operationalize any mass movement for environmental protection (Kothari, 2000). The study will certainly aim at exploring whether the rhetoric of people's, participation is being implemented in environmental management in the research area or not. If in case, people show an inhibition in this context, it is important to analyze the causes which have obscured the common people to participate in Joint Forest Management (JFM).

The Bio-Diversity bill was introduced in Lok Sabha in May 2000 under scrutiny of Parliamentary Committee on Science and Technology and stressed upon participation of local communities in environmental management. This bill was not accepted due to political opposition (Down to Earth, 2000). Non-acceptance of this bill is a great shock for the environment related scenario. People need to be invested in, in terms of funds as well as rights if they are to be made strong instruments for environmental management. Such legislation act as a means for this purpose. Along with such a legislation, there is a need to generate more funds to make the instruments of environment management available (Bhargava, 2004). 'Have the common masses witnessed any improvement in funds generation to the local bodies or not', reflects one of the objectives of the study. Not only economic efficiency of community can help manage issues related to the environment, rather the factor of awareness and the inculcation of the participation instinct are other allied concepts. The same has been explored through the study with a detailed reference to the role being played by the local governing bodies, NGOs, and the Media in environmental management.

A complex matrix exists, which leads to many sorts of problems. This complex matrix comprises of economy, environment, culture, science and technology and other allied aspects of human existence. Human activities in form of deforestation, construction of dams, industrialization, etc., have led to causation of adverse effects on the environment, which further poses many pernicious issues acting as a hindrance to a sustainable development. If the area under forests keeps on decreasing, it would lead to a situation of socio-economic panic on earth. Hence, environmental degeneration needs to be scientifically assessed, evaluated and analyzed.

In India environmental problems have attracted the attention of a wide cross-section of people especially during the past decade. People are becoming increasingly conscious of a variety of problems like global warming, acid rain, floods, scarcity of food, fodder and firewood, pollution of air, water, etc. (Shastri, 2007). No doubt India is very fortunate from the point of view of availability of natural resources; but it must be considered along with that these resources are finite. Hence, our natural resource wealth must not be wasted and it should be consumed with great care and consumed as far as possible. There is a need to select or construct methods to use and conserve the available natural resources for the purpose of which research is the strongest possible instrument for success.

Objectives

The purpose of study intends to achieve the following objectives :

1. To understand, what are the factors that have led to deforestation in a particular area;
2. To understand the extent of deforestation and its impacts on economy and social life of people involved;
3. To understand the nature of the land-use patterns, in the region, where forest cover has been eroded;
4. To understand the role played by the communities of the area in environmental management;
5. To understand the role of state and non-governmental organizations (NGOs) in Afforestation programmes and the rehabilitation of the affected people.

The present research has been undertaken to capture the following concerns:

1. To understand linkage between environment and other aspects of survival of the people of this area;
2. To understand the categorical impacts of deforestation on village communities (men, women, children);
3. To understand intensity of extinction of species in the area;
4. To understand the extent of the potential of the people to relate the environmental local issues with that of the global issues;
5. To understand the extent of the effectiveness of the policies and programmes formulated and enacted by the state or the national government; and

6. To understand the efficacy of forest department established in the area.

Significance of the Study

In the contemporary era, the cardinal emphasis of all the governing and administrative bodies is on "Sustainability". But, as a matter of fact, Sustainability can be achieved only if environmental concerns are not ignored. Paradoxically, the present developmental regime is threatening the environmental paradigm. The current target of economic growth aims at sundry processes and activities like, industrialization; urbanization; construction of dams; widening and construction of roads, etc. All these human activities directly or indirectly influence the environment. In most of the cases the influence is adverse and damaging. The ongoing developmental procedures for economic growth have, to a large extent, deteriorated the environmental frontiers. The most serious environmental consequence is 'Deforestation'. This notion attains stronger validity in context of a nation like India; where a larger part of the population dwells in rural construct and framework. The survival pattern in Indian villages enrolls 'environment' in most of all the aspects. In simple words, the rural masses depend upon the forests and the goods and services provided by the forests. Their household activities; economic life; socio-cultural and religious part of life; and even health, are dominantly related to the forests around them. Especially in the case of the villages of the remote areas, where the infrastructural development cannot be accessed by the dwellers, the forests, to a significant extent, compensate the deprivation. The reason is that forests provide fuel wood and wood for many other purposes, medicine, fruits, natural medicine for ailments and diseases, fresh air, shed, fertility to soil by controlling soil erosion. These facilities are the basic and adequate conditions for a contended survival. In such a context, deforestation becomes a haunting and alarming scenario. The contents discussed in this part of the chapter hold a greater relevance in case of Punjab. In spite of Punjab being one of the most prosperous States of India, some of its area along the border that is the sub-mountainous track of Punjab, is still backward in socio-economic facets of existence. It needs to be emphasized more upon to enhance natural prosperity and multiplicity in self-reliance.

Many villages are dependent on the forests around them. But with intense industrialization on a large scale, a lot of deforestation is being done. What are the multiple-factors causing deforestation, What effects does the process of deforestation have on the dependent rural communities and how they cope with these problems, all this needs to be a major concern of research. Indian researchers are very well acquainted with the problems of environmental issues and challenges coming out as impact of deforestation in India, but such analysis to a large extent needs to emphasize on the role of village community in forest management, hence, an in-depth study is required. Such study will help to have a multi-dimensional approach to village life in pertinence with deforestation. Policy makers, environmentalists and academicians concerned with development and even common masses need to identify the real causes and effects of deforestation and render usable advice. Such a study provides a comfortable and facilitated environment for this objective. In addition, such an analysis provides a framework for people participation in the process of achieving a sustainable society. In other words it will encourage people to stand as "Pillar Core" of sustainable development.

Limitations of the Study

Along with possessing an 'element of significance', the study suffers from a limitation also. Application of the study will have a limited impact, since it is confined only to city of Pathankot. Rather Kandi Area of Punjab includes Pathankot, Hoshiarpur and Ropar also. Further, the socio-culture conditions and the cultural pattern of the area under study and the concerned households thereon, will largely impart influence on the study.

The discussion in the preceding part of the chapter leaves no leeway to establish that Environmental Degradation in India is a fact not any fallacy. And this phenomenon is backed up by sundry social factors creating adverse conditions for the natural environment. In the encapsulation of environmental consequences, deforestation is a 'severe' effect. In a nation like India, where rural and tribal people are largely dependent on natural resources like forests for availing basic needs of survival; deforestation becomes a grave threat. Forests are being cut due to economic projects like establishing industries; construction of residences for the increasing population; expansion of old roads and building of new roads to improve the scenario of transportation; construction of dams; enlargement and expansion of already existing cities, etc. Though all the above referred chores are dire needs of human survival; but these aims should be achieved with an approach of 'Sustainability'. Until and unless the developmental regime considers 'sustainability' as a credential for the purpose, Overall growth of humanity is not possible and a dream far off. Ordinary masses can sure contribute is maintaining and preserving environment; but they cannot forward technical understanding or interpretation to the linkage between ecology and economy. This onus lies with the formal legislative and executive machinery of the nation. Hence, it is important to create balance between the economic motives and the environmental concerns. This notion needs to be specifically entrenched in the psychic of the rural people, who owe their life to natural environment. Forms of environmental degradation like Deforestation haunt the countryside dwellers more than the dwellers of the urban areas. This research work has emphasized on the rural impacts of deforestation in the realm of Kandi Areas of Pathankot Tehsil of Punjab; and those impacts are very serious. The review of literature forwarded through the first chapter of the thesis establishes the notion that there is a need of 'corporate effort' to maintain, preserve and protect environment. This 'Corporate Effort' implies joint hands of ordinary masses, local formal and informal bodies including NGOs also, and the government. Perhaps, the role of the ordinary masses is the most important instrument to achieve the set goals, because the section of demography suffering from a social issue can provide the most in-depth understanding and potential solutions to that problem.

2 Methodology of Research

Environment is the source of life on earth. It not only directs but also determines the existence, growth and development of the mankind and all its activities (Saxena, 2006). But as a matter of paradox, nature has been increasingly damaged, restorative capabilities have been progressively weakened, and human environment is deteriorated day by day to the point of affecting not only the quality of life but even the very existence of life. At this point, man realized the need to preserve and improve his environment, which is now called the 'Ecological Approach'. The importance of environment and environmental studies get even more realized and recognized in case of rural areas; as the rural population depends upon the ecological resources for sustenance more than that of the urban population. Countryside survival pattern is still not fully technologically fabricated, due to which natural resources remain indispensable for the rural life support and the sustenance system. No doubt, ecological studies view pattern of spatial distribution of population, economic activities and social institutions along with their growth, development and settlement pattern, with an emphasis on ecological processes but environmental dimension is increasingly being viewed as a part of ecological studies. Burgess Concentric Zone Theory (Burgess, 1925) refers to 'Zone of Deterioration' which occupies particular area of an urban centre due to neglect, and invasion of business and industry, the neglect of environment issues in the growth process is leading to a deterioration of quality of life. For this, the present research in particular, covers those areas which have undergone deforestation, making the dependent communities' sustenance difficult and changing their life style and life chances.

Selection of the Area

The Research work encapsulates the Kandi Area of Punjab State. Punjab, as a State, covers an area of 50,362 sq. km. The northern boundaries of Punjab State include Himalayan sub-mountainous zone (locally called 'Kandi Area' of Punjab or Shivaliks). The geological characteristics of Shivalik region have been enumerated in this Chapter to make it appositional to understand the role of the forests and the impacts of deforestation in the region. The Kandi Area covers an area of 4,600 sq. km., which constitutes nine per cent of the total area of the State. The area under research is distributed in the districts of Gurdaspur (mainly in Tehsil Pathankot), Ropar and Hoshiarpur in the Northern part of the State.

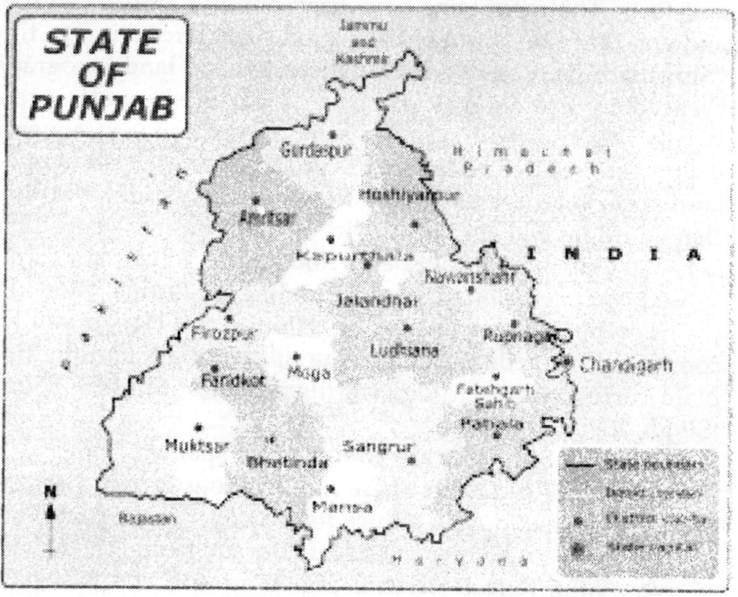

Figure 2.1: The State of Punjab

Source: http://upload.wikimedia.org/wikipedia/commons/f/fa/Punjab_district_map.png

In these areas, maximum forests belong to village people under "Mustarka Malka". This term denotes common ownership over the available forests. The population of the Kandi Area is well aware of the fact that they had a common ownership over the natural green resource, i.e., forests, due to which people had been making a multi-dimensional use of the forests. Before going further with any exploration, it becomes an important obligation of the researcher to put forth a brief view about Shivalik region and its characteristics in order to facilitate the further understanding of the geology of the area and its effects on the village and the community life.

Shivaliks : An Overview

Shivaliks are a world popular mountainous zone marked with heavy geographical characteristics and environmental mysteries and facts. The mountains have been popular allover the times and eras, but the nature of the region varied from time to time. "Shivalik hills present a highly dissected bad land topography created by ephemeral streams of various genetic types. Weathering and erosion in this semi-arid region (consequential to uncontrolled deforestation) has produced a variety of erosional land form features as rills, gulleys, scarps, spurs, variously shaped ridges and amphitheatrically made basins. Depositional features like choe terraces and flood plain scrolls are formed subsequent to erosion of the surrounding landforms. The rolling plains of the region primarily lie is Punjab and Haryana and are comprised of piedmont plain, the upland plain and the flood plain corresponding to descent ingradient of Shivalik Foothill (Singh, 1990).

Now the Shivaliks are found to be sparsely forested but according to Puri (1949), these mountainous terrain possessed luxuriant vegetation and a thick forests cover in the past times a few decades ago and owned bulk of flora and fauna. The Shivaliks of trans Satluj Punjab-Haryana region are soft and friable. The composition of deposits shows that they comprise of alluvial detritus. According to Wadia (1949) this alluvial detritus is derived from sub-aerial wastes of the inner mountainous ranges, swept down by their numerous rivers and streams and deposited at the foot.

The region as stated earlier too had a thick forest cover in the past times, which it lacks now. Deforestation has taken place at a rampant scale in the region, but still the availability of the trees in the region is remarkable. Most prominent trees available in the region are *Acacia catechu (*Katha*), A. leucophloea, A. modesta, A. nilotica (*Kikar*), Dalbergia sissoo (*Sisham or Khli*), Diospyros cordifolia, Ehretra aspera, Eucalyptus tereticornis (*Safeda*), Engenia jambolava (*Jaman*), Ficus benghalense (*Borh*), F. religiose (*Peepal*), Flacourtia indica, Grewia oppositifolia, Lagerstroemia parviflora, Nallous phillippense, Mangifera indica (*Amb*), Sizygyium cuminii, Termilia arjuna, Trewia nudiflora, Vitisnegundo, zizyphus mauritiana (*Ber), etc. Widely seen shrub in the region of Shivalik foothills is *Calotropis procera (*Desiak*)* and the one normally grown at homes is *Lantana Ịndica, Mimosa Aspericanlis, Murraya Korngii (*curry-patta*).* Other popular trees available in the Kandi belt are *Khair, Pla* and *Neem.*

The Shivalik Hills of Punjab and Haryana are very popular in context of wildlife. In the past, people watched and experienced existence of many wild species, but now the region is not that rich in wildlife. Fishes (Pisces) of about dozen types are still available in all small and large waterbodies in the area. Some prominent species available are *Catla catla (*thail*), Tor putifore (*Mahseer*) and Labeo rohite (*rohu*).* Two main types of tortoises are still available and 3-4 types of lizards are seen in the buildings, lawn and hedges. One of these has a brilliant vermilion colour during mating session. For snakes, the region is quite known in the world of geologists. Snakes in the region are of different types such as *Russels, Viper, Blind snake, Cobra, Indian Python, Sand Cobra, Pat Snake,* etc. (Sharma, 1987 and Bhoria, 1984). The species of birds consist of over 100 different kinds. Here are also migratory kinds visiting during winters from far off lands as Siberia. But those migratory kinds do not tend to extent their route to Punjab Kandi Belt, rather rests up to Sukhna Lake of Chandigarh. The estimate about the number of the migratory or visitor birds varies from 200-250 types depending upon the estimates of different years.

Mammals are also available in the region. Some of them dwell in forest zones and some are even found munching on the mountainous roads of the Kandi area and even in the lanes of the villages. Common ones available are *Grey musk, shrew monkey, langur, flying fox, tickellis bat, striped squirrel, Indian rat, common rat, house mouse, Indian porcupine, Indian horse, common mongoose, striped hyena, jackal, Indian fox, nilgai, black bucks* and *chital.* Children of the Kandi area told stories on these mammals and species. And the elderly ones were ready to tell their real life encounters and experience with the aforesaid species of fauna (http://gbpihed.gov.in). The given description of the area makes it ocular to State that the region was once upon a time very rich in the wealth of flora and fauna. The flora and fauna was the real possessed wealth which has now been eroded to a drastic extent due to deforestation making it necessary to undertake more studies in environmental context of the region falling under the Kandi belt.

Selection of the District

From all the districts falling under Kandi areas, district Gurdaspur has been selected due to its proximity to the mountainous region having thick foliage cover as compared to other districts. Secondly, many rivulets pass through it that ends up in river 'Ravi'. There has been accelerated pace of soil erosion due to deforestation and this has affected the economy of the area. Easy accessibility is another reason for the selection of this district.

Gurdaspur district has 5 Tehsils and 16 Blocks whereas Hoshiarpur and Rupnagar districts have 4 Tehsils each with 10 and 7 Blocks respectively (Table 2.1). This indicates that the area of Gurdaspur is larger as compared to other districts of Kandi area. Hence, if a study is conducted in a larger area, it automatically leads authentic results because more people are given a chance to be involved in the process of data collection and maximum possible facts can be explored and explained.

Table 2.1 : District-wise Distribution of Tehsils and Blocks of Kandi Areas

District	*Tehsils*	*Blocks*
Gurdaspur	5	16
Hoshiarpur	4	10
Rupnagar	4	7

Source : Statistical Abstract of Punjab, 2007.

From among the five (5) tehsils of Gurdaspur, Dharkalan and Pathankot tehsils fall under Kandi Area. As compared to Pathankot tehsil, the population of Dharkalan tehsil is totally rural (Statistical Abstract of Punjab, 2005; pp. 57). Therefore, Dharkalan tehsil has been selected for the study. Further, from amongst the two blocks of Dharkalan tehsil, Dharkalan block has been selected using fish bowl method. Dharkalan tehsil has 28 villages. Out of these 28 villages, five (5) villages have been selected on the basis of their respective populates.

Selection of the Villages

Tehsil Dharkalan includes 28 villages namely Darbahn, Dharkha Bangla, Sarti, Dukhnyali, Gho, Bharsudai, Dunera, Bharmlada, Nalloh, Phnagota, Dhar Khurd, Phagli Mama, Uparla Thara, Lanjera, Lohrun, Bhagatpur, Rohg, Bhanguri, Jalahar, Dharkalan, Hardo Saran, Chamrour, Thara Jhilkhla, Narainpur, Tarhari Basa, Kot Teeka Samanu, and Tureti. All these villages have variable sizes of population. These 28 villages have been categorized on the basis of their inhabited population (Table 2.2).

There are fourteen villages with population up to 1,000 persons. Only four villages have population of 4,000 or above. Realizing that many of the villages with population up to 1,000 have a small number of households, these villages have been excluded from the universe for drawing the sample. From the rest of the villages (number 14), five villages have been selected using the fish bowl method to maintain randomness.

Table 2.2 : Size of Population of the Villages of Tehsil Dharkalan

Population (in Person)	*Number of Villages*	*Names of the Villages*
Up to 1000	14	Dharbahan, Dhakhra Bungla, Dukhniyali, Bharsudai, Nalloh, Dhar Khaurd, Bhakhli Mama, Lanjera, Bhagatpur, Rohg, Jlahan, Hardo Saran, Chamrour, and Narainpur.
1000-2000	5	Gho, Bhangota, Lohrun, Bhanguri, and Dharkalan,
2001-3000	2	Dunera, and Tureti
3001-4000	3	Sarti, Thara Jhikhla, Bhamlada
4001 and above	4	Hara, Kot Teeka Samanu, Thara Uparla, and Tarhari Basa

The names of the selected villages is as follows; Kot Teeka Samanu (referred in the text as Samanu), Tarhari Basa (referred in the text as Basa), Gho, Dunera and Thara Uparla. The population of the villages Gho and Dunera is 1,625 and 2,105 respectively. Rest of the villages has population above 4,000. The exact size of population of Kot Teeka Samanu, Tarhari Basa and Thara Uparla is 5,030, 6,207 and 7,362 respectively as per information provided by Patwari of the village.

Selection of the Respondents

Our knowledge, attitudes and actions are based to a large extent on samples. This is equally true in scientific research. Due to lack of resources at the disposal of the researcher, study of a fragment of the phenomenon might advance our knowledge and provide sourced conclusions from the results. For this, sampling method has been used to select the villages as well as the respondents. The selection of the respondents has also been made on random basis. The distribution of population and households in the selected villages has been depicted in Table 2.3. The number of household in all the villages shows a significant difference. Village Gho has the smallest number and village Uparla Thara has the largest number followed by Basa.

Table 2.3: Distributions of Household of the Selected Villages

Village	*Population*	*Number of Households*	*Total Respondents Selected for Sample*
Gho	1625	375	60
Tarhari Basa	6207	1102	60
Kot Teeka Samanu	5030	973	60
Dunera	2105	482	60
Uparla Thara	7362	1284	60

From each of the selected villages, 60 respondents have been selected. This number has been fixed to each of the village in order to avoid bias. In order to avoid the over-representation/under-representation of certain villages in the sample, it was decided to give an equal weightage in terms of the number of the respondents to be selected for the study. Over-representation of a particular village may have the consequences on the generalization to be drawn for the study; particularly related to the environmental issues, which are not specific to the people but to the area itself.

Likewise the under-representation may influence the conclusion drawn from the study.

Collection of Data

The villages being covered under the research work are the victims of widespread illiteracy; and the illiterate respondents can neither read the questions nor write the responses themselves. Keeping this phenomenon of Kandi areas in mind, it was decided to use 'Interview Schedule Method'. Interview Schedule is an encapsulation of a specific number of questions with space for relative responses; which the researcher has to fill himself after he/she gets answers from the respondents. While using interview schedules for deriving responses from the respondents, the researcher can conveniently interpret and explain the questions to the respondent and get the answer, which otherwise the respondent could not have been able to forward. There is logic behind this assertion of inability of the respondent; for an illiterate respondent it often becomes a colossal task to understand the question and to forward a desirable context of response. It makes clear to the respondent about what he is expected to tell. Interview schedule as compared to questionnaire method of course demands more efforts from the researcher but still the responses drawn after using interview method hold much more authentic and meaningful substance to substantiate the reliability of data. As experienced by the researcher, Interview Schedules were an absolutely successful research method, with reference to the concerned respondent sample. The interview schedule used in this research work included 85 questions dealing with multiple themes and sub-themes related to deforestation.

The interview schedule has four sub-sections. The first part relates to the family information on variables like age, sex, education, income, etc. The second section relates to the issue of changing cropping pattern. This section is followed by the changes that have been experienced in lieu of environment, forest cover, role of women, NGOs, and others. The last part contains information of the future perspectives of their socio-economic life.

The interviews have been conducted mostly at the house of the respondents, and where the circumstances demanded, the respondents have been interviewed at their place of work. Each interview took about 40-50 minutes. The response was good and positive and hence, it was possible to interview all the respondents.

In addition to the information collected through interview schedule; data was also gathered from a few knowledgeable persons conversant with the area, its environment and the changes that have occurred over the years and the like. Certain Case Studies have been conducted to attain views from those persons/ institutions/organizations, which have not been covered as respondents but are conscious of the multi-dimensional angles of the problems. The case studies are related to members of Mahila Mandal, Sarpanch, Patwari, NGO and the activists of the NGO operating in specified village of the Kandi area, and forest official appointed in the research area.

Case Studies in the present research work were conducted by using 'Unstructured Interview' and the discussions undertaken with the subjects of the cases forwarded a lot of information regarding the causes and the effects of deforestation. Fixed number and format of questions hinder the researcher to deviate from the main track of the research theme, which sometimes becomes a pre-condition to make a complete analysis of the facts. Moreover, the respondents sometimes produce such a diverse view, which is not enumerated in case if structured interview method is being used. This makes the researcher unable to discuss it, even if it is important. Hence, unstructured interview helps to extract a wider spectrum of responses from the cases being studied. Case study is an instrument to establish 'Authenticity' and 'Originality'; which are perhaps the most important credentials to make a research work a success. Case Studies also help to attain views from those persons/institutions/organizations; who/which had not been covered as respondents during the field work. Above all, the researcher while using Case Study method of research can analyze the research theme from a multi-dimensional angle; and incorporate various institutions/organizations/persons of immense importance in the research field to cross examine the views given by the respondents in the course of the field work and research (Vaus, 2003; Singh, 2005; Mittal, 2006). On the whole, the data from the 300 respondents, as the primary sources of information has been derived by using 'Interview Schedules' and supplement with some case studies.

The field work started in the third week of February 2007 and continued till second week of April. Continuous stay in the area of research was not possible due to financial and geographic constraints; hence, all 300 respondents could not be researched in single run of visit.

Analysis of Data

The data collected was analyzed to understand the changes that have been experienced over the years. Data analysis involved various stages like preparation of Code Design, Code Sheets and Tabulation. After going through most of the interview a schedule, a code design was prepared that includes all the possible responses given by the respondents. Certain responses were categorized into a group keeping the nature of the response. The data from the interview schedule was then transferred to the code sheets using the code design.

On transferring all the data on the code sheets, single variable and double variable tables were prepared. Wherever it was necessitated multivariable tables were prepared. Percentages were calculated for the entire tables; where necessary median and correlations were also calculated. Further, bar diagrams and pie chart have been drawn to present the collected data and to highlight the comparative picture of the variation—demographic and environmental issues, the types of forests, causes and impacts of deforestation, etc., as they absorb a great deal of information.

3 Profile of the Villages

Environmental studies encompass the plight of those communities, whose sustenance depends upon the natural resources. These communities have suffered economically, socially as well as politically with degradation of the soil, air and water. Inadvertently, the tribal communities and those living in the foothills of mountains have lost their sources of sustenance more so due to deforestation, denudation of their fertile soils with upcoming of hydro-electric projects. As the present study focuses on changing climatic conditions, sustenance system and the other aspects as a consequence of deforestation, it is pertinent to have a glimpse of the study areas. In this context, the profile of the villages under study has been detailed out. There are five villages, which have been covered under the present research work. These villages are located at different heights of the mountainous tracks; some easily approachable and others have to be tracked for. These five villages exhibit certain similarities with some prominent differential features. This analysis of similarities and differences presents a detailed picture of natural as well as man-made discrimination among the study villages.

Village Gho

The village Gho is situated at a distance of eight km. from Pathankot and 20 Km. downward from Ranjit Sagar Dam. It is situated into the right-side-interior roads of Shahpur Kandi Road. The village can be divided into two divisions on the basis of its steep roads. The lower half part of the village mainly shows agricultural fields, whereas the upper half does not show such an agricultural view but comprises of built up houses. The homes made in this village possess diverse and different external features. Few of these are made with roofs of 'slates' and 'wood'; whereas most of the homes have been constructed with cement and bricks like that of the cities with flat roofs. Most of the houses have built in area of about 50 yards of construction and 10 or 20 yards of small garden like open space used for keeping cows, buffaloes, etc. However, domestication of animals has reduced to a large extent. This is because of the lack of easy availability of fodder and grazing fields in the village or nearby as per the villagers. The villages can be termed as a longitudinal one. Village lacks in proper sewage and sewerage facilities. Despite the village has four ponds of water and five wells, there is still a shortage of drinking water in the village. The reason is that all these ponds and wells are not filled with water always. The water level is very low about 180-200 feet below the earth surface. The Government has no doubt installed a tube well in the village; but the needs related to drinking water are not fulfilled adequately. The people cannot easily afford to climb up or down to the point of that government supply because the roads are sharply mountainous; due to which transporting a bucket filled with water or any other utensil from one place to another is too difficult a task. There was a time, when all these waterbodies provided drinking water adequately in the needed quantum. But now, the situation has worsened. Out of these five wells, three are completely dry and the watertable in the rest two is so low that does not provide sufficient drinking water so often. During rainy season, these wells provide water as they get filled with rain water. As far as ponds are concerned, two out of the four are completely dry and the rest are used by the stray animals and the residents of this village alike. During the field work, it was seen that from the same pond, residents were filling bottles and buckets to get drinking water and also the animals licked water from it. Hence, the condition of the availability of drinking water in the villages is deplorable both quality and quantity-wise too.

Roads are kutcha, due to which heavy rainfall results into intense soil erosion and even the moderate rainfall makes the roads slippery. The soil type of the village is clay-alluvial, due to which the roads become slippery because the water is not retained and remains on the surface of the road. As per the views given by the villages, the soil of the village used to be very fertile in the past. But its fertility has declined in the recent years. The reasons stated are deforestation and lack of rainfalls in present times. Due to deforestation, the soil erosion has increased which has further affected the fertility of the soil. As far as rainfall is concerned, villagers are very upset because heavy rains used to give them good and adequate amount of drinking water in the past; along with adequate water for irrigation purpose. Now with decreased rainfalls and fertility of soil, the agricultural produce has suffered from irreparable loss, thereby further deteriorating the economic condition of the village. Lack of rainfall has also increased the temperature of the region due to which the need for fans and coolers has further increased; adding to the economic burden of the villages. The reason is that now they have to pay comparatively heavy electricity bills, which was not the case in the past. Hence, geography of the village has altered drastically from that of the past. Earlier it possessed heavy thick deciduous forests, with fertile soil and well occupied agricultural land; but now it has less fertile soil, dispersed and an inadequate forest cover with less prosperous agricultural status.

As an addition to the explanation of the geographical profile of the village, the mountains are visible on just one side of the village. The road, alongside which the village is situated, is in zig-zag shape. From whichever point of the village someone watches, mountain are seen on just one side of the village that too seem to be far off from the land of the main village. Hence, it will not be wrong if it is said that the geographical profile of the village is not as rich as it used to be in the past.

Population of the village is more than 1,625 persons as per the latest Census conducted. Only about 2-3 per cent of the people are employed. Maximum people work as labourers in cities and towns nearby. Most of them get contract for labour work in Pathankot. The village is not that far from the Pathankot Tehsil, so the villagers easily commute daily when they are given a contract for construction or any other labour work. Literacy rate is about 20-25 per cent only. Females have even lower rate of literacy. The household burden on women is so heavy that it is difficult for them to manage it all alone; hence, assistance from another member of the house is needed. In this case the girl child is either not enrolled in the school or she gets withdrawn early in order to share the mother's burden of household tasks. This way, the literacy of women suffers in Kandi areas. As a matter of surprise, the household work burden has increased after deforestation. Cutting wood from the forests is generally a women's chore in the villages because the men are involved and busy in agricultural and labour related works. With deforestation, women consume double the time in collecting fuel wood and fodder for household purpose. Other than the collection of wood and other forest products, the females of the village are involved in the tasks like making handicrafts and also assist the male members in the agricultural tasks. A few of them are also involved in works like embroidery on shawls and carpet weaving. There is one Senior Secondary School in the village in which the children of the village and even the neighbouring villages come to study. The enrolment rate of the school is lower than the withdrawal (specifically in case of the girl child); the reason has been stated in the preceding part of the chapter. As per the views obtained while the profile of the village was being assessed; the boys are enrolled in a larger number than that of the girls. The available medical facilities in the village are just negligible but there is one 'Dispensary' (kind of a private clinic), being run by a local MBBS doctor. According to the doctor the people in this village are generally the victims of diseases like asthma; skin allergy; infections and related allergies leading to fever and cold; etc. All these diseases are prevalent due to contaminated drinking water; and secondly, because of the change in the temperature of the region. The temperature of the village has changed to a large extent, due to deforestation and the reduced rainfalls.

The village includes persons belonging to multiple castes like Bhagat, Tarkhaan, Med, Ghumiar and Brahmins. The dominant castes are Bhagat and 'Ghumiars'. There are some people belonging to high castes also but still the majority falls in Scheduled Castes category. As a matter of surprise, many people in the village were such who were not even sure of their caste belonging.

The economic profile of the village at present is very poor. In the past, people of this village were economically self-sufficient since the agricultural profile of this village was very rich. The people used to earn a lot because of a good agricultural production and the variety of the agricultural products being available due to rich and fertile soil. But now agricultural production has declined to a large extent, which has further affected the economy of the village and the villagers thereon. All this is due to decrease in fertility of soil. Those crops which could yield adequate income for the villagers are not sown and not grown now. Earlier cereals like *chana, maa, masar, kulth* and *teel* used to yield a lot of income but now only Maize and Wheat are sown. The crops like *chana, maa, masar, kulth* and *teel*, etc., used to extract a good income from the market as all these were sold in markets of other cities and towns, and also to the government. The quantity of these products was so adequate that the residents themselves also consumed these along with making a commercial use of them. With a decrease in these agricultural products in the village, the income of the villagers has, therefore, reduced; hence, affecting the all over economic standards of the village. People of the village still sow the crops like *chana, maa, masar, kulth* and *teel*, but now the produced quantity of these crops is not adequate for the commercial purpose and is just used for the self-consumption of the households. In order to compensate the 'past-present agricultural product disparity,' the people now undertake the rotation of crops like wheat and maize. It is clear that the economic profile of the village has deteriorated. The government has not even established any small scale industry in the village; so employment in village is virtually inadequate. Most of the people have constructed their homes after taking loans from the banks because they lack that optimum earning, which was a strong support for their life in the past. All these factors in an encapsulation have put a lot of economic pressure on the villagers.

People are politically very active and they are aware of the political situations around the State. Most of the people belong either to Congress (i) or BJP. No other regional political party dominates this area. There is Panchayat in the village, which holds meetings often and solves matters like minor quarrels. There are three divisions of Panchayat, (i) Mangani Panchayat, (ii) Proper Gho Panchayat, and (iii) Khwaana Panchayat. This three-fold division of Panchayat has been made due to the convenience of the villagers. People of the village reside in dispersed hamlets; which are groups of houses made on scattered points of the village land. One hamlet is just at the central point of the road stretching the village. And the rest of the two hamlets are situated on both the ends of the same road or it can also be said that these two hamlets are located at two opposite ends of the village. In case of any emergency like major quarrels or any other mis-happening; the Sarpanch or other Panchayat officials cannot rush to the place of the incident at once. This three-fold division of Panchayat is pertinent to these three geographical divisions of the village, making the Panchayat officials easily available to common masses in case of an emergency. This is the main cause of confusions regarding the administrative and demographic boundary of the villages.

Mahila Mandal also exists there, in which some women of the village participate. But as per the generally drawn view, both, Panchayat and Mahila Mandal do not address satisfactorily the problems of the common masses. Further, the environment and the water related problems of the village have worsened since in the past no attempt has been made by these political units to improve this situation. As implied through discussions undertaken with the residents of the village; and the political units and the officials thereby, there is a lack of 'will' for bringing about the general social welfare. Along with this assertion, the dwellers of the village also believe that there should be an N.G.O. working in the village to develop it because according to them the N.G.Os hold the potential to mobilize the ordinary masses into a common aim to be achieved and the procedure adopted therein.

'Environment', as expressed by the residents of village Gho, has always been the most important determinant of their livelihood. The people of this village express that 'Forests' are such environmental units, which have been catering to multiple needs of life of the people. Forests provide lots of credible products and services to the villagers, like adequate quantum of fodder for the domesticated animals; fuel and furniture wood; herbs and natural medicine for minor as well as major ailments; housing for the prominent species of the area; leaves for making *'pattals'*, which are further used for commercial purpose and for earning; forests jobs in case of some specific government owned programmes (like 'Ten years felling programme for the tree named *khair*. After every ten years the trees of *khair* are cut and the stem of the tree is processed to form into pulp and out of it *katha* is extracted which is a commercial product. But in the present times, the people of this village feel deprived of these forests produce and the services too. The reason behind this deprivation is increasing deforestation.

Deforestation is such a phenomenon, which has haunted the environmental scenario of many regions. It becomes even more alarming in case of villages as the rural people depend upon the forests for their sustenance and use many of the forest products and services for a contented survival. With excessive and uncontrolled deforestation, many activities have been affected. The adverse effects derived as a consequence of deforestation are not single dimensional rather multifaceted. All the angles of survival (health, education, economy, society and culture) of the villagers have been affected. A huge economic burden has been imposed upon the life of poor villagers with decrease in natural resources like forests. Now they have to spend a lot of amount on availing the above stated goods and services from the market, which were once available free of cost. As per the views given by the villagers, the highest amount is spent on buying material for the construction of homes; for which the forests provided enough wood in the past. Deforestation has resulted into large scale soil erosion, which consequently affected the fertility of soil. Earlier people earned a lot of income with sale of fruits like mangoes, but now the growth of mango has been affected with change in temperament (again people owe this loss to deforestation). It will be judicious to say that the residents of this village lead an economically backward life and the major reason behind this backwardness is environmental degradation. The people of the village believe that the worst form of environmental degradation is deforestation because they are the ardent sufferers of this deterioration of the environment.

Village—Samanu

The village 'Samanu' is situated 15 km. from Pathankot on Drrang Khadd Road. Samanu is directly linked to the 5.8 km. long road of the village Gho and it is through the village Gho only, that people of Samanu village access the main road. The population of the village comprises of 5,030 persons. Samanu falls extremely far from the main Shahpur Kandi Road, due to which till now, no developmental project has ever entered into its geographical boundaries. The village has been built on both the sides of a 2½ kilometres long stretch of road which is quite narrow. At certain places it is *katcha*. As a result it is difficult to drag a bullock cart sometimes, but village structure can be termed as longitudinal one.

The soil type of Samanu village is clay-alluvial. It is just the same as that of the soil type available in Gho. It does not retain water; so during rainfall, even walking on these roads becomes a tedious task because the roads become slippery making it difficult to walk. Mountains can be seen on the two sides of the village at a distance varying from half km. to 1-2 km. approximately. These mountains look dark green as they all are covered with lush green trees. The geographical profile of the village in the most probability resemble to that of the village Gho, the only difference is that in Gho, the mountains are seen on only one side of the village, but in Samanu, the mountains are seen on two sides. The houses constructed in this village are smaller than the houses in Gho, in about 30-40 sq. yards of land. The houses constructed in this village are either one room or at the most two rooms with a kitchen. There is no house with a proper toilet facility due to which the open fields around the houses are used for the excretion purposes. Very less number of houses has gardens or courtyards. Most of them start with the main door opening to one of the rooms of the house. Domesticated animals like cows and buffaloes are seen in Samanu, but in comparison to the village Gho, the number of houses owning milch cattle is low. The condition of the sewage in Samanu is very poor as it has no proper drainage system; resulting into a consistent sting in the air. There are two ponds and only one well in the village but these three waterbodies do not provide adequate water for drinking. The reason is that the ponds are dried up and the water in the well is so deep that sometimes the water cannot be reached and pulled up; so these waterbodies are insufficient to cater to the needs of drinking water of all the villagers. At only one point of the village, there is one tubewell installed by the government to provide drinking water to the people. As a matter of serious concern, the tubewell also does not function all the time and the availability of water is not adequate. However, due to a good understanding between the residents of Gho and Samanu; people of Samanu move down the road and use the water supply point installed by the government in Gho. Geographical proximity of these two villages that is Gho and Samanu is a matter of privilege for the residents of Samanu in the context of availability of drinking water. It can be said that the geographical conditions of both the villages resemble to a significant extent.

Population of the village crossed 5,030 persons in the latest Census only. The population is a mixture of people of various caste group, out of which Harijans and Rajputs are predominant. Rajputs are numerically lesser than that of the Harijans. Most of the residents of this village are Hindus and very few of them belong to Sikh religion. There is no communalism in the area. According to the people, they have never experienced any fight or quarrel in the name of religion.

In this village, there is an Elementary School but enrolment of children in school is very less. The educational profile of the village absolutely resembles to that of the village Gho. Females have very low rate of literacy. The burden of the household chores on women is so heavy that it is difficult for them to manage it all alone; hence assistance from another member of the house is needed. This is the reason for which girl child is either not enrolled in the school or she is withdrawn from school in order to share the mother's burden of household tasks. As a matter of surprise the household burden has increased after deforestation. Cutting wood from the forests is attributed to women as the men are busy in agricultural and labour related works. Women now consume at least double the time in collecting fuel wood and fodder for household purpose than they used to spend in the past when the region had thick forest cover.

The condition of health services is very poor in the village. There is no Health Centre due to which people have to move to other villages around for minor ailments and diseases. The private clinic of the village Gho is often visited by the residents of Samanu, in case they have some health related problems. The people in this village are mainly the victims of diseases like asthma, skin reactions, infections and related allergies leading to fever and cold, etc. According to the doctor, the reason is again the consumption of contaminated water; and secondly the change in the temperature of the region. The causes behind the health sufferings of the residents of Gho and Samanu are similar. The temperature of the village has changed to a large extent due to deforestation. Even the pattern of rainfall has changed. This environmental change coupled with increasing humidity and rise in temperature has affected the health of the people. Literacy Rate is very low rather the worst among all the villages under study. At the time when the field work was being conducted, there was only one girl pursuing graduation from a college in Pathankot.

The residents of Samanu claim that they lead a life of security and safety and can sleep even with open doors because there is no threat of theft or robbery in this area. Taking care of the village and the houses built therein, is not an individual's responsibility rather a collective promise of all the dwellers. This feeling has been expressed by many people from the village, proving it to be true that the Indian villages are still an epitome of strong social bonds.

Economy of Samanu is even poorer than that of the village Gho. People have no jobs and even their income from agriculture has reduced to a large extent. Earlier cereals like *chana, maa, masar, kulth* and *teel* used to yield a lot of income but now only maize and wheat are sown. The crops like *chana, maa, masar, kulth* and *teel,* etc., used to extract a good income from the market as all these were sold in markets of other cities and towns, and also to the government. The quantity of these produces was so adequate that besides using it for household consumption, they used to sell it in the market. With a decrease in the production of these crops, the income of the villagers has reduced, further affecting the overall economic standards of the village.

Most of the people are involved in labour works but their earning is so less that it hardly facilitates 'hand to mouth' pattern of survival. People do not get regular contracts or orders of labouring, due to which income is below an optimum level. But still, they believe that labour contracts are the last resort for them to earn their livelihood as they have no other option after decline in agricultural productivity of crops and changing cropping pattern. Maximum people have constructed homes after taking loans from banks, due to which they have come under severe loan stress and burden. However, people show a strong grudge against the government because till now no attempts have been made to improve the employment scenario of the village and the government has even never taken any steps to reinstate the previous prosperous agricultural conditions. With shift from traditional pulses like *maa, chana* and *teel* to wheat, the income of villagers has been affected a lot and the present crops like maize and wheat are unable to compensate that loss at all. According to the people of this area selling of mangoes was a great source of income in the past for them, but now the production of mangoes has also suffered a great loss due to change in climate of the area.

The change in temperature, decreasing soil fertility and the consistently eroding soil have all affected the production of many crops and fruits. This phenomenon does not limit the adversities here only. The current agricultural scenario is not adequately serving the needs of the people. This demands an expansion of agricultural area as the last resort. This may lead to further deforestation which is jointly taken up by the residents.

In addition to household works, women are involved in tasks like embroidery and carpet weaving. They earn a significant income from these tasks. As compared to the female of the village Gho, the females of Samanu earn better from these chores. People say that this difference exists because they spend more time on these tasks than on agriculture. But women in Gho spend more time on agriculture than on embroidery and weaving carpets. Though the family earns from agriculture, labour or handicraft but the income is just sufficient to suffice their food related intentions. The young boys of the village share the agricultural workload of the men and the young girls share the household burden of the women, making it convenient for the elderly ones to devote more time to their own tasks like agriculture, embroidery and carpet weaving respectively. According to the men of this village, they earn lesser than that of their counterparts in Gho who get larger number of labour related contracts as compared to the people of Samanu. Forwarding a reason to it, they say that Gho's people have better contacts with the constructors, developers and the builders in Pathankot. Perhaps, it is because of Gho's geographical proximity with the town. On the whole, the residents of Samanu feel relatively deprived in economic scenario, when they discuss about the conditions of the village Gho and its residents.

Just like other villages of Kandi Area, Congress (I) and BJP are the two political parties, which have engaged maximum people in the political realm. People are not so politically active otherwise, but they become politically activate during election period. The Panchayat of the village is divided into two parts, (1) Samanu Panchayat; and (2) Bhabbhar Panchayat. In fact the name of village is also pronounced as 'Samanu Bhabbhar'. Just like the village Gho, there are geographical divisions in the village also. The upper half of the village falls under the authority of Bhabbhar Panchayat and the lower half of the village (attached to Gho) falls under Samanu

Panchayat. There was no logic available as to why this two-fold division exists; it seems to be as a trend followed in the Kandi area. Watching the convenience and comfort, the people of Gho have derived from the three-fold division of their Panchayat, Samanu has also followed the same pattern. But as a matter of serious concern, people say that these political bodies are not rendering the services as they are expected to do. The functioning of Panchayat is as good as that of the Panchayat of Gho. Mahila Mandal is largely non-functional and does not cater to even minimum expectations of people. No efforts till now have been made to improve the economy, the standards of survival and the environment of the village.

Environmental scenario of the village is miserable at present. People have pathological state of sewerage and the village has no sewerage or sanitation facilities due to which garbage and the solid waste are often seen lying on the roadsides and even in the agricultural fields. The area had deciduous forests in the past about 8-10 years back. It is now converted into open fields with scant shrubs and trees. The environmental pathology of the region is featured with excessive deforestation, poor sewerage and sanitation facilities, absolutely no solid waste management and above all the lack of political will to improve the environment of the region. Even the masses do not express any intention to pool in the environmental upgradation efforts. According to them, they do not have time to spare from the agriculture and the labour related tasks. And, moreover, they completely attribute this chore to the government.

Village—Basa

Village Basa is situated at distance of about 20 kilometres from Pathankot. It is a small village with a population of 6,207 persons. This village falls at the immediate foothills of Shivalik mountains and these mountains can be seen from any point and any angle of the village. In fact, the village seems to be encircled by a ring of mountains. The inner lanes of the village are kutcha and brick lined, not conducive for vehicular traffic. The condition of the approach road exactly corresponds to Samanu and Gho. The village has been built on both the sides of the main road. The houses are built in a scattered pattern rather than a clustered format as that of the dispersed hamlets of the village Gho. There are three wells in the village which serve the drinking water needs of the people of the area. But these three wells do not meet the needs of drinking water by villagers. Out of the three wells, one has completely dried now and the rest of the two provide water only after rainfalls. The water level is low. It is available at a depth of 600-650 feet below the earth surface due to which, it is impossible for an individual household to afford submersible pump to lift the water. There are three *boulies* (a small and natural depression in the earth surface filled with the groundwater) in the village which serve as a source of drinking water for the villagers. The persons in need of water have to walk down to the *boulie*. The shape of the *boulie* is circular. But in rainfalls, it swells up and becomes difficult to reach and fill up the pitchers with water. Concluding the water related scenario it is justifiable to say that the water they get to drink, cook, or for any other purpose, is neither adequate in quantity nor is it good in quality.

The village is inhabited by a number of caste groups and the majority comprises people from the sub-caste groups 'Mahasha' followed by 'Batwaal'. A very few people of the village belong to 'Rajput' caste. The built-in houses are either one room and a kitchen set or have maximum of two rooms and a kitchen set. Some of the houses have small open courtyards, which are meant to keep the milch animals. These houses open directly into the main lanes. As compared to the houses seen in Samanu and Gho, the houses built in Basa look more traditional because most of them are built in traditional structure with 'woods', and 'slates', and a countable number of homes (nearly 8-10 houses only) have been constructed using cement, bricks, iron, etc. The infrastructural level of the village is very low. There is no school in the village. The parents send their children to the Elementary Schools in the neighbouring villages. But still, the number of children being enrolled in these Elementary Schools is just negligible.

Illiteracy is one of the biggest social issues which this village faces at present. Nearly all the young girls (in an age to attend school) are engaged in either *Pattal* making (leaf plates) task or in household chores. This task cannot be compromised as per the views given by the villagers because it gives a good income to women of Basa. As far as health services are concerned, the condition is very poor. There is no dispensary in the villages. People say that they use natural herbs for wounds and minor ailments. Just like the cases of Samanu and Gho, the residents of the village Basa have been regular victims of infection, fungal diseases, skin reactions, and asthma. For all such considerably serious health related issues, the villagers adhere to the services of the clinics/ dispensaries in the neighbouring villages. People ignore visiting cities for health services because transportation is costly besides hefty doctor's fees and expensive medicines. They simply cannot afford this heavy expense burden with their limited income. Hence, the population of the village leads a backward life which is deprived of even basic amenities of life. Girl children of the village are largely engaged in household works and making *pattals* and least get a chance to be educated. In all, the conditions of economy, health, education and infrastructure in the village are very poor and need a proper care and concern of the government.

The major reason behind the economic downfall is the deterioration of agriculture. As per the views derived from most of the respondents, earlier they used to cultivate *maa, masar, kulth, teel, chana,* and used to earn a good income. But now with decreased fertility of soil and immense change in temperature, the cropping pattern has changed and now the income has reduced to a considerable extent. Though expansion of the already available land is being undertaken; but still the earlier level of agricultural income cannot be attained because of the shift from pulses to the cereals. No doubt, cereals fetch at least the minimum remunerative price but the production is not sufficient to have marketable surplus. The agriculturists have sufficient for their family but not to market the same to earn profit.

Earlier fruits like mango and guava used to be sold in the market but now the quantity of the fruit product is not adequate for sufficient returns. The villagers owe this reduction of fruit growth to the environmental changes. As per their views, with excessive deforestation, the temperature of the village has changed to a significant extent along with increased soil erosion. Another phenomenon affecting the economy of the village is the trend of *pucca* houses and the simultaneous shortage of wood from forests due to deforestation has put high economic burden on villages. Earlier people availed wood for construction of the houses and for furnitures from the forests of the region; but with excessive deforestation, the availability of wood has decreased to a significant extent. It has further added in the expenses of the villagers because now construction of a house has become a costly affair, leading to an increase in the debt burden in many instances. All these circumstances have lowered the economic profile of the village. According to them, most of the people of the village at present are under debt.

Deforestation in many other ways also has affected the economy of the village. When forest cover was thick and dense, it provided many types of job opportunities. Forest department undertakes multiple forest related commercial projects, for examples extracting pulp from *Khair* tree to produce *Kaththa* for commercial usage; cutting dry trees to get wood for multiple purposes; afforestation programmes, etc. For completing all these tasks, the people of the villages nearby the forests are given contractual or part time jobs. These jobs are paid with good remuneration rates. In the past, persons of this village were enrolled in tasks like digging pits for sowing the seedlings and cutting of dead trees. The situation has changed now. With excessive deforestation, now the residents of the region are deprived of these jobs to a large extent affecting their earning capacity. The 'Ten Year Felling Programme' undertaken by the government, pertinent to the *khair* tree still goes on, but still, it does not enroll the same number of people into job provisions as it used to do in the past, because in present times forests have decreased to a large extent. It is not only because of Deforestation that the economic standards of the village have come down, development of technology is also blamed to be a major cause behind economic degradation of the village. In the past, say 10 years from now, the women of the area used to make an ample amount of *Pattals* for commercial usage, with the leaves of *Pla* trees. These *pattals* are the hand-made disposable plates, which are used in temples, gurudwaras, household functions, and occasions of community gatherings to distribute food etc. Women earned a good amount by selling these *pattals*. But now, disposable plastic plates are used instead of *pattals*. This has reduced the demand of *pattals*, which has curtailed in fact the family income. Hence, this phenomenon has affected the economy of the village to a large extent.

In this village, people seem to be least interested in politics, but, however, on being asked, they say just two names; these are of two major national political parties BJP and Congress (I). People are annoyed with both the parties because according to them no government has ever taken case of their village and no government officials have ever come to watch the infrastructure, forests or water related conditions of the village. No efforts have been ever made by MLA of the area to improve the economic or environmental profile of the area. Anyhow, Panchayats and Mahila Mandals are existent in the village and they hold certain meetings in the village but nothing related to forests or environment in general is discussed. However, people have a firm faith in NGOs, though they have never experienced functioning of an NGO in their region. They refer to Dunera in this context and say that Dunera is as developed as a town, and it is just because of the existence and functioning of the NGO in Dunera. The role and the profile of the referred NGO have been discussed in details in profile of Dunera. However, it can be said that people have no faith in Political institution of the region and have a stronger faith in the non-governmental organizations.

People of Basa, Gho and Samanu are though illiterate, but they possess concern for environment which an educated person sometimes does not have. According to them they have faced a great loss with deforestation around their areas. The reasons they owe to deforestation and excessive exploitation of the natural green cover by people for their individual and familial needs; and the lack of attempts being made by the government to save people from this alarming form of environmental degradation, for example programmes like 'Afforestation', etc. Forests provide lots of credible products and services to the villagers, like adequate quantum of fodder for the domesticated animals; fuel and furniture wood; herbs and natural medicine for minor as well as major ailments; house for the prominent species of the area; leaves for making *pattals* (which are further used for commercial purpose and for earning), forests jobs in case of some specific government owned programmes like 'Ten Years Felling Programme' pertinent to the tree named *Khair*, and the forests are also considered to be the most potential instrument to curtail soil erosion. Taking these extraordinarily important goods and services being provided by the forests into consideration, deforestation has affected rather threatened a glib and an adequate survival of the dependent people. With deforestation, soil erosion has increased and it has reduced fertility of the soil due to which the cropping pattern has suffered from a severe jolt, which has further forwarded dangerous repercussions for economy of the village. Moreover, the change in temperature with deforestation has further worsened the situation and has increased physical traumas and diseases. Due to increased contamination of air and drinking water, the physique of the villagers has been badly affected. The discussion rendered hereby provides enough evidence for the justification of the assertion that the village life gets sufficiently haunted by environmental degradation, that too specifically in case of deforestation.

Village—Uparla Thara

The village Uparla Thara is at a distance of 30 kilometres from Pathankot. The population of the village comprises of 7,362 persons. It is located on the roads leading to Residential Colonies of Shahpur Kandi. This village is heavily surrounded by mountains. The mountains surrounding the village are without a green cover. At a few places, cover of green plants and trees exists. The soil type of the village is alluvial. As per the views given by the people, it was very fertile in the past but the fertility level has declined in the recent years, particularly due to soil erosion.

The roads made in Uparla Thara are either bricked or even cemented; there is no kutcha road. Houses built in Uparla Thara are comparatively larger and the most of them have two floors constructed. The houses are built in land ranging from 80 to 125 square yards or more. Even the roofs of the houses are cemented. Many of these houses are cemented. Uparla Thara had thick and dense deciduous forests approximately thirty years ago, but now such forest cover is nowhere to be seen as a result of deforestation. The main cause of deforestation in the area is construction of Ranjit Sagar Dam in the nearest region and location of residential colony. Figure 3.1 shows the site of the Ranjit Sagar Dam.

This village has large number of streets on one side of Dalhousie Road, which are further sub-sectioned into different sub-streets. Out of all the villages covered under this research work, it is the only village which shows the greatest number of streets and sub-streets. As compared to the villages at a lesser distance from Pathankot; Uparla Thara has wider and larger markets having well constructed huge shops. The main shops are of clothes, utensils, cassettes, eatables, etc. Most of these are parts of houses. However, there are some people who have taken shops on rent in the neighbouring streets for earning. Well constructed houses owe much to employment generated by Ranjit Sagar Dam. At least one member of the household is employed there and it provides regular and stable income.

Figure 3.1: The Site of Ranjit Sagar Dam

Source : http://www.tribuneindia.com/2004/20040728/ed2.jpg
http://www.tribuneindia.com/2006/20060905/pun1.jpg

One Senior Secondary School is a prominent feature of the village as said by the dwellers of Uparla Thara. Enrolment of children in school is better than that of the other study villages. According to the caretakers and the teachers of the schools, mostly all the parents of the village irrespective of the sex enroll their children to the school. Most of them are either Matric or have done Plus Two.

There is a hospital in the village that provides services round the clock, but people prefer taking health related services from the doctors appointed by the Ranjit Sagar Dam site. These doctors stay in the colony constructed by the government for A-Class employees of the Dam site. Since most of the people are employed there, they easily access these doctors for treatment. People conveniently afford paying for these services due to good and regular salary. People in this village are generally the victims of diseases like asthma; skin reactions; infections and related allergies leading to fever and cold; etc. On the whole, the condition of the persons in Uparla Thara is certainly better than that of the residents of other villages.

Majority of the persons in this village are of Harijan caste. Other prominent caste groups are Brahmins and Rajputs. There is a separate colony for class IV employees of Dam Site constructed near Ranjit Sagar Dam at Shahpur Kandi. Many of the Harijans are living in these colonies after getting employment. As a result, the economic position of these low caste people is sufficiently good to afford even vehicles like scooter/motor cycle/car. In other words, there is a significant improvement in living standard after commissioning of the development project. Many women of Uparla Thara are working and do different jobs. Some of the working women are employed at the site of the Dam as Class IV and some have got jobs on compassionate grounds. Many women have shifted to the colony made near Dam Site popularly known as Jogindra Colony. Earlier many females of the village used to assist the males in the agricultural works but now, the women do not involve themselves in such hard tasks. The reason is the regular income of a male (due to the job available at the site of dam) member of their family. On overall basis, the demographic profile of the village displays a better scenario of survival, as compared to the other villages. Though the village experienced deforestation at a rampant scale just like that of the other villages of Kandi area of Pathankot tehsil; still this form of environmental degradation has not affected the economy of the area because the population of this village has proved to be the most gainful beneficiary of the construction of dam, which is in fact the main cause behind deforestation of the village. However, the adverse impact of deforestation on the health of people is speaking upon.

The village experiences a good economy in the present times as compared to the past. About 30-32 years back, the entire economy of Uparla Thara depended upon agriculture, growing and selling fruits and available forest products. Earlier crops like *chana, maa, masar, kulth* and *til* used to yield a lot of income but now only miaze and wheat are sown. Further with acquisition of the land by the government, the agricultural area has decreased considerably, and so the production of crops. Similarly the area under fruit crops like mango, guava, litchi, too has reduced thereby, affecting the production and income of the dependent communities. Deforestation, establishing of Ranjit Sagar Dam, and the construction of colonies has its bearing on the climatic conditions of the area and productivity of agricultural commodities. But the generation of employment opportunities due to developmental project has compensated the dwindling economy of the village.

The political parties popular in Uparla Thara are Congress, BJP, and BSP. But the followers of Congress and BJP still supersede than that of the BSP. Panchayat and Mahila Mandal are also the salient features of the village. Mahila Mandal is usually evolved in minor level Social Welfare Works like donating utensils on marriages of poor girls, etc. Panchayat of Uparla Thara has contributed efforts in area of water management and installed tubewells at 2-3 points of the village. But paradoxically those points are generally surrounded by homes of Panchayat people and ordinary persons do not take an adequate advantage of these tubewells because of being too far from them. People of Uparla Thara sometimes use old wells of the village to meet their drinking water needs. People get supply of water from the government installed tubewell but the supply of drinking water is irregular due to defects. Water is supplied during fixed hours in a day. The pressure of water remain slow and many of the households store water in that period which is just sufficient to meet their requirement. For the acute water shortage, people blame government, Panchayat and partially the location of the village at such a height that water does not get lifted with sufficient pressure.

The climate and temperature of the area, as per the views of the residents of Uparla Thara, have experienced intermittent changes. In the past two decades, the summers have become very hot. With the passage of time, the village is regaining a better climate. But rains are not as frequent as it used to be in the past. As per the views given by the villagers, now the rainfall situation is improving. Excess population burden, excess exploitation of natural green forest and their products followed by construction of Dam, are some of the factors which have led to incessant cutting of forests in the geographical limits of Uparla Thara. Maximum forests land was used for the purpose of construction of Dam, functioning of 'Conveyer Belt' extending up to 2-3 kilometres upto the Dam site, and the construction of colonies for the employees of Ranjit Sagar Dam etc. Undoubtedly the deforestation increased the sufferings in every aspect of life but the developed economy as a result of construction of dam has compensated the situation; and has balanced adversities with that of progressiveness. Now at present, people do realize the importance of forests and need of afforestation, but still they believe that due to construction of Dam and replacement of forest with the site of Ranjit Sagar Dam, followed by the further use of forest lands for developing residential colonies, has in all developed the economic standard of the village.

Village—Dunera

Dunera is situated at a distance of 45 kilometres from Pathankot. It has population of 2,105 persons. Dunera falls in exact mountainous laps and the residential area of the village is surrounded by mountains on its three sides. It is a compaıatively developed area of Kandi zone. Dunera has one main bazaar and other than this, there are multiple clusters of shops in whole of Dunera. This village has one Senior Secondary School and one Hospital also. Dunera is popularly known as centre of *Aampapar* (mango flakes). It has three wells, which are mostly used as a totem and spots for rituals, but not for drinking water. The reason is that unlike other villages of Kandi Area, each home in Dunera has government's water supply. Dunera has thick, dense and dark forests around it and the life in Dunera seems to be satisfactory by all means. Roads in Dunera are well made. All houses, shops and buildings are white washed with yellow tone to give a beautiful look to the village. And all the name plates hanging on the outer walls of the houses and the shops are black and white. The houses are mostly double storied. Some of these have shops on the ground floor with residence at the top. Some houses in Dunera have small gardens, where multiple fruits like litchi, mango, guava, etc., besides certain flowers are grown. On the whole, among all the villages covered under this research work, Dunera reflects comparatively more developed profile; with the most dense forest cover in its vicinity which reflects that the environment has not degraded rather preserved and maintained to a significant level. The soil of the village is alluvial and fertile as it used to be in the past. The reason is that forest cover is retained to a large extent which does not allow soil erosion in rainy season. This is one of the reasons for the sustenance of soil fertility.

Dunera has a population composition comprising of different caste bases. Some of the prominent castes in Dunera are Brahmins, Rajputs, Teeka, and Ghumiar. The numerically dominant caste group is that of the 'Harijans'. The living standard of people is good on an average. There is a school in the village with a high rate of children enrolment; not only from this village but also from the nearby villages. Many females are in the teaching profession. There is an NGO which runs computer centre in the village, offering many free of cost computer courses and, some of the courses can be done by paying a negligible amount of fees. Many people are technically proficient in computers and can take up minor works like accounting and record maintenance on the computer. There is a dispensary in the village also, and the people visit it in case of minor ailments like fever, cold, dehydration, etc. However, the incidence of fungal infection, asthma, skin allergy, etc. is low. The main reason behind this good health scenario may be the environment of the village. The strength of the village is the NGO named Bharatiya Vikas Parishad. This Parishad functions under the auspices of Jindal Foundation (A Canada based NRI NGO), founded in 2001 and since then, it has invested lakhs and probably crores of rupees on development of Dunera. This NGO specially worked on construction and maintenance of toilet complexes on the main road of Dunera. It has also worked for the widening of the narrow lanes of the village with an extension of 2-3 feet and proper drainage. Now these streets extend up to 8 to 12 feet, making convenient for the people to walk and drive. Hardly any kutcha road is seen in the village.

Just like Uparla Thara, people in Dunera are also satisfied with their economic standards. Main sources of income in Dunera are agriculture and forests. Crops like *maa*, maize, wheat are very prominent to this area and these crops are still grown and yield sufficient to meet consumption needs of the cultivators with some produce for marketing. As per the views given by majority of the respondents from Dunera, men and women both are employed or hired on contractual basis by the Forest Department for various jobs like digging holes to plant trees under Afforestation Programmes undertaken by the government, extracting *Kaththa* from *Khair* trees. Third most common source of income of Dunera people is the *shops* being run by them. These shops deal with sale of clothes, tapestry, CDs and cassettes, utensils, sweats, etc. There are a few beauty parlours, embroidery and stitching shops being run by the women of the village. Some of the women also contribute to the economy of their household by working as teachers in school located in or around the village. Due to good connectivity, it is easy for the ladies to communicate to their work place. Not only this, Jindal Foundation has also employed some people on permanent basis for the tasks like maintenance of Computer Centre, School, Hospital and has also employed some people as sweepers for cleanliness of roads. According to the people of Dunera, the NGO working in Dunera is the strongest force behind the overall developmental of the village and it is only due to the inspiration and moral force of this NGO, that developmental projects are being consistently initiated in the village either by the government or by the people themselves. In short, the economic scenario of the village depicts a level of prosperity.

Prominent political parties in Dunera are Congress, BJP and BSP. Most of the people are followers of Congress or BJP. It was difficult to derive that which of these political parties has larger number of followers. The truth is that whichever party comes in power, people hardly feel effected because the developmental projects are being undertaken by NGOs like Bhartiya Vikas Parishad and Jindal Foundations. Most of the residents of Dunera are its members and they have adopted an aim of social welfare in their own characters. These NGOs functioning in the village have made the masses so collective in approach that when the research was working on this work, people met in cluster and gave collective responses. Earlier, Panchayat and Mahila Mandal did not possess a strong political will to establish social welfare but being influenced by the success of the NGOs both these political wings have become very active. Panchayat and Mahila Mandal indulge in function pertinent to social solidarity and cohesion like

Figure 3.2: Forests in the Vicinity of Village Dunera

managing and resolving minor as well as major quarrels: maintenance of cleanliness, repair of roads, etc. But as per the views aired by the residents of Dunera, neither Panchayat nor Mahila Mandal did any work for environmental concerns. People say that forests are already being managed well and Afforestation programme continues along with the efforts of government and the public, so Panchayat and Mahila Mandal do not work on these issues. In addition to the thick forests, many trees/plants with medicinal value have been planted in the area; especially of *khair, pla, pipal, arzaan, teel* and others along with the fruit trees like mango, litchi, jamun, etc.

Though the area has thick forest, forest wood, natural medicine trees like *arzaan* and *bill,* still there has been a loss of certain species. The area has different kinds of animals as well. Panther, tiger, jackal and wild cow are found in the nearby forest areas. The forests also support avian population. Sparrow, crow, and parrots are some of the common birds. In this way, the village has a fairly well established ecosystem.

An in-depth analysis of the profile of the area under study makes it convenient and facilitates to understand and interpret various phenomenon related to the research. The description of demographic, economic, political, social and environmental profile of the villages under study in fact forwarded a strong platform for bringing about a detailed exploration of the research themes. Without analyzing the profile of an area, it becomes impossible to gauge out the hidden facts related to the livelihood pattern of the people. It has been noticed that the Gho, Samanu and Basa resemble a lot in the context of their socio-economic and environmental profile with minute differences thereon. But the villages, Dunera and Uparla Thara show a significantly different scene. The economy, society and the environment of Gho, Samanu and Basa are featured with similarity. The people of these three villages largely depend upon labour related tasks for their sustenance. The deterioration in the agricultural scenario has haunted the allover survival of the villagers and has deregulated the economy of the villages. These three villages are victims of immense penury; which has further got aggravated due to the cutting of forests in the region.

Deforestation is global threat but its impacts are even more threatening for the communities which are directly dependent upon the goods and services being provided by the forests. In apposition to the discussion, it has been observed that after deforestation in the region, the economy of these three villages has become instable rather burdened. Villagers used to save a lot of money by availing goods and services from the forests free of cost. But now due to forests being in scarcity; people have to spend money to avail the same goods and services. Deforestation has not only deprived the masses of valuable forest produce but it has also affected the climatic conditions of the region; further playing havoc with the agricultural productivity. The end of the traditional crop in the region has also given a drastically affected the earning of the villagers. According to the residents of these three villages the cutting of the forests for multiple purposes has disrupted their overall living standards. But the condition is not at all similar in the other two villages under study. Dunera and Uparla Thara present entirely a different scenario.

Cutting of forest took place in Uparla Thara too, but the impacts are not as worse as that in Gho, Samanu and Basa. People of Uparla Thara have experienced economic development in the recent years. The construction of Ranjit Sagar Dam in the region has improved the employment scenario, further improving the economic conditions of the villagers. The residents of Uparla Thara say that deforestation has affected the temperature of the region; but this has not further influenced any aspect of their life negatively. These people do not depend upon agriculture as they are well settled due to the jobs they have got at the dam site.

The village Dunera possesses the most distinct features. It is blessed with a strongly maintained environment and a facilitated infrastructural scenario. The villagers have not experienced deforestation in their region rather the forest cover has been maintained and preserved. It is only in Dunera out of all the villages under study that people are found satisfied with the local environmental condition. People say that the region has good infrastructural level too. The villagers owe these good conditions of survival to the NGO functioning in their village. According to the residents, even the political units of the village have been encouraged by this NGO and now these units are more conscious of general social welfare of the residents than they used to be prior to the coming up of the NGO. But the other villages under study feel relatively deprived in the context because they neither have any NGO working in their regions nor do the political units perform in a desirable manner.

Concluding the discussion, it can be said that Gho, Samanu and Basa are experiencing a deteriorated environmental and economic conditions but Uparla Thara and Dunera have a better economy; rather Uparla Thara has the best economic standards amongst all the villages under study. The difference does not exist only in the context of economy; rather it is also noticed in the conditions related to the infrastructure; enrolment and literacy rates; role of forests for the communities and the area in all; importance of agriculture as a source of sustenance; role of the governmental bodies in upliftment of the living standards of the villages; and the role of the ordinary masses and NGOs in the improvement paradigm.

4 Profile of the Respondents

Communities and the groups have relationship with environment in different proportions and in different ways. Communities dependent upon the nature for their sustenance view differently the causes and the impact of an environmental occurrence and the lately coming changes. Women, men, and the children, all view environment through a different perspective and they respond to the environmental changes with different approaches. Likewise, old people who have growth under direct social interaction with nature provide a strong footing to the causes of deforestation and the impacts thereon. On the contrary, young men not being so aware of the negative consequences of deforestation as their source of sustenance, as a matter of convenience have shifted from the primary to secondary/tertiary sources. Likewise women have opinion different from men. It is in this context that the socio-economic profile of the respondents assumes significance. Various variables like sex, age, caste and income have been considered to explain the socio-cultural profile of the respondents. Though 'caste' is not a factor considered for selecting the sample, still caste is an important social variable due to its relationship with occupation, status, and inter-caste relationship. A detailed categorization has been made on the bases of the above-mentioned variables, which is being presented below. All the factors of analysis have been enlisted and explained with a database in the coming part of the chapter.

Sex

Gender may not be so dominant part of a study being undertaken in a developed urban area; but it becomes a pre-condition for an authentic research work in case of rural areas or the related studies. About 60 per cent of the respondents are males and the females constitute 39.6 per cent of the sample (Table 4.1).

Table 4.1: Sex-wise Distribution of the Respondents

Sex-wise distribution	*Name of Villages*					*Total*
	Gho	*Samanu*	*Uparla Thara*	*Basa*	*Dunera*	
Male	39 (65.0)	37 (61.6)	36 (60.0)	34 (56.6)	35 (58.3)	181 (60.3)
Female	21 (35.0)	23 (38.3)	24 (40.0)	26 (43.3)	25 (41.6)	119 (39.6)

The category of male respondents include 65 per cent of the respondents from 'Gho' village; 61.6 from Samanu; 60 from Uparla Thara; 56.6 from Basa and; and 58.3 from Dunera. The female respondents comprised of 35 per cent from Gho; 38.3 from Samanu; 40 from Uparla Thara; 43.3 from Basa and; 41.6 from Dunera. Although women constitute a considerable proportion of the total number of respondents, still they show reluctance to respond, as they are not confident of the knowledge they possess and its relative adequacy.

Age

Age is a crucial component for the analysis of various community related themes. The responses derived from various members of a community vary depending upon their ages. Youth, middle aged people and the old people hold different views and distinct notions about the subject of the study. Similarly, 'Environment' as a concept is interpreted in specific ideological domains of these age groups. Youths, which has not seen the natural environment in 'its own youth', and has been a part of the era of consistent environmental degradation, generally undermines the importance of environment. On the other hand, the zone of senility (that is the old aged people) has been a witness to the 'radically donating' nature of environment. They have seen the times when life as a whole was dependent on natural environment and the sustenance of humanity predominantly relied on the natural resources.

Understanding environment and the related contents like, importance of natural resources; attitude of the community towards environment; chances of environmental preservation and maintenance, etc., cannot be undertaken in completion until and unless people belonging to all the age groups are taken into consideration. The majority of the respondents fall in the age group of 30-60 years which constitutes 45.7 per cent of all the respondents (Table 4.2). The village-wise distribution of this percentage is 56.7 per cent respondents in Basa; 55 per cent in Gho; 53 per cent in Uparla Thara; 33.3 per cent in Samanu; and 30.3 per cent in Dunera.

Table 4.2: Age-wise Distribution of the Respondents

Age	*Name of Villages*					*Total*
	Gho	*Samanu*	*Uparla Thara*	*Basa*	*Dunera*	
Up to 30 Years	8 (35.0)	31 (51.7)	25 (41.7)	12 (20.0)	33 (55.0)	122 (40.7)
30-60 Years	33 (55.0)	20 (33.3)	32 (53.0)	34 (56.7)	18 (30.0)	137 (45.7)
60 and Above	6 (10.C	9 (15.0)	3 (5.0)	14 (23.3)	9 (15.0)	41 (13.7)
Total	60 (20.0)	60 (20.0)	60 (20.0)	60 (20.0)	60 (20.0)	300 (20.0)

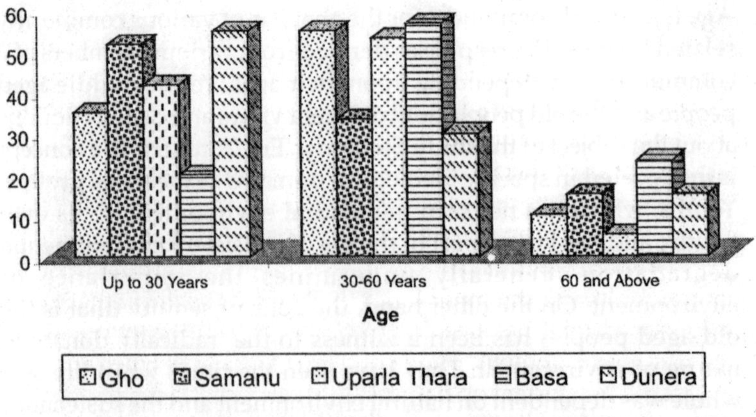

Figure 4.1: Age-wise Distribution of the Respondents

In a descending order of the respondents' strength, the next age group comprises of the persons up to 30 years of age constituting 40.7 per cent of all the respondents. The village-wise distribution of all such respondents shows that Dunera has the largest proportion (55.0%); followed by Samanu (51.7%); Uparla Thara (41.7%); Gho (35.0%); and Basa (20.0%).

Further, there are only 13.7 per cent of all the respondents whose age is 60 years or above. The village-wise distribution of this percentage is 23.3 per cent respondents in Basa; 15.0 per cent in Samanu and Dunera each; 10.0 per cent in Gho and 5.0 per cent in Uparla Thara. Dunera has the largest proportion of respondents in the age group of up to 30 years, whereas Basa has those of the age group 30-60 years and 60 years and above.

Caste

Caste occupies a pivotal position in the sociological research. It is a crucial factor which largely influences the socio-cultural choices of individuals; forms attitudes in the process of socialization of individuals; determines choices and decision-making too. Caste implies an extreme form of social class organization, in which position of individual in the status hierarchy is determined by birth. This definition given by Anderson (2009) cardinally puts forth the elements of 'differentiation and levelling' amongst human groups. Sharma (1982) emphasizes on Caste as a composite feature of society by saying, "a combination of concept with analytic synthesis may ensure a deeper and realistic understanding of Social Stratification in India'. This clearly reflects how caste is related to other factors of survival, making it an important part of studies. Not only the multiplicity of Caste implications, rather its historicity is its strength as stated by Singh (1974 and 1981). Mukherji (1957) stated that class and power along with caste are treated as economic and political dimensions of social inequalities and hierarchy.

Many scholars defined and interpreted Caste from their own perspective. The notions were positive as well as negative too. Some defined Caste as a constructive feature of Indian society, some labelled it as a destructive feature whereas some gave a neutral interpretation.

After having an intense flow of intellect to define Caste by the academicians, anthropologists, philosophers and sociologists from all over the world even prior to the mid of the earlier century, G.S. Ghurey (1950) opined that even after having a significant labour of many minds, the exact definition of Caste has not been derived. For this task, that is, to understand the term 'Caste', the best way is to examine various factors underlying Caste System like endogamy, hereditary, social cultural disabilities, etc. Caste system is extremely elaborate and it varies in its structure from area to area so much that it does not really constitute all "systems" at all, but implies a losely connected diversity of varying beliefs and practices (Chopra, 2007). Weber cited from Bettille (1969) though defines Caste as status group but for him, these status groups are based on the notion of purity and pollution that makes it distinct from class which is based on ownership of the means of production.

Caste in rural survival is largely linked to the factors like occupations and income. Not only this, Caste and Class structures around an individual pave a way for formation of his views about various aspects of survival like environment, economy and society. All these factors make 'caste' a crucial component of the analysis of the profile of the respondents.

The Sample was selected irrespective of the caste, but still caste remains one of the most crucial base of differentiation and stratification in society. In the Interview Schedule, 'Caste' has been one of the contents used to explain the personal and social profile of the respondents. The social profile of the 300 respondents has been characterized in three broad divisions, i.e., (1) High Castes, (2) Backward Castes, and (3) Scheduled Castes, on the bases of their castes.

However, the sub-castes prominent in various villages have been referred to in detail in the profile of each village separately. The majority constituting 42.3 per cent of all the respondents belong to the lower caste group (Table 4.3) and they constitute the majority in Uparla Thara (61.7%); followed by Samanu (41.7%) and Gho (40.7%) with a negligible difference.

Of 37.3 per cent of all the respondents from Backward Castes out of which the majority is from Gho (46.7%) and the minimum proportion is from the village Uparla Thara (26.7%). Even Basa (43.3%) shows a significant percentage of Backward Castes. The percentage of respondents belonging to lower and backward caste groups in Dunera is coincidentally exactly the same.

Table 4.3: Caste-wise Distribution of the Respondents

Caste	*Name of Villages*					*Total*
	Gho	*Samanu*	*Uparla Thara*	*Basa*	*Dunera*	
Upper Caste	8 (13.3)	16 (26.7)	7 (11.7)	16 (26.7)	14 (23.3)	61 (20.3)
Backward Caste	28 (46.7)	19 (31.7)	16 (26.7)	26 (43.3)	23 (38.3)	112 (37.3)
Lower Caste	24 (40.7)	25 (41.7)	37 (61.7)	18 (30.0)	23 (38.3)	127 (42.3)
Total	60 (100.0)	60 (100.0)	60 (100.0)	60 (100.0)	60 (100.0)	300 (100.0)

Regarding the high caste group, it constitutes the smallest proportion of the sample that is 20.3 per cent of all the respondents. The highest proportion of such respondents is seen in Samanu (26.7 per cent each) and Basa (26.7%); followed by Dunera (23.3%); Gho (13.3%); and Uparla Thara (11.7%). The data thus shows that maximum respondents in the lower caste are from Uparla Thara whereas majority of the Backward Caste is seen in Gho. High Castes respondents have the largest strength of respondents in the villages namely Samanu and Basa. Whatever the derivations forward, one fact remains intact that the majority of people residing in the villages under study belongs to the lower castes and a very few belong to the High Castes.

Moreover, Indian caste system not only defines the status of individual, it is equally linked with the occupation. Caste groups are economically homogeneous and perform particular economic functions. The caste system is so structured that it is sustained and perpetuated even under the changing economic order. So, caste not only remains a salient feature of the social morphology, it is still manifestly correlated with every form of Social Stratification, whether based on Wealth, Occupation, Education or some other criterion. This system with its vices acts as a balancing factor in Ecology through its principle of 'Ecological Space'. According to it, natural resources can only be used by a particular occupational group. This resource partitioning helps to reduce the inter-caste competition over scarce natural resources (Sahoo, 1996).

The rural-urban divide is largely an outcome of different resource use and shift in caste based occupational structure. In spite of this, India with its dominant agrarian economy, is growing industrially and for this reason, there is a shift in the caste based occupational structure although it has not losened its hold over society despite industrialization (Gill, 1991). Hence, it is an important socio-cultural variable.

Analyzing the relationship between Caste and Occupation shows that the majority of the respondents from the lower castes are agricultural labourers (30.7%, Table 4.4). They also have a large proportion among the construction labourers (20.5%). Some of them are engaged in cottage industry (13.4%). Not only that lower caste respondents are engaged in low prestige occupations such as agriculture, construction and industry labour; some of them are traders (16.5%) and cultivators as well (3.1%).

Even majority of the backward caste respondents are agricultural labourers (21.4%); followed by construction labour (19.6%) and industrial labour (13.4%). Still, a good proportion of them are cultivators (7.1%); Traders (20.5%) and Servicemen (17.9%). In this way, the backward caste respondents are comparatively better placed than that of the low caste respondents.

Among the respondents belonging to upper castes, again the majority of them are agricultural labourer (24.6%); followed by cultivators and labourers in cottage industry (16.4%) each; traders and construction labourers (14.8%) each; and Servicemen (13.1%). So, cultivators and servicemen are mostly the members of upper castes whereas construction and agricultural labourers are in majority from Backward and Scheduled Castes. Gill (1991), Kaur (2007) too have found the same in their studies.

Like caste, occupations too have a prestige depending upon the notion of income and purity. The occupations which defile or pollute, such as tanning, scavenging, etc., are considered to have low prestige as compared to the other occupations. Gill (1991) categorized occupations into various different prestige categories. Keeping that into consideration, the occupation of the respondents is segmented as high, medium and low prestige occupations. This data is compared with the caste categories (Table 4.5).

Accordingly, the upper caste respondents have a high proportion in the high prestige occupations like cultivation and cottage industry. Of course, many of them have medium (16.7%)

Table 4.4: Distribution of the Respondents by Caste and Occupation

Caste \ *Occupation*	*Cultivator*	*Agricultural Labour*	*Construction Labour*	*Servicemen*	*Traders*	*Cottage Industry*	*Total*
Upper Caste	10 (16.4)	15 (24.6)	9 (14.8)	8 (13.1)	9 (14.8)	10 (16.4)	61 (20.3)
Backward Caste	8 (7.1)	24 (21.4)	22 (19.6)	20 (17.9)	23 (20.3)	15 (13.4)	112 (37.3)
Lower Caste	4 (3.1)	39 (30.7)	26 (20.5)	20 (15.7)	21 (16.5)	17 (13.4)	127 (42.3)
Total	22 (7.3)	78 (26.0)	57 (19.0)	48 (16.0)	53 (17.7)	42 (14.0)	300 (100.0)

and low prestige occupation (17.8%). Further, a large proportion of the backward castes fall in the medium prestige occupation (41.7%). Likewise, majority of the lower castes have low prestige occupation (48.1%). It does not mean that the respondents belonging to backward or the lower castes are invariably practicing the medium or low prestige occupations.

However, the data reveals that most of the upper caste respondents have high prestige occupation. The statistical analysis reveals that castes status and occupational prestige are significantly related ($X^2 = 4.85$, d f = 4, significant at 0.05 Level). This shows that most of the upper caste respondents have high prestige occupations whereas most of the low castes respondents have low prestige occupations. Bhattacharya (1969), Trivedi (1976), Gill (1991), Kaur (2007) too concur the above findings.

Table 4.5 : Distribution of Respondents according to their Caste and Occupation

Occupations / *Castes*	*High Prestige Occupations*	*Medium Prestige Occupations*	*Low Prestige Occupations*	*Total*
Upper Caste	29 (24.8)	8 (16.7)	24 (17.8)	61 (20.3)
Backward Caste	46 (39.3)	20 (41.7)	46 (34.8)	112 (37.3)
Lower Caste	42 (35.9)	20 (41.7)	65 (48.1)	127 (42.3)
Total	117 (39.0)	48 (16.0)	135 (45.0)	300 (100.0)

Occupation

'Occupation' stands as one of the important criterion to analyze profile of the respondents under any study being conducted for socio-economic analysis. It is the basic determinant of the economic status of the individuals. In the study area, there exist six occupational groups; those are Cultivators, Agricultural Labourers; Construction Labours; Servicemen, Traders and those engaged in one or other cottage industry.

Out of the six occupational categories, majority of the respondents are agricultural labourers (26.0 per cent, Table 4.6);

followed by construction labourers (9.0%). Cultivators and traders comprise respectively 7.3 per cent and 13.3 per cent of the respondents. These engaged in cottage industry constitute 14 per cent of all the respondents.

Servicemen constitute 16 per cent of all the respondents. Among the labourer category, agricultural labourers are more in villages Dunera (33.3%), followed by Gho (31.7%) and Basa (28.3%). They have the lowest proportion in village Uparla Thara. Construction labourers are found to be more in Gho and Samanu (28.3% and 26.7% respectively), than that in Basa, Dunera and Uparla Thara.

In all, labourers of different categories found to be more in villages Gho and Samanu as compared to the others. Further, cultivators have high proportion in Basa (13.3%) and Samanu (11.7%). On the other hand, the number of traders in the sample is found to be more in Dunera (26.7%) as compared to the other villages under study. From this, it is clear that the proportion of respondents engaged in primary activities is more in Gho and Samanu, whereas those engaged in tertiary sector is more in Uparla Thara. The proportion of those respondents taking up secondary activities is almost the same in all the villages, except Uparla Thara.

Table 4.6: Occupation-wise Distribution of the Respondents

Occupation	*Name of Villages*					*Total*
	Gho	*Samanu*	*Uparla Thara*	*Basa*	*Dunera*	
Cultivator	4 (6.7)	7 (11.7)	—	8 (13.3)	3 (5.0)	22 (7.3)
Agricultural Labour	19 (31.7)	16 (26.7)	06 (10.0)	17 (28.3)	20 (33.3)	78 (26.0)
Construction Labour	17 (28.3)	16 (26.7)	6 (10.0)	9 (15.0)	9 (15.0)	57 (19.0)
Service	4 (13.3)	3 (5.0)	31 (51.7)	3 (5.0)	7 (11.7)	48 (16.0)
Trade	8 (13.3)	8 (13.3)	12 (20.0)	9 (15.0)	16 (26.7)	53 (17.7)
Cottage Industry	8 (13.3)	10 (16.7)	5 (8.3)	14 (23.3)	5 (8.3)	42 (14.0)
Total	60 (100.0)	60 (100.0)	60 (100.0)	60 (100.0)	60 (100.0)	300 (100.0)

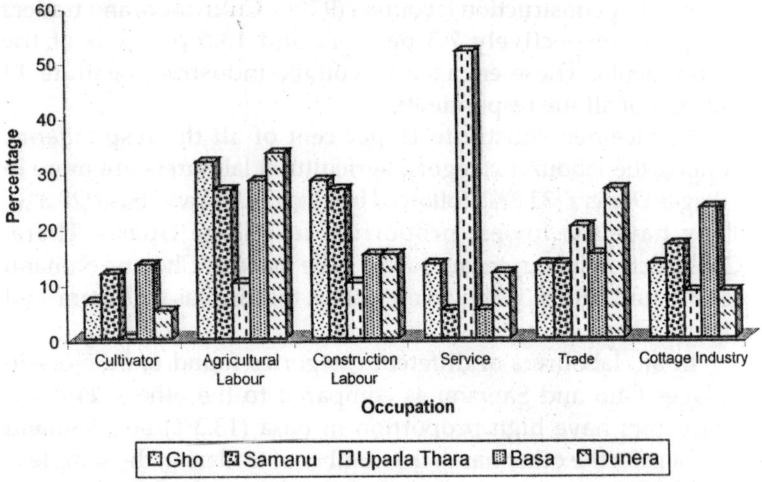

Figure 4.2: Occupation-wise Distribution of the Respondents

Further, after collecting and analyzing the database of all the given occupational categories, it becomes evident that the majority of the respondents in the sample are labourers of different sorts. As most of the respondents are doing one or the other kind of labour, it is pertinent to analyse the economic standing of the respondents.

Income

So as to understand the socio-economic status of any group, the level of income is very essential because the income is the most decisive factor in defining one's status in society. Income does not provide prestige which caste does but still it determines the intentions and capacity for use or misuse of the natural resources around him.

The status of an individual in the group differs on account of income variation even within the same occupation. According to Tripathi (1987), income is a crucial factor in determination of power, prestige, consumption pattern, control of services and utilities. Studies (Sharma, 1996; Iyer, 1996) show that the consumption of the resource and income levels is inter-related. Although environmental Kuznets Curve (EKC) Theory in general is not accepted by the environmentalists but still it has its own importance. This theory emphasizes that if we want to improve the environmental quality, then per capita income should be high. The theory goes that as the citizens get richer, it helps to clean the environment and conserve the natural resources. According to this theory, the best way to treat environmental problems is to get rich first, clean up later (cited from Martinez, 2007). In this context, income level becomes an important variable study. When respondents were asked about their income, they had a vivid picture of their annual income.

After receiving responses from the units of sample, 'income-groups' have been constituted. Since majority of the respondents are labourers, the income status of the respondents ought to show significant variations. Data with regard to income reveals that majority of the respondents (33.7%) have annual income between Rs. 5001 to Rs. 10,000 (Table 4.7). Respondents from Samanu (63.3%) constitute the majority of such respondents, followed by Dunera (38.3%). Such respondents have their least percentage in the village Uparla Thara (11.7%).

Further, 25.7 per cent of all the respondents earn an annual income of Rs. 10,001 to Rs. 15,000. From all, the village Dunera has the highest proportion (45.0%) and the lowest proportion is from Samanu (15.0%). These respondents who have the highest annual income varying from Rs. 20,001 and above, constitute 18 per cent of all the respondents. In this category, Uparla Thara (46.7%) has the largest proportion, followed by Basa and Gho. However, there is a small proportion of such respondent in Samanu (5.0%) and no such respondent is found in Dunera.

The respondents having annual earning up to Rs. 5,000 comprise of a very small number; only 5 per cent of the total sample. Such respondents have high proportion in Basa (11.7%) followed by Gho (5.0%); Samanu and Uparla Thara (3.3% each). Dunera has only 1.7 per cent of the respondents having income less than Rs. 5,000. The data thus shows that the respondents from Dunera and Uparla Thara earn higher income than that of the respondents from the other three villages. After analyzing the income related profile of the respondents, the median income of the villages under study has been calculated; of course on the basis of the data provided by the respondents.

Considering the annual median annual income of all the villages separately, a hierarchy of the villages has been observed.

Table 4.7: Income-wise Distribution of the Respondents

Income	*Name of Villages*					*Total*
	Gho	*Samanu*	*Uparla Thara*	*Basa*	*Dunera*	
Up to Rs. 5,000	3 (5.0)	2 (3.3)	2 (3.3)	7 (11.7)	1 (1.7)	15 (5.0)
Rs. 5,001 - Rs. 10,000	15 (25.0)	38 (63.3)	7 (11.7)	18 (30.0)	23 (38.3)	101 (33.7)
Rs. 10,001 - Rs. 15,000	14 (23.3)	9 (15.0)	14 (23.3)	13 (21.7)	27 (45.0)	77 (25.7)
Rs. 15,001- Rs. 20,000	17 (28.3)	8 (13.3)	9 (15.0)	10 (16.7)	9 (15.0)	53 (17.7)
Rs. 20,001 and above	11 (18.3)	3 (5.0)	28 (46.7)	12 (20.0)	— —	54 (18.0)
Total	60 (100.0)	60 (100.0)	60 (100.0)	60 (100.0)	60 (100.0)	300 (100.0)

Accordingly, Samanu stand at the bottom of this hierarchy with the median annual income of Rs. 7,339.2. In contrast, the village Uparla Thara with annual median income of Rs. 22500.50 occupies the top position. Other villages fall in between depending upon the position with the hierarchy, Basa (Rs. 14821.60); Dunera (10,295.05); and Gho (12, 500.50) hold respective position.

Income and occupation have been discussed individually, as prominent factors of analysis of the profile of the respondents. But both these factors are interrelated as well. Studies (Gill, 1991; Kaur, 2008) points out that the income level of the labourers is lower than those of the cultivators or manufacturers.

This variation also arises due to seasonal or temporary nature of certain activities, especially in the primary sector. The analysis of the data shows that of agricultural labourers (47.4%) and construction labourers (40.0%) earn an annual income varying between Rs. 5,001 to Rs. to 10,000 per year (Table 4.8). Those engaged in cottage industry too have a high proportion in the above category.

About 23 per cent of the cultivators have their annual income between Rs. 5,000 to Rs. 10,000. The proportion of cultivators in the category of those having annual income less than Rs. 5,000 is also high (13.6%).

None of the construction labourers has yearly income less than Rs. 5,000. Data further provides that most of the traders (32.1%) have high annual returns between Rs. 10,001 to Rs. 15,000. Many of the agricultural labourers are having this much annual income (28.2%). Servicemen have the highest percentage among those earning more than Rs. 20,001 per annum (45.8%). None of the cultivators has this much yearly income.

Table 4.8 : Distribution of the Respondents by Occupation and Income

Occupation \ Income	Up to 5,000	5,001-10,001	10,001-15,000	15,001-20,000	20,001 and above	Total
Cultivator	3 (13.6)	5 (22.7)	3 (13.6)	11 (11.0)	—	22 (7.3)
Agricultural Labour	2 (2.6)	37 (47.4)	22 (28.2)	12 (15.4)	5 (6.4)	78 (26.0)
Construction Labour	—	23 (40.0)	15 (26.3)	10 (17.5)	9 (15.8)	57 (19.0)
Servicemen	1 (2.1)	7 (14.6)	11 (22.9)	7 (14.6)	22 (45.8)	48 (16.0)
Trader	4 (7.5)	10 (18.9)	17 (32.1)	10 (18.0)	12 (22.6)	53 (17.7)
Cottage Industry	5 (11.9)	19 (45.2)	9 (21.4)	3 (7.1)	6 (14.3)	42 (14.0)
Total	15 (5.0)	101 (33.7)	77 (25.7)	53 (17.7)	54 (18.0)	300 (100.0)

Further analysis reveals that majority of the respondents in territory sector has the highest income level (Table 4.9). A significant proportion of the respondents in the secondary sector earn yearly income above Rs. 20,000. On the other hand majority of the respondents engaged in primary sector has yearly income level between Rs. 5,001 to Rs. 10,000.

Table 4.9 : Distribution of the Respondents by Income and Occupation Category

Occupation \ Income	Up to 5,000	5,001-10,001	10,001-15,000	15,001-20,000	20,001 and above	Total
Primary	5 (5.0)	42 (42.0)	25 (25.0)	23 (23.0)	5 (5.0)	100 (33.3)
Secondary	9 (5.9)	52 (34.2)	41 (26.9)	23 (15.1)	27 (17.8)	152 (50.7)
Tertiary	1 (2.1)	7 (14.6)	11 (22.9)	7 (14.6)	22 (45.8)	48 (16.0)
Total	15 (5.0)	101 (33.7)	77 (25.7)	53 (17.7)	54 (18.0)	300 (100.0)

Likewise, most of the respondents (34.2%) engaged in secondary sector have income between Rs. 5,001 to Rs. 10,000. Many of them have yearly income ranging between Rs. 10,001 to Rs. 15,000 (26.9%). Interestingly, the proportion of respondents in the lowest income category is high among those engaged in secondary sector as compared to those in primary sector.

On the basis of above analysis, it is hypothesized that higher the income level, the higher will be the prestige of the occupation held by an individual. The data in this regard has been computed in Table 4.10. Accordingly, majority of the respondents in high income category has the higher percentage in the high prestige occupations (39.3%) followed by those in low prestige occupations (33.6%). Not only this, the majority of the medium income group respondents (54.5%) has low prestige of occupation.

Table 4.10 : Distribution of Respondents by Occupation and Income

Income / Occupation	*High Prestige Income*	*Medium Prestige Income*	*Low Prestige Inome*	*Total*
High Prestige Occupation	42 (39.3)	63 (35.4)	12 (80.0)	117 (39.0)
Medium Prestige Occupation	29 (27.1)	18 (10.1)	1 (6.7)	48 (16.0)
Low Prestige Occupation	36 (33.6)	97 (54.5)	2 (13.3)	135 (45.0)
Total	107 (35.7)	178 (59.3)	15 (5.0)	300 (100.0)

A considerable proportion of the medium income respondents are found to have high prestige occupation. Further, the percentage of low income respondents is high in the high prestige occupations (80.0%). The correlation between the income category and occupation prestige is found to be insignificant (29.91, d.f. = 4, p=.05); thereby showing that high income is not necessarily related to high prestige occupation and *vice-versa*.

As no significant relationship exists between income and occupation, it was assumed that income may have a positive relation with caste. Keeping this in mind income and caste status has been tabulated (Table 4.11). Data in this regard reflect that majority of the upper caste respondents (37.0%) has high annual income (Rs. 20,001 and above). Nearly an equal percentage of low castes respondents has high per annum income level that is above Rs. 20,000. As compared to it, a high proportion of the backward caste respondents (46.7%) earn very less, that is up to Rs. 5,000 a year.

At the same time, 43.3 per cent of the backward castes respondents have annual income between Rs. 15,001 to 20,000. Further, majority of the respondents from lower castes (49.5%) earn Rs. 15,001– Rs. 20,000. The proportion of low caste respondents earning Rs. 20,001 and above is also significant (35.2%), which is more than that of the respondents earning the same income in backward caste respondents. In all, it is clear that the economic status of the low caste respondents is far better than that of the other respondents from the other two castes.

Table 4.11 : Distribution of the Respondents by Income and Caste

Caste / Income	Upper Caste	Backward Caste	Lower Caste	Total
Up to Rs. 5,000	4 (26.7)	7 (46.7)	4 (26.7)	15 (5.0)
Rs. 5,001 - Rs. 10,000	18 (17.8)	37 (36.6)	46 (45.5)	101 (33.7)
Rs. 10,001 - Rs. 15,000	15 (19.5)	30 (39.0)	32 (41.2)	77 (25.7)
Rs. 15,001 - Rs. 20,000	4 (7.5)	23 (43.3)	26 (49.5)	53 (17.7)
Rs. 20.001 and above	20 (37.0)	15 (27.8)	19 (35.2)	54 (18.0)
Total	61 (20.3)	112 (37.3)	127 (42.3)	300 (100.0)

It is also seen that from all the three caste groups, a small proportion of respondents fall in the income group up to Rs. 5,000 per year; whereas in upper caste respondents (26.7%) and the lower caste respondents (26.7%) are in the same proportion and the backward caste respondents (46.7%) hold the highest strength. The analysis thus provides that income is not necessarily related with caste status despite the fact that a high proportion of the upper castes have higher income level but its *vice versa* is not true.

Education

Education is crucial factor of analysis. Awareness level; participation rates; and efficiency of the respondents to address environment or the related issues, etc., are such contexts which largely get affected with the level of education of an individual. Though education does not provide the solutions to environmental degradation and the allied issues directly but it does help to create environmental conscience in individuals, whereby one becomes intellectually equipped to realize the importance of environment and its units. Keeping such a functionality of 'education' into consideration, it has been added as a factor of profile analysis of the respondents.

Majority of the respondents constituting 50.3 per cent of all are illiterates (Table 4.12). The highest proportion of illiterate respondents is from Dunera (68.3%); followed by Uparla Thara (50.0%); Gho (46.7%); and Samanu and Basa (43.3% each). This indicates that there is not much difference in condition related to illiteracy in the villages under study which is prevalent in most of the rural areas of India.

Table 4.12 : Education-wise Distribution of the Respondents

Educational Status	*Name of Villages*					*Total*
	Gho	*Samanu*	*Uparla Thara*	*Basa*	*Dunera*	
Illiterate	28 (46.7)	26 (43.3)	30 (50.0)	26 (43.3)	41 (68.3)	151 (50.3)
Up to 5th Standard	5 (8.3)	—	1 (1.7)	7 (11.7)	2 (3.3)	15 (5.0)
Up to 8th Standard	—	—	—	8 (13.3)	8 (13.3)	16 (5.3)
Up to Matric	27 (45.0)	34 (56.7)	19 (31.7)	16 (26.7)	9 (15.0)	105 (35.0)
Up to Twelfth (+2)	—	—	10 (16.7)	3 (5.0)	—	13 (4.3)
Total	60 (100.0)	60 (100.0)	60 (100.0)	60 (100.0)	60 (100.0)	300 (100.0)

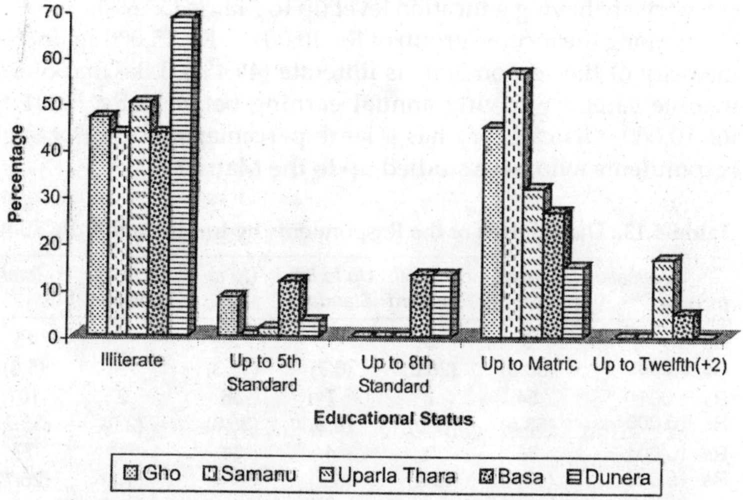

Figure 4.3 : Education-wise Distribution of the Respondents

Another 35 per cent of all the respondents have studied up to matric level. The proportion of such respondents has been the highest in Samanu (56.7%), followed by Gho (45.0%). Dunera has the least percentage of such respondents. Very few respondents are found to have studied above tenth.

Those who have studied up to twelfth (+2) are the respondents from village Uparla Thara (16.7%) and Basa (5.0%) only. None of the respondents from other villages in the sample have educational level above matric. Another feature of the area under study is that most of the respondents are either illiterates or have studied up to Matric. The percentage of the respondents who have studied below Matric is very small in all the villages.

An attempt has been made to analyze the interrelationship between education and income. It is largely believed that high educational status results into high income status. But the other facet of the phenomenon is also observed in many instances. People with high qualification standards are victims of trauma of inadequate income and economic dependency too; on the contrary, higher income is earned by people with lower educational standards. To understand the relationship between 'Income' and 'Education' in the study area, Table 4.13 has been incorporated. The majority of all the respondents earning between Rs. 5,001 to Rs. 10,000 per year are illiterate (53.5%). Many of the respondents in this income category are having education level up to Matric (35.6%).

Among the income group of Rs. 10,001 to Rs. 15,000 again, the majority of the respondents is illiterate (49.4%). Like that of the income category having annual earning between Rs. 5,001 to Rs. 10,000, this category has a large percentage (40.3%) of such respondents who have studied up to the Matric.

Table 4.13 : Distribution of the Respondents by Income and Education

Education / *Income*	*Illiterate*	*Up to 5th Standard*	*Up to 8th Standard*	*Up to Matric*	*Up to Twelfth (+2)*	*Total*
Up to Rs. 5,000	9 (60.0)	3 (20.0)	1 (6.7)	2 (13.3)	—	15 (5.0)
Rs. 5,001- Rs. 10,000	54 (53.5)	2 (2.0)	7 (6.9)	36 (35.6)	2 (2.0)	101 (33.7)
Rs. 10,001- Rs. 15,000	38 (49.4)	3 (3.9)	4 (5.2)	31 (40.3)	1 (1.3)	77 (25.7)
Rs. 15,001- Rs. 20,000	27 (50.9)	4 (7.5)	3 (5.7)	16 (30.2)	3 (5.7)	53 (16.7)
Rs. 20.001 and above	23 (42.6)	3 (5.6)	1 (1.9)	20 (37.0)	7 (13.0)	54 (18.0)
Total	151 (50.3)	15 (5.0)	16 (5.3)	105 (35.0)	13 (4.3)	300 (100.0)

A similar trend is seen in the other income groups with regard to educational level. Thus, respondents' income level does not show any consistency with their educational level. Of course, those having higher qualifications, i.e., above Matric are from the higher income group. In addition, the proportion of illiterates is high in the low income category. But the overall analysis does not show much consistency between education and income.

Marital Status

The discussion of the Marital Status of the respondents is inclusive of three categories. Those are respondents who are (i) Married; (ii) Unmarried; and (iii) Widow/Widower. The majority of all the respondents (80.0%) are married. Out of all such respondents, the largest proportion is from Basa (90.0%), followed by Gho (88.3%). The proportion of the unmarried is found to be more in Samanu (28.3%) and Dunera (26.7%) (Table 4.14).

Table 4.14 : Distribution of the Respondents by Marital Status

Marital Status	*Name of Villages*					*Total*
	Gho	*Samanu*	*Uparla Thara*	*Basa*	*Dunera*	
Married	53 (88.3)	42 (70.0)	48 (80.0)	54 (90.0)	43 (71.6)	240 (80.0)
Unmarried	7 (11.7)	17 (28.3)	9 (15.0)	6 (10.0)	16 (26.7)	55 (18.3)
Widow/ Widower	—	1 (1.7)	3 (5.0)	—	1 (1.7)	5 (1.7)
Total	60 (100.0)	60 (100.0)	60 (100.0)	60 (100.0)	60 (100.0)	300 (100.0)

The category of widow/widower holds the minimum strength (1.7%) of all the respondent. However, no respondent from Gho and Basa comes under this category. There are 5 per cent of such respondents from Uparla Thara and 1.7 per cent in Samanu and Dunera each.

Family Type

India, in context of its social institution is popular worldwide for joint family prominence. Specifically in rural areas of India, it is seen that joint family still dominates the pattern of affinal and consanguine groupings. But the pattern of existence of Social Institutions in Kandi area has been found to be variant from the general notion. Most of the households encompassed in the present study have nuclear set-ups. Joint family is not seen as the dominant preference in the social set-up of villages under study.

Data pertaining to family type reveals that the majority of all the respondents (69.3%) live in Nuclear families (Table 4.15). Out of all the five villages under study, the largest proportion of nuclear households is seen in Uparla Thara (81.7%), followed by Dunera (80.0%) with not a much difference. Gho has the smallest percentage of nuclear family households (50.0%).

In this case of the joint family set-ups, most of the respondents in Gho have joint families. This is followed by those from Samanu (38.3%). Some of the households have extended families and their proportion is very small and that too is found in Basa (3.3%) and Gho (1.7%). The analysis thus shows that a significant proportion

Table 4.15 : Distribution of the Respondents by Family Type

Type of Family	*Name of Villages*					*Total*
	Gho	*Samanu*	*Uparla Thara*	*Basa*	*Dunera*	
Nuclear Family	30 (50.0)	37 (61.7)	49 (81.7)	44 (73.3)	48 (80.0)	208 (69.3)
Joint Family	29 (48.3)	23 (38.3)	11 (18.3)	14 (23.3)	12 (20.0)	89 (29.7)
Extended Family	01 (1.7)	—	—	02 (3.3)	—	03 (1.0)
Total	60 (100.0)	60 (100.0)	60 (100.0)	60 (100.0)	60 (100.0)	300 (100.0)

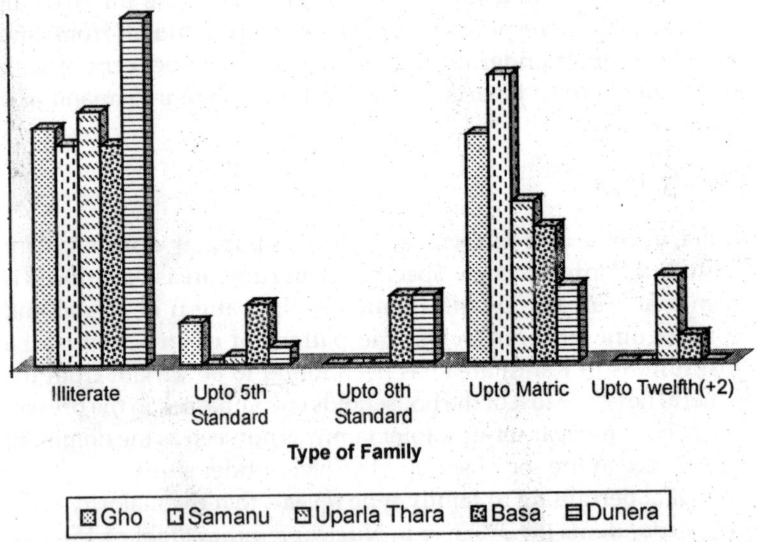

Figure 4.4 : Distribution of the Respondents by Family Type

Note: The numbering of Tables is different and the numbering of Diagrammatic figures is different. For example Table are running like 4.1 to 4-2... 4.14 and Diagrammatic Figures are running like 4.1 to 4.2, 4.3... etc.

of the respondents from Uparla Thara is from nuclear families and that from the village Gho is from joint family set ups. The data depicts an extreme difference in family pattern in the village

Gho and Uparla Thara. This oculor polarization is not seen in any other couplet of villages under the present study.

The analysis of the profile of the respondents depicts recognizable differences in the economic, marital, social, and educational profile of the respondents from different villages under study: a few instances of similarities between respondents from two or more villages are being observed in different contexts of discussion, but in general, various respondents possess invariably distinct features.

5 Deforestation and its Impacts

In contemporary era, where economic development has become a cardinal aim of the nations, environmental consequences are a serious concern. Deforestation is such an effect of developmental procedures undertaken by the government aggravated by the ignorance as well as civil negligence of the masses, which affects multiple aspects of human life. Kandi area falling under Pathankot tehsil, has also experienced deforestation in the recent years. The environmental profile of these areas has changed over the last ten years, but now the situation is deteriorating incessantly. Under this study, an attempt has been made to interpret environmental circumstances of the past and the present to forward the transformations in the environmental variables. The respondents have been asked questions regarding availability of tree/plants in the area over the past ten years and those at the present. This factor of analysis has been further linked with multiple other factors. The forthcoming part of this chapter deals with the causes of deforestation and its impacts on rural life and communities surviving thereon. While collecting data, sundry facts were discovered, which played an instrumental role in understanding and interpreting the environmental conditions of the Kandi area and further, it helped to interpret the consequences of environmental alterations which have taken place in the region.

Availability of Trees/Plants

Trees are a wealth of the nation. It is the type of trees grown in an area that provides the inhabitants a source of sustenance, income, fodder, timber and the like. Any change in the forest cover has a direct bearing on the life of the people. Secondly the composition of flora and fauna changes with the change in climatic conditions. Deciduous plants are being replaced with coniferous plants with rise in temperature and humidity. It is in this context that the availability of trees is being evaluated.

Respondents on being asked about the prominent types of trees and plants available in the area over the past ten years, majority of the respondents comprising of 97 per cent of them say that pipal, pla, khair, and mango trees have been prominently available in the area (Table 5.1). This view has been supported by 85 per cent respondents from Gho and 100 per cent of the respondents from the other four villages under study. Availability of these trees has been facilitation for the villages like Samanu, Uparla Thara, Basa and Dunera; but Gho has not been a beneficiary of this natural wealth like the other four villages under study.

Table 5.1 : Prominent Types of Trees/Plants available in the Area in the Past Ten Years

Prominent Trees	*Name of Villages*					*Total*
	Gho	*Samanu*	*Uparla Thara*	*Basa*	*Dunera*	
Pipal, Pla, Khair, Mango	51 (85.0)	60 (100.0)	60 (100.0)	60 (100.0)	60 (100.0)	291 (97.0)
Jamun, Leechi, Guava	—	41 (68.0)	60 (100.0)	—	20 (33.0)	121 (40.3)
Harar, Ber, Aamla	—	—	—	—	60 (100.0)	60 (20.0)
Taali, Arzaan	—	—	—	—	9 (15.0)	9 (3.0)

On the other hand, 40.3 per cent of the respondents state that trees of fruits like jamun, litchi and guava have been available in the region over the last ten years. The village-wise distribution of such respondents is 68 per cent in Samanu; 100 per cent in Uparla Thara and; 33 per cent in Dunera. Respondents from Gho and Tarhari Basa did not endorse this view at all, which makes it quite clear that these fruits were not available in these regions as that in villages like Uparla Thara and Samanu. However, the percentage of the respondents from Dunera falling in this category is also not as high as that of Samanu and Uparla Thara. In all, only 20 per cent of all the respondents comprising of ail the respondents from Dunera opine that Harar, Ber, Amla have been the prominent trees about ten years back. All the 100 per cent respondents from Dunera forward this view. It shows that there has been ample availability of fruits and herbal trees in Dunera; whereas other four villages under the study did not enjoy this ample availability. A negligible percentage of the total respondents, that is only 3 per cent are of the opinion that trees like Taali and Arzaan were the prominent ones about ten years back and the view is held by 15 per cent of the respondents, all of them are from Dunera village. The analysis shows that Dunera has been the richest village in the context of natural forests wealth. It had Pipal, Pla, Khair, Taali, Arzaan along with Harar, Ber, Amla, Mango, Litchi, Guava, and Jamun also over the past ten years. According to the villagers, the region had been rich in production of fruits as well as of wood, fodder, medicine and other products for commercial usage. The villages like Gho and Basa present the worst picture; only trees like Pipal, Pla and Khair have been there about ten years back. These villages lacked trees like Litchi, Guava, Jamun and herbals like Amla, Harar, etc. Herbal trees such as Harar, Amla, Ber, Arzaan never existed on the forest scene of Gho, Kot, Uparla Thara, and Basa. It shows that over the past 10 years the prominent trees available in the region have been Pipal, Pla, Khair and Mango, whereas certain fruits and herbal trees were exceptional to the area.

While having a discourse in the same context, 100 per cent of the respondents have stated that Khair, Pipal, Pla and Mango are available in the present times as well (Table 5.2). This view is held by respondents from Gho; Samanu; Uparla Thara; Basa and Dunera. Another 16.3 per cent of all the respondents say that Tali, Kikkar and Arzaan are the main trees at present. The village-wise distribution in this regard is 65 per cent in Uparla Thara and 16 per cent in Dunera. Further, 9 per cent of the respondents from the sample hold that Litchi, Jamun and Guava are available in the present times as well. The percentage of such respondents is 1.7 per cent in Samanu and 43.3 per cent in Dunera.

Availability of Amla, Harar and Ber at present has been supported by 20 per cent of all the respondents and all such respondents are from Dunera only. It is evident that Dunera still remains the richest in case of natural forests wealth comprising of trees like Khair, Pipal, Pla, Mango, Taali, Kikar, Arzaan, Amla,

Table 5.2 : Prominent Types of Trees and Plants available in the Area at Present

Prominent Types	*Name of Villages*					*Total*
	Gho	*Samanu*	*Uparla Thara*	*Basa*	*Dunera*	
Pipal, Pla, Khair, Mango	60 (100.0)	60 (100.0)	60 (100.0)	60 (100.0)	60 (100.0)	300 (100.0)
Taali Kikkar, Arzaan	—		39 (65.0)	—	10 (16.6)	49 (16.3)
Litchi, Guava, Jamun	—	1 (1.7)	— —	— —	26 (43.3)	27 (9.0)
Amla, Harar, Ber	—		—	—	60 (100.0)	60 (20.0)

Harar, Ber, Litchi, Guava, and Jamun also; though not uniformly found in other villages under study. From this it may be inferred that fruit trees are largely axed to meet the needs of the inhabitants. In spite of this mango tree continue to sustain because of the cottage industry that is "Aam Papad" flourishing in Dunera. Even the medicinal trees once found in abundance in Dunera, have been cut down. It is quite evident from the decrease in the strength of the response. On the other hand, trees largely maintained by the forests department such as Taali, Arzaan and Khair still occupy the prominent place in the forest cover. Peepal is also prominent because of its religious prominence among the people who are largely Hindus. The data collected for this very discussion makes it quite evident that the availability of multiple trees has remained intact in Dunera, but the other villages under the study have experienced a loss in this context over the passage of time.

On being asked about the reasons behind the change in the availability of these trees and plants over the past ten years, 49.6 per cent of the total respondents said that change in temperature, population pressure, and the consequent misuse and over-exploitation of the natural resources are the main reasons for the change in the forests cover (Table 5.3). These reasons have been forwarded by 46.7, 1.7 and 100 per cent of the respondents from Gho, Basa, Samanu and Uparla Thara respectively.

It is seen that a negligible quantum of respondents contribute to this response category from the village Basa in contrast to the

Table 5.3 : Reasons behind Changing Availability of Prominent Trees/Plants

Reasons	*Name of Villages*					*Total*
	Gho	*Samanu*	*Uparla Thara*	*Basa*	*Dunera*	
Change of temperature, population pressure	28 (47.7)	60 (100.0)	60 (100.0)	1 (1.7)	—	149 (49.7)
Soil Erosion, deceased soil fertility, deforestation	32 (53.3)	12 (20.0)	29 (48.3)	59 (98.3)	10 (16.7)	132 (44.0)

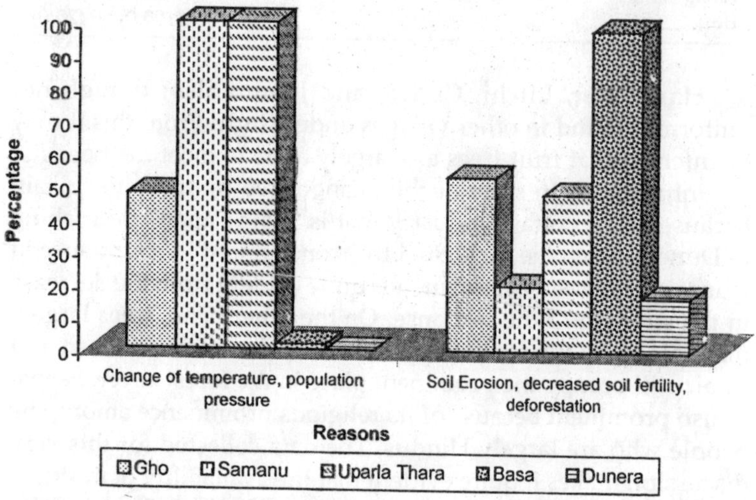

Figure 5.1 : Reasons behind Changing Availability of Prominent Trees/Plants

proportion of the respondents from Samanu and Uparla Thara. According to them, there has been a drastic change in the temperature of the region. They owe this temperature change to lesser rainfalls and even deforestation. In addition, they blame the ever increasing population of the region which has put a demand for more timber resulting in cutting of trees/plants that do not get replanted or regenerated. When asked about the reason of felling these trees, Mohinder Pal Singh, Sarpanch of Mangani Panchayat in Gho says that it is ignorant attitude, illiteracy and environment apathy of the villagers which has created the present unhealthy environmental circumstances. According to him, the people cut forests in an uncontrolled manner not thinking even once about repercussions of this act for the coming generations. According to his view, increasing population and its ignorant concern for the environmental maintenance are the main causes behind the present uncontrolled cutting of trees.

On the other hand, 44 per cent of the respondents express that soil erosion and deforestation are the main reasons for decline in the forest cover. The village-wise distribution of respondents under this response category is 53.3 per cent in Gho; 20 per cent in Samanu; 48.3 per cent in Uparla Thara and 98.3 per cent in Basa and 16.7 per cent in Dunera. According to these respondents, deforestation resulting into excessive soil erosion and followed by decline in the soil fertility are the main causes behind the changing availability of the trees/plants in the region.

Deforestation has taken place on a rampant scale in the region, due to which temperature has increased, thereby affecting the type of trees and crops grown in the region. As stated in chapter 3, the villagers have reported a change in the species grown in the region ten years back and now due to climatic change. Ignoring any of these factors is difficult task as somewhere or the other, these factors interplay in a complex matrix resulting into the stated decline in the availability of flora and fauna.

Nevertheless, deforestation and population pressure are associated with environmental changes and the consequent decline of the forest wealth, it is pertinent to know the benefits of the trees from the respondents point of view. Trees and plants cater to multiple needs of individuals and communities of those areas. According to 75.7 per cent of all the respondents, these trees and plants are crucial because people get fuel wood to cook, fodder for the domesticated animals and even medicines from some of the trees (Table 5.4). The village-wise distribution of the percentage shows that all the respondents from the village Samanu, Uparla Thara and Basa endorse this response; whereas it is only 78.3 per cent respondents from the village Gho who have forwarded the same view.

Many household domesticate cows and buffaloes for which there is a dire need of fodder to feed those animals. People consider it as on of the biggest advantages of trees and plants that they can avail the fodder without any cost.

Table 5.4 : Benefits of the Trees/Plants for Your Community

Benefits	*Name of Villages*					*Total*
	Gho	*Samanu*	*Uparla Thara*	*Basa*	*Dunera*	
Fodder + Fuel - wood	47 (78.3)	60 (100.0)	60 (100.0)	60 (100.0)	—	227 (75.7)
Earning and Employment	13 (21.7)			—	(60) (100.0)	73 (24.3)
Total	60 (20.0)	60 (20.0)	60 (20.0)	60 (20.0)	60 (20.0)	300 (100.0)

Further, 24.3 per cent of all the respondents add that the major benefits of the trees and plants for the communities dwelling in the Kandi region have been earning and employment. This view has been constituted by 21.7 per cent of the respondents from Gho and all the 100 per cent respondents from Dunera. The fruits are sold in the market and wood from Taali and Arzaan is used for lumbering industry. Katha processed from Khair trees provides handsome earning. Government has initiated 'Ten Years Felling Programme' in the area, which provides employment to the people. In this way, trees provide part-time and full-time employment opportunities to the residents. These trees are very important source of income for the inhabitants of the region. Trees are also a source of fodder for domesticated animals and raw material for the industry.

Effects of Changing Availability of Flora

There is an alarming rate of decline of forests cover in the tropical countries like India, Indonesia, Malaysia, etc. This has become a problem for environment and ecosystem. Deforestation has changed the micro environment of the region, soil erosion, loss of fertility and the like. In this regard, the respondents have been asked to elaborate the changes in their areas and its effect on community and the region. On being asked about the effects of this change on the area on community level, respondents forwarded two-fold responses. Nearly 62 per cent of the respondents say that with the decreasing availability of these trees and plants, there has been an adverse impact on availability of fodder for domesticated animals; earning of the individuals; agricultural productivity; availability of herbal medicine; and *pattal* making activity of the women of the region (Table 5.5).

Table 5.5 : Effects of the Changing Availability of Prominent Trees/Plants on the Community

Effects	*Name of Villages*					*Total*
	Gho	*Samanu*	*Uparla Thara*	*Basa*	*Dunera*	
Reduced Fodder and availability; lesser earning; lesser agriculture medicine, reduced *pattal* working	43 (78.7)	60 (100.0)	22 (36.7)	60 (100.0)	—	185 (61.7)
Weakening of Social bond	17 (28.3)	3 (5)	37 (61.7)	—	—	57 (19.0)

People could earn money by selling fruits and *pattals* made from broad leaves of the trees. With cutting of forests, the availability of natural medicines and herbs has also decreased which had been very useful for healing wounds or to cure minor ailments. This response has been forwarded by 71.7 per cent of the respondents from Gho, 100 per cent from Basa and Samanu, and 36.7 per cent from Uparla Thara. However, the respondents of Dunera did not opine under this response as they have not experienced any decrease in the availability of the trees/plants in their region.

On the contrary, Samanu Basa, Gho and Uparla Thara have been a great losers in this context. In the preceding part of this chapter, it has been pointed out that the level of deforestation in Dunera is extremely low; thereby it maintains its rich diversity of trees. Rest of the respondents constituting 19 per cent say that the decreased availability of trees and plants in their areas has weakened the social bonds of the villagers. Percentage distribution is 28.3 per cent in Gho; 5 per cent in Samanu and 61.7 per cent in Uparla Thara.

Perhaps, it can be said that this effect has been manifestly realized by respondents from these three villages only, unlike that of the respondents from Dunera. People are largely old and irrespective of their sex have expressed that trees like Peepal, Mango and other huge trees were the meeting points of the residents. People used to share information and pass time by gossiping with each other for hours together. In this way, the trees served the purpose of social bondage among individuals and families. Leaving aside other factors, cutting of such trees has affected the interaction process and thereby weakened the social bonds. Uparla Thara has experienced the deforestation the most as is evident from the data. It is presumed as a social loss for the villages and the communities living thereon the main source of these products were forest trees.

Analyzing the impact of the decreased availability of trees and plants at village level, various eye catching responses have been derived. Approximately 43.3 per cent of the total respondents say that it has led to aggravation of poverty (Table 5.6).

Table 5.6 : Effects of Changing Availability of Prominent Trees/Plants on Village Level

Effects	*Name of Villages*					*Total*
	Gho	*Samanu*	*Uparla Thara*	*Basa*	*Dunera*	
Increased Poverty	20 (33.13)	54 (90.0)	14 (23.3)	42 (70.0)	—	130 (43.3)
Fertility of soil has reduced	40 (66.7)	14 (23.3)	56 (93.3)	—	—	110 (36.7)
Weakend Social Bonds	17 (28.3)	3 (5.0)	37 61.7)	—	—	57 (19.0)
Income has reduced	—	—	—	18 (30.0)	—	18 (6.0)

People used to earn by selling fruits and *pattals* and the main source of the raw material were the forest products. They could also save money by collecting leaves, twigs, and grass from the forests to be used as fodder for the domesticated animals but now they have to depend upon the market. The percentage of the respondents sharing this view is 33.3 per cent in Gho; 90 per cent in Samanu; 23.3 per cent in Uparla Thara and 70 per cent in Basa. Another 36.7 per cent of all the respondents state that the major impact of decline of forest cover on the villages is the decline fertility of soil and increased temperature. The village-wise distribution of such respondents is 66.7 per cent in Gho;

23.3 per cent in Samanu; and 93.3 per cent in Uparla Thara. The inhabitants of Basa and Dunera do not support the above connotation. In their views, soil fertility and temperature have not been affected so far. Further, even among the respondents who state decline of fertility and rise of temperature, there is a variation. As compared to Kot, the percentage of respondents from Uparla Thara and Gho is more of those who find a decline in soil fertility and temperature shift further affecting the agricultural productivity. This may be attributed to the level of deforestation occurred in these villages.

Other 19 per cent of all the respondents assert that other major effect of this change is the weakening of the social bonds. This percentage has been constituted by the 28.3 per cent respondent from Gho; 5 per cent from Samanu and 61.7 per cent from Uparla Thara. In case of villages like Basa and Dunera this phenomenon has not been noticed. Further, as per the data collected for the study, 6 per cent of all the respondents comprising of 30 per cent from Basa only, opine that the major impact of this change has been on the income level of the villages; as the decreased individual income has largely affected the regional income too.

As far as the effect of the decreasing availability of plants and trees on individual level is concerned, only 52.3 per cent of all the respondents have recorded their response. Out of these, 48.4 per cent respondents say that the effects of this changing availability of trees/plants on an individual are not specific ones (Table 5.7). This response has been constituted by 46.6 per cent of the respondents from Gho and 80 per cent from Basa. However, the respondents from Samanu, Uparla Thara and Dunera do not opine under this response category.

Table 5.7 : Effects of the Changing Availability of Prominent Trees/Plants on Your Own Self

Effects	*Name of Villages*					*Total*
	Gho	*Samanu*	*Uparla Thara*	*Basa*	*Dunera*	
Not any Specific effect	28 (46.7)	—	—	48 (80.0)	—	76 (48.4)
Increased Economic Burden	32 (53.3)	15 (25.0)	22 (36.7)	12 (20.0)	—	81 (51.6)
Total	60 (38.2)	15 (9.6)	22 (14.0)	60 (38.2)	—	157 (52.3)

On the other hand, 51.6 per cent of the respondents express that this environmental change has increased their economic burden. This view is shared by 53.3 per cent of the respondents from Gho; 25 per cent from in Samanu, 36.7 per cent from Uparla Thara and in 20 per cent from Basa. There is a small difference between the percentage of the respondents from Samanu and Basa under this category. However, the largest proportion of the respondents supporting this view is from Gho, followed by Uparla Thara. Garib Das, Patwari in Gho says that many people living in the villages in proximity to the forests get forest job on contractual basis many times in a year. Nature of such forest jobs is digging holes for replantations, collecting wood for government based project, extracting medicinal leaves or liquids from some specific forest trees like Bel (*Bel Pattar*) and Arzaan, etc. He tells that a tree named 'Khair', from which *kaththa* is extracted after 10 years growth of the tree. The government extracts *kaththa* from trees of *Khair* after their stem attain a radius of 2½ feet. People of the nearly villages are employed for cutting, pealing those huge stems and extracting that semi-solid, which is boiled afterwards to produce Kaththa. Garib Das said that this business fetches a lot of income for the people employed by forest department. Another benefit stated by him is in context of the tree 'Pla' which provides huge leaves used by the women of Kandi area to make *Pattals* (in regional language known as *pattar*, disposables used to serve food at huge gatherings, especially in Gurudwaras for *langar* which is Holy Communion). Garib Das said that women of his village used to earn an optimum amount per year with sale of these hand-made *pattals*. But, with immense cutting of forests these trees are not available in ample quantity and at convenient distance as they used to be available in the past. Hence, this environmental degradation has affected the economic standards of the people and consequently that of the village too.

As discussed in the preceding part of this chapter also, the trees and plants available in the region provide many products and services to the people, with which people could save a lot of money and some could also earn from them. For example there was never a need to spend money on availing fodder for the domesticated animals; fuelwood for household purpose; fruits and herbal medicine, etc. But with decrease in quantum of trees/plants in the region, the availability of these goods and services has been largely affected. Residents of these villages have to spend money on availing these goods and services. In other words the economic self reliance of the region and the dwellers thereon has largely been affected.

Role and Importance of Forests

Forests have always been a popular source of sustenance for the rural and tribal masses. Forests acts as service providers goods producers, and carbon-sink also. Metz (2007) has also opined that plantation can contribute positively, for example to employment, economic growth, and export renewable energy supply and poverty alleviation, therefore, renders an empirical hand and supports the notions discussed in this part of the chapter. A significant proportion of the sample holds the belief that if more plantations are undertaken the environmental conditions of the region can improve thereby improving the economic scenario too.

The abovestated qualities of forests are well acknowledged by the residents of Kandi area of Punjab. Though literacy rate in the villages of Kandi area and also that of the villages under research is very low, but still the residents are adequately aware of the environmental circumstances around them. They understand and interpret the general importance of forests and trees with environmental consequences. All the respondents irrespective of village category find that forests are a crucial component of survival for the people of the villages (Table 5.8).

Table 5.8 : Benefits of the Trees and Forests for Your Village

Benefits	*Name of Villages*					*Total*
	Gho	*Samanu*	*Uparla Thara*	*Basa*	*Dunera*	
Control Temperature; Soil Fertility Maintenance; Economic Stability	60 (100)	60 (100)	60 (100)	60 (100)	60 (100)	300 (100)
Wildlife Protection	—	1 (1.7)	—	—	60 (100.0)	61 (20.3)
Health Maintenance	—	3 (4.8)	—	—	60 (95.2)	63 (21.0)

The reason in their opinion is that forests preserve soil fertility. Secondly, thick cover of forests acts as an instrument to maintain temperature. Temperature remains moderate in an area, where forest cover is adequately spread. Above all, people hold a view that forest help mankind to maintain economy because many forest products are available free of cost, which otherwise need a lot of expenditure, if bought from a commercial place. In addition, the respondents say that forests maintain fertility of the soil by controlling soil erosion in the region. Maintained fertility further contributes to agricultural production; thereby strengthen the economy of the communities associated with cultivation. If agriculture is flourishing and agriculture produce is being available in ample, it obviously results into good income. There is another addition to the importance of forests that has been forwarded by only 20.3 per cent of the respondents who hold that forests protect and maintain wildlife in general. This view is held by 1.7 per cent of the respondents from the Samanu. In addition to this, 21 per cent of all the respondents and all from Samanu say that forests help to maintain a good health because these absorb all the pollutants and toxicating gases to release fresh air. This view is held by all the respondents from Dunera and 5 per cent from Samanu and all the 100 per cent respondents from Dunera. The variation in the data forwarded by these two villages show that the respondents from Dunera are a manifest beneficiary of the forest and the forests products with no exception.

No doubt, people are aware of the general use of forests, it becomes crucial to know the specific advantages of forests for the area and the people dwelling thereon. All the 100 per cent respondents hold a similar view. Forests help the people by providing fodder for their animals which is one of the most crucial features of forests according to them (Table 5.9).

With this facility, villagers are able to get fodder for the cattle. They do not have to commute to cities for getting it. It saves a lot of time and money both. Another advantage of forests for people living in the area is the easy availability of fuelwood and medicine. According to these people, these goods and services are a boon for them because they are their daily needs without which their life cannot run. Fuelwood is required everyday to cook food in households. Natural medicine in the form of wild herbs or some specific forests plants helps them to prepare home remedies for

Table 5.9 : Advantages of Forests for the Area and the People Living Here

Advantages	*Name of Villages*					*Total*
	Ghc	*Samanu*	*Uparla Thara*	*Basa*	*Dunera*	
Provision of Fodder, Fuel Wood, Temperature Control	60 (100.0)	60 (100.0)	60 (100.0)	60 (100.0)	60 (100.0)	300 (100.0)
Maintain quality of atmosphere	–	–	23 (38.3)	–	18 (30)	41 (13.6)
Generate Employment	50 (83.3)	57 (95.0)	45 (75.0)	60 (100.0)	60 (100.0)	60 (20.0)

treatment minor ailments or diseases. Protection of wildlife is another function of the forests as held by 13.7 per cent of all the respondents. This percentage comprises of 38.3 per cent respondents from Uparla Thara and 30 per cent from Dunera. People feel a sense of belongingness with the wildlife too. According to them, there are some specific species which are available in the Kandi region only. They also feel pride over this regional possession. According to other 20 per cent of all the respondents, forests are a source of generating employment. This view is held by 100 per cent of the respondents from Dunera. No respondent from any other village has reported this function of the forests.

According to the dwellers of Dunera, people living in the areas situated near forests or in variable proximity get jobs on part-time or *ad hoc* basis whenever the government undertakes any forest based project or programme. NGO working in the region undertakes afforestation programmes which again gives job opportunities to the people living in the nearby villages. Moreover, 90.7 per cent of all the respondents find that another important function of forests is to maintain quantity of the atmosphere. This view is expressed by 83.3, 95 and 75 pre cent from Gho, Samanu and Uparla Thara and all the respondents from Basa and Dunera. So, provisions of fodder, fuelwood, and employment, preservation of the wildlife and maintenance of the good quality of atmosphere are the main functions of the forests.

Impact of Deforestation

Environmental studies (Aggarwal, 2002; Saxena, 1996; Speth, 2004) undertaken in the recent decade made it ocular to the world that deforestation has rendered irreparable losses to the mankind; and has forwarded conditions of panic for the survival of the forest dependent communities. There exists a variation in the global, regional and national environmental consequences of deforestation; depending upon the variability of dependency of the respective region on the natural environment and its units. The consequences of deforestation in case of developing and under-developed nations take even a serious form. There are large number of communities dependent on forests for their sustenance and get drastically affected by deforestation. The rural belt of Kandi region is a manifestation of such dependence. The dwellers of this region depend upon the natural environment especially forests for maintaining their economy, organizing household activities and for many other purposes like getting herbal medicine, fuelwood and wood for construction purpose, fodder for domesticated animals, etc. With no leeway left, it becomes clear that deforestation is a threat for survival of the residents and prosperity of the region. This has been manifested in the following discussion.

With decreased availability of forests, many activities have been affected. Multiple changes have been bought in lives of the dwellers with decreased forest cover in the region as 80 per cent of the respondents say that the routine activity of collecting fuel-wood and fodder has been affected largely (Table 5.10).

This view is supported by 100 per cent of the respondents from Samanu, Gho, and Uparla Thara; whereas 66.7 per cent and 33.3 per cent of the respondents from Basa and Dunera support this view. Earlier the forests were available at a shorter distance, hence these activities like collecting fodder and fuelwood consumed less time and less physical efforts as well. But now, the distance between the forests and the villages has increased with deforestation. People take more time to collect fuelwood and fodder from the forests than what they used to spend in the past. In many cases, people have stopped collecting these goods from the forests rather; they spend money to buy/hire the goods from the market. All the respondents from the selected villages have stated that forests and soil fertility are interlinked; deforestation has been responsible

Table 5.10 : Deforestation and its Impacts

Impact of deforestation	*Name of Villages*					*Total*
	Gho	*Samanu*	*Uparla Thara*	*Basa*	*Dunera*	
Maintenance of Soil Fertility	60 (100.0)	60 (100.0)	60 (100.0)	60 (100.0)	60 (100.0)	300 (100.0)
Availability of Fuel Wood and Fodder	60 (100.0)	60 (100.0)	60 (100.0)	40 (66.7)	20 (33.3)	240 (80.0)
Religious activities	—	3 (5.0)	—	—	—	3 (1.0)
Medicinal Plants	30 (50.0)	26 (43.3)	16 (26.7)	22 (36.7)	—	94 (31.3)
Female Literacy	—	—	—	—	60 (100.0)	60 (20.0)
Health Maintenance	—	—	—	—	60 (100.0)	60 (20.0)

for decline of soil fertility. A very negligible percentage that is only 1 per cent of all the respondents says that decreased availability of forests has also affected religious activities. This group constitutes 5 per cent of the respondents from Samanu only. No respondent from any other village under study say anything in context of 'Totemism'. It is a practice in which a tree in particular, plant, an animal, is considered as an object of reverence and it is worshipped as a sacred part of life. According to the residents of Samanu, earlier the dwellers of these villages would worship forests as a 'God' and the some trees or species of birds and animals available inside forests as totems; but now this practice has nearly come to an end. People have now been mentally detached from forests as a spiritual entity. People attribute this phenomenon of mental change to excessive cutting of forests and trees. They say that many forms of worship have ended with cutting of forests and non-availability of many trees.

Discussing another important context, 31.3 per cent of the respondents constitute 50, 43.3, 26.7 and 36.7 per cent respondents from Gho, Samanu, Uparla Thara and Basa express that earlier extracting medicine from wild herbs, plants and trees was very prominent in the regions. But now, with reduced forest cover, this activity has been affected. There is almost negligible quantity available of ayurvedic/natural medicine. As per the views given by the people the communities in the past entirely depended upon the ayurvedic and herbal medicines for minor as well as major ailments, but now they depend upon allopathic medicines in the absence of adequate availability of herbal shrubs and plants. Further, 20 per cent of the total respondents (all such respondents from village Dunera) have stated that the maintenance of the forests cover in their region has made female literacy possible in addition to better health condition. Thus, deforestation has been responsible for lack of availability of fuelwood, fodder, medicinal plants and change in the soil fertility levels as a result, their monthly expenditure have been affected.

According to the respondents, the monthly expenditure of the residents of the villages of Kandi areas has increased ranging from less than Rs. 500 to more than Rs. 2,000 due to reduced availability of forests. It is only 0.6 per cent of the total respondents comprising of 3.3 per cent respondents from Gho, tell that now they spend between rupees 100-500 to avail those goods and services from market which were once available through the forests (Table 5.11).

Table 5.11 : Per Month Increase in Expenditure due to Deforestation

Per Month Increase	*Name of Villages*					*Total*
	Gho	*Samanu*	*Uparla Thara*	*Basa*	*Dunera*	
Rs. 100–500	2 (3.3)	—	—	—	—	2 (0.7)
Rs. 500–1000	2 (3.3)	21 (35.0)	13 (21.6)	14 (23.3)	—	50 (16.7)
Rs. 1000–1500	30 (50.0)	32 (53.3)	—	46 (76.7)	—	108 (36.0)
Rs. 1500–2000	26 (43.3)	6 (10)	37 (61.7)	—	—	69 (23.0)
Rs. 2000–2500	—	2 (3.3)	10 (16.7)	—	—	12 (4.0)

Other 16.7 per cent of all the respondents say that their expenditure has increased between Rs. 500-1000. The percentages of such respondents in the selected villages is 3.3 from Gho, 35.0 from Samanu, 21.6 from Uparla Thara and 23.3 from Basa. Another 36 per cent of the total respondents say that their expenditure on buying these goods and services ranges between Rs. 1,000 to lesser than Rs. 1,500. The distribution of such respondents in the selected

villages is 50 per cent in Gho, 53.3 per cent in Samanu and 76.7 per cent in Basa. Forwarding a more intense response, 23 per cent of the respondents express that their monthly expenditure has raised by more than Rs. 1,500 to lesser than Rs. 2,000. Such respondents constitute 43.3, 10 and 61.7 per cent from Gho, Samanu and Uparla Thara respectively. Only 4 per cent of the total respondents state that their expenditure for the goods that they get from forests has increased by Rs. 2000. The hereby mentioned category includes 3.3 per cent respondents from Samanu and 16.7 per cent from Uparla Thara. Interestingly, the respondents from Dunera village have not reported increase in expenditures. This is the village which has sufficient forest cover. From the above discussion it can be inferred that no doubt deforestation has occurred in whole of the Kandi areas but still the intensity or dimensions of its economic impact is not similar. In some cases people spend about more than Rs. 100 on availing the goods and services from markets, which were available absolutely free of cost in an adequate quantum from the forests.

On the contrary, expenditure of some of the households has increased to more than Rs. 2,000 a month for availing similar products and services. Probably this difference is backed by several factors like, the number of the animals being domesticated by the household; distance from the neighbouring forests affecting the convenient collection of fuelwood and fodder; distance of the village from the markets from which the goods and services can be bought/ hired; standard of living of the individual households; income of the household, etc. Those are such factors which have largely influenced the monthly expenditure of the residents. On the whole, deforestation has affected the economic stability of the life of the residents of Kandi area. Chattopadhyay (2004) also opines that environmental degradation has severe consequences on the economic well-being of the people along with other aspects of life.

In apposition to the discussion, 80 per cent of all the respondents said that this change has affected the economic standard of the area because it has led to increase in economic burden and poverty (Table 5.12). This view has been forwarded by 100 per cent respondents from the villages Gho, Samanu, Uparla Thara and Basa. On the contrary, 20 per cent of all the respondents inclusive of all the respondents from Dunera say that their economic standards have raised. In the past, villagers could extract fuelwood; wood for construction of houses and for furnitures; natural herbs and medicines; fodder for their domesticated animals, etc., but as a matter of serious concern, with increased deforestation, the availability of these forests products has decreased and the villagers now need to spend huge amount to avail those goods and services from the market, due to which their monthly budget has drastically been affected.

Table 5.12 : Deforestation and the Overall Economic Standard of the Area

Impact	*Name of Villages*					*Total*
	Gho	*Samanu*	*Uparla Thara*	*Basa*	*Dunera*	
Decreased	60 (100.0)	60 (100.0)	60 (100.0)	60 (100.0)	—	240 (80.0)
Not affected	—	—	—	—	60 (100.0)	60 (20.0)
Total	60 (20.0)	60 (20.0)	60 (20.0)	60 (20.0)	60 (20.0)	300 (100.0)

In addition, deforestation has led to increased loan burden on the villagers. Earlier they could construct their houses with the wood available from the forests and now they have to buy it. To cater to this need, they adhere to taking loans from banks and come under a severe debt strain. Now people want to have brick-lines houses as compared to the earlier type. This may be another factor contributing to the escalated cost of the houses as all the building material has to be bought from the market. The respondents in addition express that due to rampant deforestation, the temperature of the region has changed which has further affected the productivity, further affecting the income of the villagers from commercial use of agricultural products. All this has made the economy of the households as well as villages unstable. And in case of Dunera there has been no deforestation as that in case of other villages under study; due to which the economic standards have not been affected much so far.

Factors behind Deforestation

In present times, deforestation is that form of environmental degradation, which is ruining mostly all the parts of the developing and underdeveloped world (although lesser in developed part) but the factors behind deforestation are different in each region. Though the cutting of forests in developing world is undertaken for the crucial developmental purposes like industrialization; expansion of residential areas, expansion of commercial centres, etc. but the environmental consequences directly have not the sustainability criteria. In an apposition, people of Kandi areas express that there is a play of different factors contributing to deforestation. A response group comprising of 40.7 per cent of all the respondents say that deforestation took place because of excessive population pressure on the natural resource followed by unregulated exploitation of forests by the people (Table 5.13). The percentage in the selected villages is 43.3 per cent in Gho; 81.6 per cent in Samanu; and 78.3 per cent in Basa. There lies a significant difference between the response statistics derived from Gho and that of Samanu and Basa. A lesser proportion of people from Gho support this particular factor.

Table 5.13 : Main Causes behind Deforestation

Main Causes	*Name of Villages*					*Total*
	Gho	*Samanu*	*Uparla Thara*	*Basa*	*Dunera*	
Excessive exploitation by + ever increasing Population	26 (43.3)	49 (81.7)	—	47 (78.3)	—	122 (40.7)
Corruption and Lack of Vigilance by the forest department	—	31 (51.7)	—	10 (16.7)	—	41 (13.7)
Construction of Dam	—	—	50 (83.3)	—	—	50 (16.7)
Construction of Residential Colonies in Dam site	8 (13.3)	—	28 (46.7)	—	—	36 (12)
Agricultural Expansion	46 (76.7)	19 (31.7)	—	32 (53.3)	—	97 (32.3)

The ever expanding population consistently exploits the natural resources for availing goods and services for the survival. The main reason behind this overuse and exploitation of natural resource is saving of money. People do not have to spend money on those things which are availed from the forests. Another view has been constituted by 13.7 per cent respondents who hold that the main reason behind in uncontrolled cutting of forests is careless government and corruption in the forest department. All such respondents strongly believe that had corruption not been there, the condition of the environment in their region and the status of the infrastructure would have been better. The study conducted by Tihiliani (2008) also supports the same finding. This response encapsulates 51.7 per cent of the total respondents from Samanu and 16.7 per cent from Basa. People believe that had the government undertaken programmes of afforestation or had the forest officers and forest guards been strict and honest, the conditions of forests in Kandi areas would not have been so worse and deplorable as it is in the present times. Other 16.7 per cent respondents constitute 83.3 per cent respondents from Uparla Thara say that deforestation has taken place due to the construction of Ranjit Sagar Dam at the Shahpur Kandi. Nonetheless, another 12 per cent of the total respondents express that the problem of deforestation has further got intensified due to expansion of residential area in the rural regions; which is again a consequence of the growing population. The percentage of such respondents in the selected villages is 13.3 per cent (Gho) and 46.7 per cent (Uparla Thara). Respondents from Uparla Thara say that firstly forests have been cut to use the land for the construction of Dam; and secondly, it further reduced because of construction of three residential colonies to provide residence to the employees of dam site. This colony has three types. Many people of Uparla Thara who got employed in the project of Ranjit Sagar Dam have now shifted to this colony with their families. Though construction of this colony and provision for the convenient survival of the dwellers symbolize adequate infrastructural development; but the environmental loss cannot be ignored.

Expansion of agriculture is another reason behind deforestation. The global forest cover is on a consistent decline, rendering multiple non-manageable survival related issue for the dependent communities and regions. "Most relevant for the carbon cycle is that between 2000 and 2005, gross deforestation continued at a rate of 12.9 million ha/yr, mainly as a result of converting forests into agricultural land, and also due to expansion of settlements and infrastructure, often for logging" (Metz, 2007).

Similar notion forwarded by Panda (2007) along with Metz, find a concrete reflection in the responses given by the respondents as a group of 32.3 per cent of all the respondents asserts that it is due to the expansion of the agriculture that forests have been cut incessantly; supported by 76.7 per cent of the respondents from Gho; 31.7 per cent from Samanu; and 53.3 per cent from Basa. Coincidentally, these three villages have resembling economic conditions, but still agricultural expansion has not been undertaken in Samanu in the same intensity as it has been done in villages like Gho and Basa.

Like many other villages of Kandi areas, these three villages have also suffered from immense economic deterioration due to declining agriculture affluence. Earlier the agricultural products like maa, chana, til, kulth were available in adequate quantity. The soil of these regions was so fertile that people easily fetched a reliant amount from these commercial goods and, hence, earned a lot of income. Later on, with the passage of time, sundry factors resulted into a degradation of soil fertility, followed by decline in the quantum of agricultural products. These factors are decreased rainfall; increased soil erosion and change in the temperature of the area. Moreover, the cultivators are not properly applying fertilizers due to poor economic conditions. With all these factors, the agriculture production has decreased. According to the people of Kandi area, when agricultural production reduced, they realized a need to expand the agricultural fields. In such a situation, forest lands are exploited and get converted into agricultural lands easily.

Just like the causes of deforestation, the effects are also not the same in different regions. Various activities got started in the region after deforestation. Not all, but 76.7 per cent of all the respondents contributed responses to the discussion, out of which 73.9 per cent say that after deforestation the vacated land is being used for agricultural activities (Table 5.14). This view has been held by 100 per cent of the respondents from Gho and Basa; and 83.3 per cent of the respondents from Samanu.

On the other hand, 26.1 per cent of the respondents (all such respondents from Uparla Thara) say that deforestation has occurred due to construction of Dam in the region. The site of Ranjit Sagar Dam is situated in Shahpur Kandi region, which is in proximity to the village Uparla Thara. A huge mass of land has been deforested for the purpose of construction of Dam. The construction of dam after deforestation contributed to the economic development of the area as a market has come up along with improvement in health and educational facilities.

Interestingly, Dunera has not witnessed deforestation on a large scale. The reason is that in their region, deforestation has not taken place at all. The region still has a thick forest cover. It can be deduced that with deforestation, efforts to increase agriculture in the area has contributed to raising productivity and improving economic status. On the other hand, construction of dam also has motives related to economic development as establishment of the colony and dam has made infrastructural development of the area.

Table 5.14 : Activities started in your Region after Deforestation

Activities	*Name of Villages*					*Total*
	Gho	*Samanu*	*Uparla Thara*	*Basa*	*Dunera*	
Agriculture	60 (100)	50 (83.3)	—	60 (100)	—	170 (73.9)
Construction of dam	—	—	60 (100)	— —	— —	60 (26.1)
Total	60 (26.1)	50 (21.7)	60 (26.1)	60 (26.1)	— —	230 (76.7)

It is amply justified from the analysis of the impacts these activities have had on the area. Forwarding a response to the context, 35.8 per cent of the total respondents comprising of 26.7 per cent from Gho, 6.7 per cent from Basa, and 93.3 per cent from Uparla Thara say that these activities have uplifted their economic condition (Table 5.15).

Table 5.15 : Impact of that Activity on Your Area

Impact	*Name of Villages*					*Total*
	Gho	*Samanu*	*Uparla Thara*	*Basa*	*Dunera*	
Economic Upliftment	16 (26.7)	—	56 (93.3)	4 (6.7)	—	76 (35.8)
Further degradation of economy	8 (13.3)	22 (36.7)	—	52 (86.7)	—	82 (38.7)
Not specific	36 (60.0)	14 (23.3)	—	4 (6.7)	—	54 (25.4)
Total	60 (28.3)	36 (17.0)	56 (26.4)	60 28.3)	—	212 (70.7)

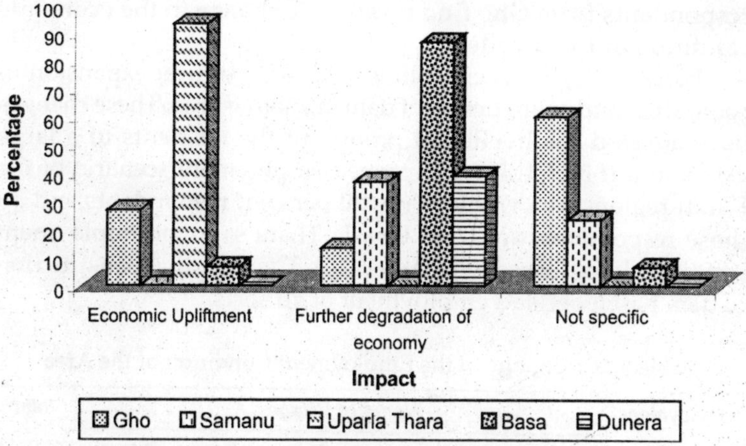

Figure 5.2 : Impact of that Activity on Your Area

In case of Uparla Thara, it is quite evident from the preceding discussions that construction of Dam in the region has improved the employment scenario and infrastructural facilities. On the other hand, due to expansion of agricultural, there has been a positive change in agricultural productivity. On the contrary 38.7 per cent of the total respondents say that with increased deforestation in the region the economic conditions have further deteriorated. The percentage of such respondents in the selected villages like Gho, Samanu and Basa is 13.3, 36.7 and 86.7 per cent respectively. In their opinion, people now have to spend a huge amount of money on availing all those forest products and services, which were availed free of cost in the past when the green cover was available in a significant quantum.

However, 25.4 per cent of the total respondents say that they have not experienced any specified impact of deforestation. They say that they have neither realized any economic upliftment in the region, nor they experienced any further downfall in the economic standards of the area. This category includes 60 per cent of respondents from Gho; 23.3 per cent from Samanu and 6.7 per cent from Basa. Thus, the majority of the respondents from Uparla Thara find that activities started after deforestation has uplifted their economy. On the other hand, the majority of respondents from Basa find degradation of their economy related to deforestation. Many of the respondents form Gho find no specific change in the economic condition of the dwellers.

Forests have been cut followed by agricultural expansion in some areas and construction of dam in another area. These changes have affected the livelihood pattern of the residents to a large extent, but it has still not improved employment scenario of the Kandi regions as a whole. Only 20 per cent respondents and all those respondents are from Uparla Thara say that employment condition have improved (Table 5.16). They say that construction of dam has generated employment of all sorts.

Table 5.16 : Change in the Employment Condition of the Area

Employment	*Name of Villages*					*Total*
	Gho	*Samanu*	*Uparla Thara*	*Basa*	*Dunera*	
Same	—	—	—	—	60 (100.0)	60 (20.0)
Increased	—	—	60 (100.0)	—	—	60 (20.0)
No at all	60 (100.0)	60 (100.0)	—	60 (100.0)		180 (60.0)
Total	60 (20.0)	60 (20.0)	60 (20.0)	60 (20.0)	60 (20.0)	300 (100.0)

Rests of the respondents in the sample have not experienced any improvements in the employment scenario. They say that employment opportunities were neither available in the past nor have seen any improvement in employment scenario of the region in the recent times. Of course, respondents from Dunera have ample employment opportunities because of its being on the main transport artery with a number of trade activities. So for them, there is no change in employment related opportunities.

Extinction of Species

Fauna in the region is in fact the regional wealth of the area. Types of mammals, snakes, rabbits, birds and insects available in the region are a pride possession of that particular land. Maximum of wildlife is preserved by the forests. So it becomes clear that with deforestation the fauna of the region also gets affected adversely.

According to the respondents, the species of animals available in Kandi area over the past 10 years are not available or seen now. They owe this bio-diversity loss to deforestation. Adding contents to the discussion, 100 per cent respondents express that about ten years back, their region has been very rich in case of species wealth (Table 5.17). Prominent species available in the area about ten years back were Peacock, Tiger, Deer, and Neel Gaye. Respondents say that they have either themselves seen these species or heard about their presence in the region.

Table 5.17 : Prominent Species/Animals which have been available in your Area in the Past Ten Years

Prominent Species	*Name of Villages*					*Total*
	Gho	*Samanu*	*Uparla Thara*	*Basa*	*Dunera*	
Peacock + Tigers + Deer + Neel Gaye	60 (100.0)	60 (100.0)	60 (100.0)	60 (100.0)	60 (100.0)	300 (100.0)
Tittar	—	—	11 (18.3)	—	—	11 (3.7)
Snakes	—	—	52 (86.7)	—	—	52 (17.3)
Rabbits	—	—	—	—	50 (83.3)	50 (16.7)

Other 3.7 per cent respondents comprising of 18.3 per cent respondents from Samanu state that Tittar has been a prominent species of the area about ten years back. Further, 17.3 per cent respondents comprising of 86.7 per cent respondents from Samanu say that snakes have also been a prominent reptile available in the region. Other 16.7 per cent of the respondents say that 'Rabbits' were also seen in the region over the past ten years. This category includes 83.3 per cent respondents from Dunera. Hence, by making an encapsulated analysis, prominent species of animals, which have been available in the region under research about ten years ago are Peacock, Deer, Tiger, Neel Gaye, Tittar, Snakes, and Rabbits. The discussion on species got featured with heavy emotional responses. The respondents while telling about the presence of species in their areas narrated various real stories of their combat with those animals with exclamatory gestures and notes of

excitement. The wild species near the villages would many times intrude and even attack the residents of the region. Mr. Joginder Singh, a trader from Uparla Thara also endorsed this fact that with deforestation, the region has lost many of the distinct species which used to be its rich possession about a decade ago. Another resident of village Gho Garib Das, Patwari by profession also expressed the same notion that with the loss of the wildlife due to cutting of the forests in their region, the area has lost its significant wealth.

The species might have been a substance of danger for the residence, but still those constituted an important part of their ecosystems and the presence of such species has been a matter of the real, ecstasy, excitement and knowledge for the villagers. But now the condition is not the same rather it has deteriorated as all the respondents say that those species are no more available in abundance. So deforestation is cause of ecological threat to the region. They further hold that the forests provide shelter and breeding ground for the wild species and hence the species suffer from an irreparable loss in case of deforestation.

Firstly they were extinct because they die and perish when dislocated and displaced; and secondly, further breeding of those species got inhibited. These respondents also added that hunting has been another cause behind extinction of species. Hence, it becomes clear that deforestation is a threat not only for the residents and villagers but also for the species of that region also. The situation being discussed in this chapter in fact indicates the threat to biodiversity imbalance and broadly speaking an ecological morose. Of course, efforts have been made for afforestation but these are limited to the villages Uparla Thara and Dunera (Table 5.18). In other villages, no sincere efforts have been done for planting trees or preserve wildlife.

Causes might have been any of the abovestated ones, but a fact remains intact that the region has been an ardent victim of deforestation in the recent decades. It is only Uparla Thara where the post-deforestation activities have benefited the region's dwellers, but in all the rest of the villages under study no such advantage has been rendered to the masses. Forests were cut to expand the agricultural fields but still, the results are not such as were expected to be. Loss of species has been a composite effect of deforestation along with the loss of employment opportunity. Even the afforestation plans are not coming concrete; which has been

Table 5.18 : Do you think Efforts are being made to Plant the Trees

Afforestation	*Name of Villages*					*Total*
	Gho	*Samanu*	*Uparla Thara*	*Basa*	*Dunera*	
Yes	—	—	60 (100.0)	—	60 (100.0)	120 (40.0)
No	60 (100.0)	60 (100.0)	—	60 (100.0)	—	180 (60.0)
Total	60 (20.0)	60 (20.0)	60 (20.0)	60 (20.0)	60 (20.0)	300 (100.0)

endorsed by the data collected hereby too. In all conditions, the situation related to the availability of green cover is pathetic and still no concrete anticipation of any edification can be laid down.

Availability of Water in Kandi Area

Kandi area has always been in discussion due to immense scarcity of water. Many projects undertaken by the government in context of Kandi region refer to either of the issues related to water. Provisions for ample water are in fact pre-condition for human welfare. Adequate and clean water for drinking and irrigation is a prerequisite for maintaining health of the people and the economy of the region respectively. But the situation is quite pathological in Kandi area of Punjab. The water for drinking as well as for irrigation is not adequately available. This scarcity is a consequence of the lack of sources of water. In all 21.3 per cent of all the respondents say that the main source of drinking water in the area is Government supply (Table 5.19). The percentage in the selected villages is 38.3 per cent in Gho and 68.3 per cent in Uparla Thara.

Other 58 per cent of all the respondents say that government supply points along with the available wells and ponds in the region are the three main sources of water. The percentage of such respondents is the highest in Samanu and Basa (100%), followed by Dunera (26.7%). Uparla Thara has the least percentage of such respondents that is only 8.3 per cent. As a contrast, other 13.7 per cent of the total respondents say that wells and ponds are the only sources of drinking water in their village and the people depend upon these natural sources of water to avail drinking water. It is

Table 5.19 : Source of Drinking Water Availability in Your Area

Source	*Name of Villages*					*Total*
	Gho	*Samanu*	*Uparla Thara*	*Basa*	*Dunera*	
Government Supply	23 (38.3)	—	41 (68.3)	—	—	64 (21.3)
Wells, Ponds and Government Supply	33 (55.0)	60 (100.0)	5 (8.3)	60 (100.0)	16 (26.7)	174 (58.0)
Only Wells + Ponds	24 (40.0)	—	14 (23.3)	—	3 (5.0)	41 (13.7)
Private Connection	—	—	51 (47.2)	—	57 (52.8)	108 (36.0)

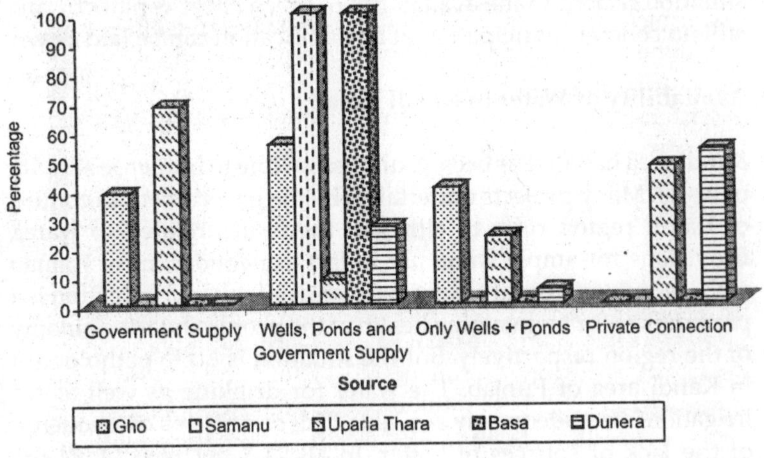

Figure 5.3 : Source of Drinking Water Availability in Your Area

particularly true for 40 per cent of the total respondents in Gho; 23.3 per cent in Uparla Thara and only 5 per cent in Dunera. For 36 per cent of the total respondents, the main source of drinking water in the area is the private connections of water. Uparla Thara village has the highest percentage of respondents owing a private water source (95.0%). This is followed by the respondents from the village Dunera. It is clear that the majority of the respondents consider that the wells and ponds as major sources of drinking water in the region. The respondents from all the five villages in variable percentage express that the natural waterbodies owned by a specific village act as providers of water for drinking and for other household purposes. The residents of Gho, Samanu and Basa are very poor; hence they cannot afford to have private connections of water in household. This makes them entirely dependent upon ponds and wells. The water available from the ponds and wells is though contaminated, but still it serves crucial needs of the villagers. On the other hand, some of the residents of Uparla Thara and Dunera have private connections for water. The study shows that the economic status of the residents of Dunera and Uparla Thara is better than that of the residents of Gho, Basa and Samanu due to which the residents of these villages can afford private meter connections. Having a private connection serves the needs of the villagers or not, is another issue as the water usually supplied during fixed hours, and that too, subject to supply of electricity to run the tubewell meant for this is available.

According to the respondents of Uparla Thara, the private water connections do not supply drinking water regularly. Sometimes the gap between the last supply of water and the next one extends up to 24 hours, making the conditions pathetic for the villagers. Sometimes residents do not get water for household need and drinking purpose for full one day. People invariably, store water in buckets and other utensils for kitchen purpose. However, in Dunera people have not complained about scarcity or crisis of drinking water.

Panchayat and an NGO have made recognizable efforts to improve the provision of drinking water, which is quite satisfactory. Analysing the collected information, it can be said that except Dunera, all the rest four villages selected for this study *vis-à-vis* Gho, Samanu, Basa and Uparla Thara, face severe scarcity of drinking water. In Gho, Samanu and Basa, the respondents say that along with wells and ponds, Government supply is also available, but still the crisis is not solved. In these villages the wells are dry and it is only during rainfalls that these wells get recharged. As far as ponds are concerned, many of those ponds available in these villages have dried up and turned to mud lands. Even if water is available in some ponds; the quality is so worse that it cannot be consumed but still people use the same contaminated water. The reason behind this compromise is the absence of another better or lesser alarming alternative. The condition in Gho and Samanu is even more pathetic.

The ponds, from which the residents avail drinking water and water for cooking purpose, are often visited by the stray animals like dogs, cows, buffaloes, goats and sheep, such ponds are sources of water for human beings and animals alike. The villagers acknowledge that they are consuming polluted and contaminated water. The condition of availability of water has worsened than the past. Earlier these ponds and wells had sufficient water because rains were adequate and the population of these villages was very less. But in present times, the situation has worsened. Rainfall has reduced up to an appreciable extent.

As a matter of global concern, the population has drastically increased in the recent decades, resulting into magnificent increase of the need of water. The same phenomenon is noticed in Kandi region also. Hence, the need of water has increased up to a significant level. But the availability of the same has reduced. Lowering of watertable and the increasing demand of water therein has affected the life of the dwellers of the region adversely. In this context, 95.7 per cent of all the respondents have forwarded their response out of which; 24 per cent respondents say that they used to consume less than 1 hour to collect drinking water ten years ago (Table 5.20). The response group comprises of 15 per cent of the respondents from Uparla Thara and 100 per cent in Basa.

Table 5.20 : Time consumed by Villagers to collect Drinking Water 10 Years Ago

Time used to collect water (in hours)	*Name of Villages*					*Total*
	Gho	*Samanu*	*Uparla Thara*	*Basa*	*Dunera*	
1	—	—	9 (15.0)	60 (100.0)	—	69 (24.0)
1-2	40 (66.7)	30 (50.0)	13 (21.7)	—	14 (23.3)	97 (33.8)
2-3	20 (33.3)	15 (25.0)	38 (63.3)	—	35 (58.3)	108 (37.7)
Above 3	—	2 (3.3)	—	—	11 (18.3)	13 (4.5)
Total	60 (20.9)	47 (16.4)	60 (20.9)	60 (20.9)	60 (20.9)	287 (95.7)

Other 33.8 per cent of the respondents express that it used to take more than 1 but less than 2 hours to collect water for drinking.

The percentage of such respondents in the selected villages is 66.7 per cent in Gho; 50 per cent in Samanu; 21.7 per cent in Uparla Thara and 23.3 per cent in Dunera. Further, 37.7 per cent of the total respondents say that the time spent was more than 2 hours and less than 3 hours. These respondents in the selected villages comprises of 33.3 per cent respondents in Gho; 25 per cent in Samanu; 63.3 per cent in Uparla Thara and 58.3 per cent in Dunera.

Forwarding another viewpoint, 4.5 per cent of all the respondents constituting 3.3 per cent of the respondents from Samanu and 18.3 per cent from Dunera; say that the people used to spend more than 3 hours to collect drinking water. It shows that the maximum time spent over the past 10 years to collect water for drinking was more than 3 hours. But the situation has drastically altered in the present. The phenomenon has experienced a significant variation with the passage of time.

The time spent on collecting drinking water at present has increased from that of the past. Out of the total sample, 2 per cent (comprising of 11.1 per cent of the respondents from Samanu) say that now the people take 2 to 3 hours to collect drinking water (Table 5.21).

Table 5.21 : Time consumed by Villagers to collect Water at Present

Time consumed (in hours)	*Name of Villages*					*Total*
	Gho	*Samanu*	*Uparla Thara*	*Basa*	*Dunera*	
2-3	—	6 (11.1)	—	—	—	6 (2.0)
3-5	33 (55.0)	20 (37.1)	—	26 (43.3)	19 (15.3)	98 (33.3)
5-6	27 (45)	2 (3.7)	15 (25)	26 (43.3)	—	70 (23.9)
More than 6	—	26 (48.1)	16 (26.6)	—	26 (43.3)	68 (23.1)
24 hrs./ day	—	—	29 (48.3)	8 (13.3)	15 (25.0)	52 (17.7)
Total	60 (20.4)	54 (18.4)	60 (20.4)	60 (20.4)	60 (20.4)	294 (98.0)

Another 33.3 per cent of all the respondents say that the time duration to collect water is now more than 3 hours and less than 5 hours. The percentage of such respondents is the highest in Gho (55.0%) followed by Basa (43.3%) and Samanu (37.1%). Dunera

has the least percentage of such respondents (15.3%). Further, 23.9 per cent respondents from the total sample say that it takes nearly 5 to 6 hours to fetch drinking water. The percentage of these respondents is quite high in Basa as compared to Uparla Thara and Samanu.

Those who say it takes more than 6 hours to collect drinking water constitute 23.1 per cent of the total respondents. This group comprises of 48.1 per cent of the respondents from Samanu; 26.6 per cent from Uparla Thara; and 43.3 per cent from Dunera. So, collecting/fetching water for household activities is becoming a tedious task for the residents of Samanu, Uparla Thara and to a lesser extent of Basa. Some of the respondents hold that many a time, water supply gets interrupted and they have to wait for a day even. The percentage of such respondents is more in Uparla Thara as compared to Basa and Dunera. The data shows that the time spent to collect drinking water 10 years ago was lesser than that of the time spent at present times.

Population pressure is the main reason for the decrease in water availability and increase in time to fetch water (Table 5.22). Studies conducted by Watkins (2006), Briscoe and Malik (2006) also support the same finding, while talking about the reasons behind the shortage of water. Majority of the respondents from Uparla Thara account population pressure as the main reason for the shortage of water and more time consumed to get the supply (73.3%). Residents from Basa and Samanu too find population pressure as one of the main reasons. The proportion of such respondents is smaller in Dunera as compared to the other selected villages.

On the other hand, 40.3 per cent of the total respondents attribute the changes to the variations in rainfall. In their opinion, due to shortage of rainfall and the duration of rainfall, the ponds and the wells do not get recharged thereby affecting the availability of water. This view is held by quite a large proportion of respondents of the selected villages, that is, 41.6 per cent respondents from Gho; 30 per cent from Samanu; 46.7 per cent from Uparla Thara; 46.7 per cent from Basa and 36.7 from Dunera. Poverty as a factor affecting the availability of water is held by only 13.3 per cent of the total respondents and the view is largely advanced by the people of Gho, Samanu and Basa as compared to those of Uparla Thara.

Though enumerable governmental efforts have been undertaken in this context, but the desired results have not been attained. In order to combat with this alarming scarcity, people store water whenever there is supply of water and it is true in the case of respondents of Uparla Thara. Because of hilly terrain, people have to walk down to the source of water and it takes a lot of time. According to the people of the region, sometimes they have to visit the neighbouring villages to avail water from the government supply points. There is one such water supply point in village Gho, where from the residents of Basa and Samanu also avail water. So the respondents attribute the shortage of water to the population pressure, change in rainfall pattern and poverty. Deforestation as a main cause has not been reported but on probing, they, of course have pointed the relation between forests and rainfall.

Table 5.22 : Reasons for the Shortage

Reason	*Name of Villages*					*Total*
	Gho	*Samanu*	*Uparla Thara*	*Basa*	*Dunera*	
Population pressure	27 (45.0)	31 (57.7)	44 (73.3)	30 (50.0)	24 (40.0)	156 (52.0)
Change in Rainfall Pattern	25 (41.7)	18 (30.0)	28 (46.7)	28 (46.7)	22 (36.7)	121 (40.3)
Poverty	23 (38.3)	16 (26.7)	3 (5.0)	11 (18.3)	9 (15.0)	62 (20.7)

The conditions related to availability of water for irrigation even do not depict any positive picture. It is as grave as that of the condition of water for drinking purpose. All the respondents say that the source of water for irrigation purpose is one that is 'rainfall'. There is no provision of wells for irrigation. The villagers have to depend upon the rainfalls for irrigation and it is due to this only, that the agricultural situation of the villages under study has not improved because to have a good agricultural produce adequate amount of water is needed, which they do not have. Watkins (2006), Briscoe and Malik (2006), and Tihillian (2008) also concur this finding through their studies. Earlier the Kandi region received sufficient rainfalls to have one good crop but the situation is not the same as before. According to 81 per cent of the total

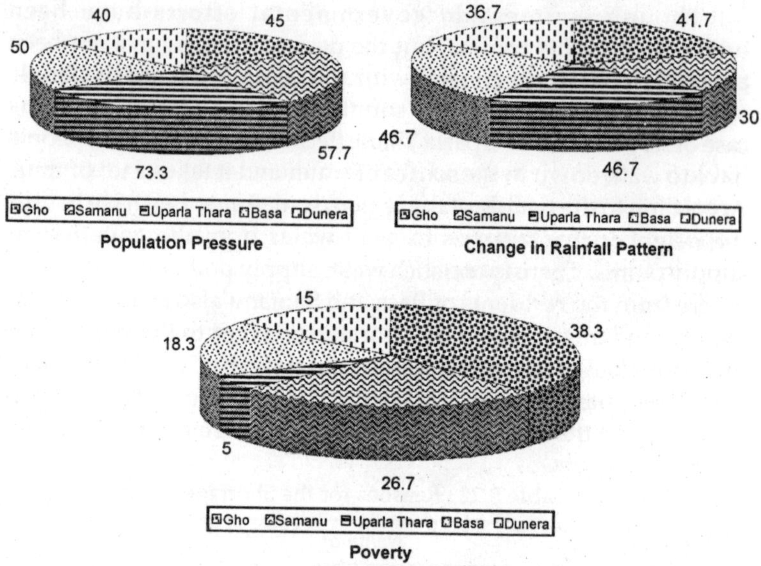

Figure 5.4 : Reasons for the Shortage

respondents, the availability of water has reduced in their region over the past ten years (Table 5.23). All the respondents respectively in Gho, Samanu, Uparla Thara and Basa hold this view. It is only 5 per cent of the respondents in Dunera village that accord the above view.

Table 5.23 : Availability of Water in the Past Ten Years

Availability of water	*Name of Villages*					*Total*
	Gho	*Samanu*	*Uparla Thara*	*Basa*	*Dunera*	
Reduced	60 (100.0)	60 (100.0)	60 (100.0)	60 (100.0)	3 (5.0)	243 (81.0)
Water for drinking increased and for irrigation decreased	—	—	—	—	57 (95.0)	57 (19.0)
Total	60 (20.0)	60 (20.0)	60 (20.0)	60 (20.0)	60 (20.0)	300 (100.0)

Further, 95 per cent of the respondents (from Dunera village) are of the opinion that though availability of drinking water has increased but for irrigation purpose, it has decreased. The village

Dunera though has sufficient coverage but they attribute this change to the overall climatic changes in the region and government's efforts to provide water to the villagers.

As a matter of crucial concern, 83.3 per cent of the total respondents say that the water level in the area has decreased (Table 5.24). All the respondents from the villages Gho, Samanu, Uparla Thara and Basa hold this view. As compared to this proportion, only 16.7 per cent respondents from Dunera contribute a nod in this response category.

The above fact is further corroborated because all the respondents except of Dunera hold a view that the groundwater level of the region was not as low in the past as it is now. They say that the major reason behind this fall in water level is lack of rainfalls, excessive population pressures, and construction of dam and diversion of water.

Table 5.24 : Change in Water Level

Change	*Name of Villages*					*Total*
	Gho	*Samanu*	*Uparla Thara*	*Basa*	*Dunera*	
Decreased	60 (100.0)	60 (100.0)	60 (100.0)	60 (100.0)	10 (16.7)	250 (83.3)
To some extent	—	—	—	—	50 (83.3)	50 (16.7)
Total	60 (20.0)	60 (20.0)	60 (20.0)	60 (20.0)	60 (20.0)	300 (100.0)

The receding water level is responsible for decrease in availability of water for drinking, irrigation and other purposes. Water shortage is the biggest issue being faced by the people of Kandi Area. Even 83.3 per cent of the total respondents from Dunera states that watertable is decreasing to some extent, show that the area lacks in water availability.

Causes of Falling Watertable

Regarding causes of falling watertable, a group of respondents comprising 74.3 per cent say that the main reasons behind the falling water level is excessive population pressure rendering limitless use of water utilizations and lack of rainfalls are the main reasons behind water scarcity (Table 5.25). These are the main reasons for falling watertable according to all the respondents from Gho, Basa and Dunera; whereas 65 per cent of the respondents from Samanu hold this opinion. On the contrary, just 6.7 per cent of the respondents in Uparla Thara find these as the main reason for falling watertable.

Construction of dam in the region is also one of the causes behind falling water level (25.7%). It is true for the respondents in Uparla Thara (93.3%) and those in Samanu (35.0%). Respondents from Gho, Basa and Dunera do not find this as a main reason for falling watertable.

Table 5.25 : Causes behind the Change in Water Level

Causes	*Name of Villages*					*Total*
	Gho	*Samanu*	*Uparla Thara*	*Basa*	*Dunera*	
Excess Utilization due to Population Pressure, lack of rain	60 (100.0)	39 (65.0)	4 (6.7)	60 (100.0)	60 (100.0)	223 (74.3)
Construction of Ranjit Sagar Dam	—	21 (35.0)	56 (93.3)	—	—	77 (25.7)
Total	60 (20.0)	60 (20.0)	60 (20.0)	60 (20.0)	60 (20.0)	300 (100.0)

According to the people, after the construction of Ranjit Sagar Dam in the region, the economic status of the villagers of Uparla Thara has enhanced due to the provision of part-time/contractual/ permanent jobs; but it has also forwarded some adverse consequences out of which, decreased availability of water is the most serious one.

As explained and accepted by the people of Uparla Thara, deforestation has not affected their lives as adversely as the reduced availability of water has done. The reason is that if forests are now not available and the people do not avail goods and services from them; but people earn good salaries and income from the jobs at the construction site and hence, can afford to buy all those goods and services from the market. But the decreased availability of water has to a large extent affected their life and pattern of survival. On the other hand, the respondents from Samanu accept that the

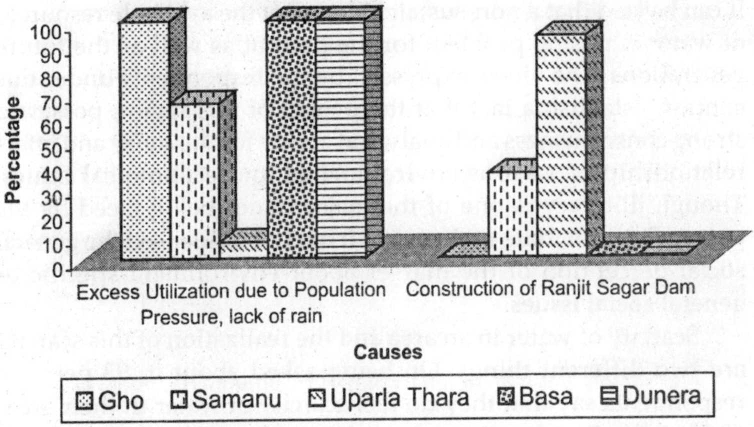

Figure 5.5 : Causes behind the Change in Water Level

construction of dam is one of the causes behind falling level of water. But unlike the residents of Uparla Thara, the construction of dam has not benefited the life of the residents of Samanu. The reason is that the residents of Samanu are not the beneficiaries of the improvements in the job scenario forwarded by this developmental project.

In addition, people hold that lack of rainfall is another cause behind the scarcity of water in the region. People of these villages are economically poor and cannot afford to have private connection of water and even cannot afford to install or buy any technological provision for extracting groundwater. Due to all this they depend entirely upon rainfalls. Over the past two decades, the rainfall has reduced hence the issue of water scarcity has aggravated. Earlier the area used to experience intermittent and heavy rainfalls, but now it does not receive rainfalls in similar quantum. Decreased rainfall has resulted into drying up of many waterbodies like ponds and wells. The average annual rainfall is lower by about 50 per cent from 1990 to 2004 in Punjab, for districts of Ropar, Hoshiarpur and Gurdaspur, part of which forms the Kandi belt, the Average Rainfall has come down by 45 per cent from 1990 to 2004 (Saini, 2008).

Population pressure, lack of rains and misuse of water besides construction of dams are responsible for falling water in the region.

It can be said that a non-sustainable use of the available resources of water is posing problem for the present as well as the future generations. The views expressed by the respondents under this context, establish a fact that the people of this region possess a strong consciousness and analytical ability for the cause and effect relationship of various environmental and economical issues. Though illiteracy is one of the major issues being faced by the people living in these regions; but it has not influenced the general social perception of the masses about environment specific or general social issues.

Scarcity of water in an area and the realization of this scarcity are two different things. On being asked about it, 93 per cent respondents say that they do feel scarcity of water in their areas (Table 5.26). Besides 65 per cent of the respondents in Dunera, all the respondents in Gho, Samanu, Uparla Thara and Basa find scarcity of water.

Table 5.26 : Scarcity of Water in Your Area

Scarcity	*Name of Villages*					*Total*
	Gho	*Samanu*	*Uparla Thara*	*Basa*	*Dunera*	
Yes	60 (100)	60 (100)	60 (100)	60 (100)	39 (65.0)	279 (93.0)
No	—	—	—	—	21 (35.0)	21 (7.0)
Total	60 (20.0)	60 (20.0)	60 (20.0)	60 (20.0)	60 (20.0)	300 (100.0)

The rest, 7.0 per cent of the total respondents (Constituting 35 per cent of the respondent in Dunera) express that they do not realize the scarcity of water in the region. Exploring the reason, they attribute this to a NGO named 'Bhartiya Vikas Parishad' that has contributed in improving the condition of water availability in the area to a large extent. This NGO has installed tubewells in the region and has also made the residents of Dunera aware of the sustainable use of these natural resources. Prior to this, the residents used to face the scarcity of water.

Further explaining the intensity of the issue related to scarcity of water, the residents of Kandi area say that there are specific months in the year when the issue of water scarcity becomes even aggravated. Not all but 93 per cent respondents have contributed response herein. It is during the summer that in May to July when the scarcity of water affects the most (59.5 per cent, Table 5.27). Village-wise distribution shows 100 per cent respondents in Gho and Basa; 20 per cent in Samanu; 50 per cent in Uparla Thara; and 10.3 per cent in Dunera.

Table 5.27 : Months of the Year in which Scarcity of Water is felt the most

Months	*Name of Villages*					*Total*
	Gho	*Samanu*	*Uparla Thara*	*Basa*	*Dunera*	
May-July	60 (100)	12 (20.0)	30 (50.0)	60 (100.0)	4 (10.3)	166 (59.5)
May-August	—	—	30 (50.0)	—	—	30 (10.7)
July-August	—	48 (80.0)	—	—	35 (89.7)	83 (29.7)
Total	60 (21.5)	60 (21.5)	60 (21.5)	60 (21.5)	39 (14.0)	279 (93.0)

Further, 10.7 per cent respondents constituting 50 per cent of the respondents from Uparla Thara only, say that the scarcity of water is felt more in the months of May-August. Another 29.7 per cent of all the respondents forward a different view. They say that it is in the months of July-August that people face the scarcity of water more than the rest of the year. This very view has been forwarded by 80 per cent of the respondents from Samanu and 89.7 per cent respondents from Dunera. It is evident that the condition of water availability in the region becomes pathological in the summer seasons, specifically in the months of May to August. This is perhaps the time of the year when water is needed the maximum; especially for drinking and other uses due to high temperature of summer. The residents of Kandi area feel scarcity of water the whole year, but certainly in these months the repercussions are even worse. Moreover the agricultural fields need more water for irrigation purposes. All these factors make the deprivation of people in the context of water even more prominent. As a matter of paradox, these months include parts of monsoon season also. The reason is explained in the previous part of the chapter that the rainfalls in the region have decreased than the past and now due to less rainfall, the ponds and wells remain dry.

People do not have any strong defense mechanism against the shortage of water. There are 93 per cent of all the respondents who have contributed a response in this very discussion. A group comprising of 35.8 per cent of all the respondents say that they fetch water from ponds and wells to fulfil their individual and household related needs of water (Table 5.28). Majority of the respondents from Gho and Basa (70.0%) rely on ponds and wells for their water related needs. Nearly 27 per cent of the respondents in Uparla Thara make use of the ponds and wells during the months of water scarcity.

Table 5.28 : Mechanism for Water Scarcity Management

Mechanism	*Name of Villages*					*Total*
	Gho	*Samanu*	*Uparla Thara*	*Basa*	*Dunera*	
Use of ponds and well	42 (70.0)	—	16 (26.7)	42 (70.0)	—	100 (35.8)
Wait for Government Supply	18 (30.0)	60 (100.0)	44 (73.3)	17 (28.3)	38 (97.4)	177 (63.4)
No solution to it	—	—	—	1 (1.7)	1 (2.6)	2 (0.7)
Total	60 (21.5)	60 (21.5)	60 (21.5)	60 (21.5)	39 (14.0)	279 (93.0)

Another way to meet such eventuality is to wait for supply by the government installed submersible pumps in their village (63.4%). Respondents of village Samanu (100.0%), Dunera (97.4%), and Uparla Thara (73.3%) are supplied water from the tubewells installed in their villages. Some of the respondents have stated that there is no solution to this problem (0.7%). This view has been constituted by 1.7 per cent respondent from Basa and 2.6 per cent respondents Dunera. Moreover, there is not any fixed time as to when the water will be available there.

It is clear that the conditions related to water availability in the region is deplorable and efforts have been made to solve it.

Still people want the panchayats/government to play a significant role to mitigate water crisis especially during summer. In the view of 66.3 per cent of the total respondents, the government/panchayat has played no role to improve or solve the existing water crisis in the area (Table 5.29). Majority of the respondents in the village Gho (71.7%); Samanu (83.3%); Uparla Thara (40.0%); and in Basa (100.0%) state that panchayats/government has not made efforts to manage water crises in their villages. On the contrary, majority of the respondents in Dunera (79.5%) and Uparla Thara (60.0%) hold that government/panchayat installed some tubewells and submersible pumps to meet the water needs of the people. This response category also includes 28.3 per cent and 16.7 per cent of the respondents from Gho and Samanu respectively. While justifying this gesture of these formal bodies, they referred to the surrounding villages.

Table 5.29 : The Role of the Government/Panchayat in managing Water Crisis

Role	*Name of Villages*					*Total*
	Gho	*Samanu*	*Uparla Thara*	*Basa*	*Dunera*	
No Role at all	43 (71.7)	50 (83.3)	24 (40.0)	60 (100)	8 (20.5)	185 (66.3)
Some tube-wells	17 (28.3)	10 (16.7)	36 (60.0)	—	31 (79.5)	94 (33.7)
Total	60 (21.5)	60 (21.5)	60 (21.5)	60 (21.5)	39 (14.0)	279 (93.0)

Thus majority of the respondents believe that the government or panchayat has not put much effort to solve the crisis of water in the region. The other traditional crops of the region include Mash, Til, Kulth, and Chana. All those crops can be sown and grown only with adequate availability of water. A respondents category (33.7 per cent of all the respondents) says that though negligible, but still efforts have been made by government and panchayat to assist people in combating the issues related to the scarcity of dinking water. However, they do not say that the steps taken by the government or panchayat are adequate; but they do not even deny the efforts made by the governmental bodies.

Impacts on Agricultural Productivity

The discussion about availability of water is relevantly related to the discourse on fertility of soil. Respondents constituting 78.7 per cent of all, agree with the notion that soil fertility in their areas has decreased (Table 5.30). This response has been forwarded by 100 per cent of all the respondents from the villages Samanu, Uparla Thara and Basa and 93 per cent respondents from Gho. Bhalla (2006) also concurs this finding of the present study.

Environmental degradation resulting into adverse impacts on the fertility of soil has serious repercussions on the agricultural productivity, which needs to be taken ardently serious (GOI, 2000; Athavala, 2003; Vyas, 2003; Nath, 2004; Anant, 2006; Sarkar, 2007; and Mamoria, 2007).

Table 5.30 : Change in the Soil Fertility in Area

Change	*Name of Villages*					*Total*
	Gho	*Samanu*	*Uparla Thara*	*Basa*	*Dunera*	
Decreased	56 (93.3)	60 (100.0)	60 (100.0)	60 (100.0)	—	236 (78.7)
Remained same	4 (6.7)	—	—	—	60 (100.0)	64 (21.3)
Total	60 (20.0)	60 (20.0)	60 (20.0)	60 (20.0)	60 (20.0)	300 (100.0)

On the contrary, 21.3 per cent of all the respondents say that the fertility of the soil of their region has remained the same. The percentage of such respondents in Dunera is the highest (100.0%) and the least in Gho (6.7%). According to these respondents, the soil fertility in their region to a large extent has remained intact.

Forwarding an empirical addition to the discussion, 81.3 of the respondents say that the main factors behind decreasing soil fertility are decreased rainfalls, deforestation and soil erosion (Table 5.31). This view is held by all the respondents from Gho and Basa; followed by 96.7 per cent from Samanu. All of the respondents from Dunera though have said that the soil fertility in their area has not declined but still hold the above factors responsible for the decline in the fertility in the region (63.3%).

Some of the respondents from Dunera attribute change in temperature for declining fertility in the region (36.7%). This view is largely held by the respondents from Uparla Thara (53.3%) and some of them from Samanu (28.3%). In all, 23.7 per cent of the respondents believe that change in temperature of the region is the major cause of decreased soil fertility.

Table 5.31 : Causes behind the Decreased Fertility of Soil

Causes	*Name of Villages*					*Total*
	Gho	*Samanu*	*Uparla Thara*	*Basa*	*Dunera*	
Decreased rainfalls, deforestation, and soil erosion	60 (100)	58 (96.7)	28 (46.7)	60 (100)	38 (63.3)	244 (81.3)
Change in temperature	—	17 (28.3)	32 (53.3)	—	22 (36.7)	71 (23.7)

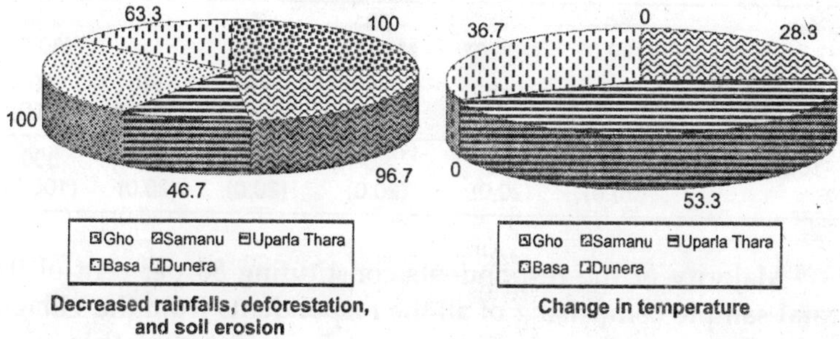

Figure 5.6 : Causes behind the Decreased Fertility of Soil

These respondents say that no doubt factors like lack of rainfall, soil erosion and deforestation contribute to decline in the agricultural productivity, but the change in temperature is a manifest cause. The villages in Kandi areas are largely dependent upon forests and agriculture. The forests provide them multiple facilities/goods/services and the agriculture acts as a main source of income for the people of the area. The economy of these villages has largely been structured and supported by agriculture; hence any degradation in the soil fertility leads to degradation in the overall village economic life thereby directly affecting the economy of the region. People assert that the change in soil fertility has affected the cropping pattern of the area, which has further forwarded multiple adversities for the survival of the dwellers. The change in levels of soil fertility has a direct implication on cropping pattern of any region.

From this, it may be concluded that shortage or change of rainfall has affected the productivity of the region with its consequence on economy. Parry (2007) too, has concluded that rainfall pattern affected by deforestation results in decline of soil fertility, agricultural production leading to immense degradation of economic standards of the villages and the communities.

Table 5.32 : Effects of Decreased Soil Fertility on the Cropping Pattern

Effects	*Name of Villages*					*Total*
	Gho	*Samanu*	*Uparla Thara*	*Basa*	*Dunera*	
Yes	60 (100.0)	60 (100.0)	60 (100.0)	60 (100.0)	—	240 (80.0)
No, It is still the same	—	—	—	—	60 (100.0)	60 (20.0)
Total	60 (20.0)	60 (20.0)	60 (20.0)	60 (20.0)	60 (20.0)	300 (100.0)

Majority of the respondents constituting 80 per cent of the total sample comprising of all the respondents from the villages Gho, Samanu, Uparla Thara and Basa support this view (Table 5.32). On the contrary, other 20.0 per cent of the total respondents (100.0 per cent respondents from Dunera) say that they still grow the crops, as they did in the past.

To further illustrate the context, the discussion shifts to the pattern of cropping over the last ten years. Nearly 68 per cent of the total respondents tell that *Til, Maa,* Gram, and *Kulthi* have been the prominent crops about 10 years ago (Table 5.33). All the respondents in Gho, Samanu and Basa corroborate the above whereas only 38.3 per cent of the respondents in Dunera support it. Further all the respondents from Uparla Thara and 61.7 per cent from Dunera hold that Rice, Maize and Wheat have been the main crops of their area about 10 years ago. The total percentage of the respondents in the same is 32.3.

Table 5.33 : Crops Sown before in the Past Ten Years

Crops	*Name of Villages*					*Total*
	Gho	*Samanu*	*Uparla Thara*	*Basa*	*Dunera*	
Til, Gram, Kulth, Maa	60 (100.0)	60 (100.0)	—	60 (100.0)	23 (38.3)	203 (67.7)
Rice, Maize, Wheat	—	—	60 (100.0)	—	37 (61.7)	97 (32.3)
Total	60 (20.0)	60 (20.0)	60 (20.0)	60 (20.0)	60 (20.0)	300 (100.0)

So, most of the respondents in the study villages used to sow oilseeds and pulses except those in Uparla Thara and some in Dunera who used to take Cereal crop like Maize, Wheat and Rice. Contrary to the cropping pattern that was prevalent 10 years ago,the region has experienced different scenario now. Wheat and Maize are the main crops at present (68.3 per cent, Table 5.34). Gho, Samanu and Basa have altogether a changed cropping pattern. Instead of growing oilseeds and pulses, the respondents in these villages now grow cereal crop.

In apposition to his view, other 3.7 per cent of all the respondents comprising of 18.3 per cent respondents from Uparla Thara say that they now grow fruits only. The production of fruits at present is not meant for commercial purpose, though the intention to use the produce commercially always remains intact in manifest or in latent terms.

Table 5.34 : Crops Sown at Present

Crops	*Name of Villages*					*Total*
	Gho	*Samanu*	*Uparla Thara*	*Basa*	*Dunera*	
Wheat, Maize	60 (100.0)	60 (100.0)	25 (41.7)	60 (100.0)	—	205 (68.3)
Only fruits	—	—	11 (18.3)	—	—	11 (3.7)
All Same	—	—	24 (40.0)	—	60 (100.0)	84 (28.0)
Total	60 (20.0)	60 (20.0)	60 (20.0)	60 (20.0)	60 (20.0)	300 (100.0)

Further, 28 per cent of all the respondents say that there is no change in the cropping pattern they continue the crops that they used to sow about 10 years ago. This view is supported by all the respondents form Dunera and 40 per cent from Uparla Thara. According to them, the soil fertility has decreased in their region but it has not altered cropping pattern of their region.

As far as the yield of the crops is concerned, 83.3 per cent of all the respondents express that it has decreased. Such decrease in the crop yield is experienced by all the respondents from Gho, Samanu, Uparla Thara and Basa (Table 5.35). A few respondents from Dunera too have experienced a decreased in the crop yield (16.7%). But most of the respondents of this village continue to have an average yield of not a good income (83.3%).

Table 5.35 : Yield of Crops in the Region

Yield of Crops	*Name of Villages*					*Total*
	Gho	*Samanu*	*Uparla Thara*	*Basa*	*Dunera*	
Decreased	60 (100.0)	60 (100.0)	60 (100.0)	60 (100.0)	10 (16.7)	250 (83.3)
Average	—	—	—	—	50 (83.3)	50 (16.7)
Total	60 (20.0)	60 (20.0)	60 (20.0)	60 (20.0)	60 (20.0)	300 (100.0)

On the whole the people of Kandi area say that the yield of crops has decreased; which is certainly a matter of serious concern for them, as agriculture is one of the main sources of livelihood. In such circumstances, the use of the agro chemicals increases. But, the use of fertilizers/pesticide is not so prominent in Kandi area. Out of the total sample, only 87.7 per cent of the respondents forwarded a response for this discourse. Out of them, a group comprising of 47.5 per cent respondents say that the people in their area now use fertilizers/pesticides (Table 5.36). Whereas 52.5 per cent of the total respondents say that people of the area do not use fertilizers/pesticides. All the respondents of Dunera followed by those of Uparla Thara (51.7%) and Samanu (38.3%) now use fertilizers. Some of the respondents from Gho have started using fertilizers whereas, most of the respondents (81.7%) do not use chemical fertilizers. Likewise, all the respondents from Basa do not find any use of fertilizers. Thus, respondents of Dunera followed by Uparla Thara and Samanu have started using more of fertilizers.

Table 5.36 : Use of Agro Chemicals by the People of the Region

Use of agro chemicals	*Name of Villages*					*Total*
	Gho	*Samanu*	*Uparla Thara*	*Basa*	*Dunera*	
Yes	11 (18.3)	23 (38.3)	31 (51.7)	—	60 (100.0)	125 (47.5)
No	49 (81.7)	—	29 (48.3)	60 (100.0)	—	138 (52.5)
Total	60 (22.8)	23 (8.7)	60 (22.8)	60 (22.8)	60 (22.8)	263 (87.7)

Continuing the discussion related to the use of fertilizers, out of the total sample only 97.3 per cent of the respondents has contributed a response. They say that earlier cow dung was the only manure that was in use as a growth inducing variable. Now people increasingly use urea and other agro chemicals in addition to cow dung manure.

In this context, 52.1 per cent of the respondents explain that now people use urea as a fertilizer in the field but earlier it was not used at all (Table 5.37). The use of urea is now being done by all the respondents of Dunera. Except few of the respondents in Gho (18.3%), most of all the respondents in selected villages now increasingly use urea. Only these respondents of Uparla Thara could not specify the fertilizers being used by them.

Table 5.37 : Particular Types of Fertilizers are used by People at Present

Particular Type	*Name of Villages*					*Total*
	Gho	*Samanu*	*Uparla Thara*	*Basa*	*Dunera*	
Not Specific	—	—	3 (5.0)	—	—	3 (1.0)
Urea	11 (18.3)	23 (44.2)	31 (51.7)	27 (45.9)	60 (100.0)	152 (52.1)
Cow Dung	49 (81.7)	29 (55.8)	26 (43.3)	33 (55.0)	—	137 (46.9)
Total	60 (20.5)	52 (17.8)	60 (20.5)	60 (20.5)	60 (20.5)	292 (97.3)

However, there are 46.9 per cent of the total respondents who say that still people use cow dung for the purpose of increasing fertility of the soil. This response group includes 81.7 per cent of the respondents from Gho; 55.8 per cent from Samanu; 55 per cent from Basa; and 43.3 per cent from Uparla Thara. So, people have recently started using urea to increase the crop yield and to counter the declining fertility of soil.

Further, regarding the change in the quantity of the use of fertilizers, 46.1 per cent of all the respondents say that the quantity of fertilizers being used in the region has increased (Table 5.38). This view is forwarded by 88 per cent respondent from Uparla Thara and 63.3 per cent from Dunera. Villagers of Uparla Thara say that they can afford to buy fertilizers because of the employment generated with the construction of dam. The savings can be reinvested in increasing the agricultural productivity. The respondents in Dunera have not forwarded the above opinion; rather they hold that trading activities have increased in their area which gives them sufficient return to their farm products especially *Aam Papar* and this income they divert to buy fertilizers for raising crop yield.

Table 5.38 : Change in the Quantity of Fertilizers being used in the Area

Change in quantity	*Name of Villages*					*Total*
	Gho	*Samanu*	*Uparla Thara*	*Basa*	*Dunera*	
Increased	—	—	22 (88.0)	—	38 (63.3)	60 (46.1)
Decreased	25 (41.7)	3 (15.0)	—	—	—	28 (21.5)
Remained Same	—	17 (85.0)	3 (12.0)	—	22 (36.7)	42 (32.3)
Total	25 (19.2)	20 (5.4)	25 (19.2)	—	60 (46.2)	130 (43.3)

As compared to the past, now people use more fertilizers in the agricultural field due to declined fertility. Other group of people giving a contrary version is inclusive of 21.5 per cent of the total respondents (including 41.7 per cent respondents from Gho, and 15.0 per cent from Samanu) opine that the use of fertilizers in the region has rather decreased. The reason behind this decrease is consistently intensifying poverty. People earned a good income in the past from agriculture and the thick forests of those times used to provide them a lot of good and services free of cost. But now agricultural production has declined and deforestation has also haunted the survival pattern to a large extent. Hence, they cannot afford to buy fertilizers now.

Other 32.3 per cent of all the respondents believe that the quantity of the fertilizers being used in the area has neither increased nor decreased. Such respondents group comprises of 85 per cent of the respondents from Samanu; 12 per cent from Uparla Thara; and 36.7 from Dunera. According to this group of respondents, the people used to apply fertilizers as well; and the quantity of this use has remained same to a great extent.

The respondents have also been asked about the reasons behind this change. Those who say that the quantity of fertilizer being used has decreased believe that the main reason is poverty (28.9 per cent, Table 5.39). The percentage is the highest among the sample of village Gho and (89.3%), followed by those of Samanu (10.7%). This shows the poverty is quite rampant in Gho and the earlier analysis too points it out.

Table 5.39 : Reasons behind this Change in the Use of Fertilizers

Reasons	*Name of Villages*					*Total*
	Gho	*Samanu*	*Uparla Thara*	*Basa*	*Dunera*	
Poverty	25 (89.3)	3 (10.7)	—	—	—	28 (28.9)
Economic Upliftment	—	—	22 (36.7)	—	19 (63.3)	41 (42.3)
Decrease in Soil Fertility	—	—	—	—	28 (59.6)	28 (28.9)
Total	25 (25.8)	3 (3.1)	22 (22.7)	—	47 (48.5)	97 (32.3)

Other 42.3 per cent of the total respondents (inclusive of 36.7 per cent of the respondents from Uparla Thara; and 63.3 from Dunera) opine that the quantity of fertilizers being used has increased and they attribute this to improvement in their position. Another 28.9 per cent of the respondents say that decline in soil fertility is responsible for the increased use of fertilizers and all the respondents represent Dunera village.

Analyzing the contents, it is derived that group of respondents who say that the use of fertilizers/manures in the region has either increased or decreased; particularly due to improvements of economic conditions or poverty respectively. Declining soil fertility is another reason for change in the use of fertilizers.

There are two contradictory views but the responses derived hereby have potential to justify. The villages like Basa, Samanu and Gho possess, economically low profile and people are very poor in these villages. Earlier they used to earn good amount of money and had a good standard of survival, but now the agricultural status of the regions have fallen down. This has adversely affected the potential of the people to buy fertilizers/ manures and use it for agricultural upliftment. On the other hand, the second category of respondents hold contrary notion. According to them the use of fertilizers/manures in the region has increased and the reason is the economic upliftment of the residents of the region. This fact is typically related to the people of Uparla Thara because they are the greatest beneficiaries of the construction of Ranjit Sagar Dam and have got good jobs at the site. With these jobs the economic position of the respondents has enhanced to a significant extent. They themselves are not too much engaged in agriculture now, but they believe that those who are engaged use more fertilizers than in the past. They relate the quantity of fertilizers/manures being used, directly to the income people earn. Similarly, a large proportion of the respondents from Dunera attribute the increased use to the change in crop varieties though they still are cultivating the same crops. The new varieties require constant use of agro chemicals.

According to them as the people earn good income; they afford more use of fertilizers/manures than what they used in the past. The third response given hereby, states that there has neither been a change in the use of fertilizers nor any change in the quantity of fertilizers being used. This view is pertinent to the village Dunera and Samanu. According to the villagers, soil fertility in Dunera has remained intact and hence, there has been no change in context of use of fertilizers but in Samanu, people have not been able to use fertilizers even with decline of soil fertility and change of cropping pattern. They attribute it to their low economic status. People in Dunera still grow the same crops as they have not experienced much decline in the fertility level of the soil.

With the changing cropping pattern and adoption of new varieties, that is more susceptible to insects and pests, the use of pesticides increases. Out of the total respondents, 99.0 per cent of the respondents have contributed a response to this discussion.

Interestingly, 31 per cent of the respondents have reported the use of pesticides in their region (Table 5.40). The consumption of pesticides is the highest in Dunera (100.0%), followed by that in Uparla Thara (36.9%). Another fact is that respondents in Basa have not reported about the use of fertilizers but some of them are aware of the use in their region (18.3%).

Table 5.40 : Use of Pesticides in the Region

Use of pesticides	*Name of Villages*					*Total*
	Gho	*Samanu*	*Uparla Thara*	*Basa*	*Dunera*	
Yes	—	—	21 (36.8)	11 (18.3)	60 (100.0)	92 (31.0)
No	60 (100.0)	60 (100.0)	36 (63.1)	49 (81.7)	—	205 (69.0)
Total	60 (20.2)	60 (20..2)	57 (19.2)	60 (20.0)	60 (20.2)	297 (99.0)

On the other hand, 69 per cent respondents out of the sample say that they do not use pesticides and are not used in their region. This category constitutes 100 per cent of the respondents from Gho and Samanu. A large proportion of respondents from Basa (81.7%) and Uparla Thara (63.1%) too are not aware of the use of pesticides in their region.

On being asked about the type of pesticide being used, only 16.3 per cent of all the respondents (all such respondents from Uparla Thara) say that there is not any specific type of pesticide which people use. The people of the region are not aware of the particular type of pesticide being used in their region. Whichever the type of pesticide they find available in the nearby markets on cheaper rates, they buy and use that. In this discourse only 47 per cent of the respondents from the sample have contributed a response. This percentage in the selected villages is 14.9 per cent in the village Uparla Thara and 42.5 per cent in villages Basa and Dunera (Table 5.41). Of these, 51.1 per cent of the respondents have said that the use of the pesticides has increased in their region whereas the rest hold that it is almost the same. The use of pesticides has increased mostly in Dunera (62.2%). Only 9.7 per cent of the respondents in Basa say that pesticides use has increased. Similarly, 29.2 per cent of the respondents in Uparla Thara say about the increased use of pesticides. This again supports the inference that people in Uparla Thara and Dunera are comparatively better off than the other villages under study and for that reason, the use of pesticides has increased.

Table 5.41 : Change in Quantity of Pesticides used in the Region

Change in quantity	*Name of Villages*					*Total*
	Gho	*Samanu*	*Uparla Thara*	*Basa*	*Dunera*	
Increased	—	—	21 (29.2)	7 (9.7)	44 (62.2)	72 (51.1)
Remained Same	—	—	—	53 (76.8)	16 (23.2)	69 (48.9)
Total	—	—	21 (14.9)	60 (42.5)	60 (42.5)	141 (47.0)

On the contrary 48.9 per cent respondents comprising of 76.8 per cent respondents from Basa and 23.2 per cent respondents from Dunera opine that the quantity of the pesticides being used in the area has remained the same as that of the past. Change of cropping pattern and the awareness among the cultivators about the effect of the insects/pests attack crop yield seems to be the main reason for increased use of pesticides, etc. Of course, the use of agro chemicals depends upon one's economic status as well.

Employment Scenario

The economic status of the regions under study and the standard of living of the people thereby, ought to be a serious concern for the administration. The target of the government needs to be shifted to employment paradigm and such efforts should be made that are helpful to upgrade the economy of the region and economic standards of the masses. But in the Kandi areas no attempts have been made to compensate the losses occurring due to deforestation or agricultural degradation. The position of the masses dwelling in the Kandi area of Punjab, along with their living standards is being worsened due to absence of any constructive step being taken by the government. The whole sample in totality (all the respondents from all the villages) express that even in case of excessive economic turmoil of economy of the region.

Forests are such a natural resource for the rural people of Kandi area that provide them uncountable valuable goods and services besides generating employment and income. People can save a lot of money if forest cover is available inplenty, but with deforestation their life has been victimized directly. Instead of cutting forests for economic development; forests could have been used for the purpose of generating employment. Forest based industry can strengthen the economy of the region but no forest based industry has been established till now. No efforts have been contributed to the zone which possess the potential to ameliorate the circumstances. There are 33.3 per cent of all the respondents who assert that the employment in the region has changed and improved (Table 5.42). This change is experienced the most in Uparla Thara (100.0%) and Dunera (65.0%).

Table 5.42 : Change in the Employment Rate in the Region

Change	*Name of Villages*					*Total*
	Gho	*Samanu*	*Uparla Thara*	*Basa*	*Dunera*	
Improved	—	—	60 (100.0)	—	39 (65.0)	99 (33.3)
No Improvement	60 (100.0)	60 (100.0)		60 (100.0)	21 (35.0)	201 (67.7)
Total	60 (20.0)	60 (20.0)	60 (20.0)	60 (20.0)	60 (20.0)	300 (100.0)

On the other hand, 67.7 per cent of all the respondents say that there has been no change in the employment scenario. This view has been forwarded by all the respondents from Gho, Samanu and Tarhari Basa; and 35 per cent of the respondents from Dunera. It is evident that the residents of Uparla Thara and Dunera only have realized some improvement in the employment scenario. The discussion has already been referred to in a laconic manner, in the chapter explaining the profile of the villages and respondents. The residents of Uparla Thara have got benefited in context of job

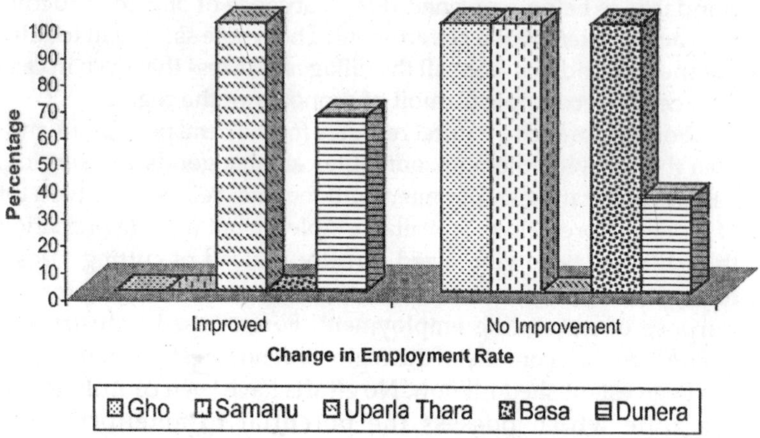

Figure 5.7 : Change in the Employment Rate in the Region

opportunities due to the construction of Ranjit Sagar Dam. On the other hand, the people of Dunera have been benefited in the same context with the efforts made by the Canada Based NGO, named 'Jindal Foundation'. This NGO has improved the infrastructure in the village and to maintain services like sewage, sewerage, solid waste management, clean roads in streets, care taking of the school, maintenance of Computer Lab, etc.; many residents of the village have been appointed on regular bases. Hence, certainly the employment conditions of Uparla Thara and Dunera have improved.

While contributing a response in context of the reason behind the stated changes in the employment scenario, out of all the 99 respondents who have contributed a response, 60.7 per cent respondents (all such respondents from Uparla Thara) say that the geographical proximity of their region to the dam constructed recently, has played a dominant role. In comparison to it, 65 per cent of the respondents from Dunera say that it is due to the maintenance, preservation and the regulated use of the forest cover that has sustained employment opportunities. A Study conducted by Vyas (2001) also supports the finding that if forests are maintained, they can be a source of generating employment for the people thereby can make people economically sound and empowered.

People from Dunera say that forests give them a lot of chances to earn through partime/daily wage basis/seasonal and *ad hoc* jobs. Government undertakes many projects pertaining to forests and other natural resources, for example. Afforestation programmes, cutting of trees for commercial purposes, 10 years felling programmes, etc. People are employed for works like cutting trees, digging pits and the like.

Analyzing details here, it can be said that employment scene has improved only in two villages out of the five under research, i.e. Dunera and Uparla Thara. Residents of other three villages say that it has not improved at all and the employment opportunities are less. Further, the change in employment scenario as stated by people of Dunera and Uparla Thara has not affected all the people equally. There are same communities or groups which have benefited more than the rest.

With regard to the group or communities getting benefits of employment only respondents from Uparla Thara and Dunera have responded; none from the other villages under study has made a mention of employment in their region/area (Table 5.43). Out of the total, 29 per cent of the respondents say that only youth have been benefited with the increase in employment opportunities. On the other hand 3.7 per cent and 30 per cent of the respondents say that it is women and men respectively. But majority of the respondents irrespective of gender and caste, all have been benefited by the developments in their regions.

Village-wise analysis depicts that it is the youth (66.0%) that has been benefited the most by the developmental activities in Dunera. On the other hand, majority of the respondents in Uparla Thara find all have been benefited by the development process and have got jobs in Ranjit Sagar Dam project.

Further, some of the women in Uparla Thara (6.7%) have got employment at Ranjit Sagar Dam project. Women are not the beneficiary of the development initiated in Dunera. Those who find the men are the beneficiary of the development project by getting employment are more in Uparla Thara (31.7%) than those in Dunera (2.7%).

A comparison of the two villages benefited by development process in the form of employment reveals that youth are able to get jobs in Dunera whereas it is not any specific group or community in case of Uparla Thara. Secondly, women have been able to find a place in Uparla Thara. In all, Ranjit Sagar Dam has

Table 5.43 : Specific Community getting Employment

Specific Community	*Name of Villages*					*Total*
	Gho	*Samanu*	*Uparla Thara*	*Basa*	*Dunera*	
Youth	—	—	—	—	31 (66.0)	31 (29.0)
Women	—	—	4 (6.7)	—	—	4 (3.7)
Men	—	—	19 (31.7)	—	13 (27.7)	32 (30.0)
All	—	—	37 (61.7)	—	3 (6.4)	40 (37.4)
Total			60 (56.1)		47 (43.9)	107 (35.7)

been able to generate employment opportunities for all without any gender or age bias.

As a consequence of this change in employment, the lifestyle of the people of Kandi areas has also been affected. However, 11 per cent of the respondents say that their lifestyles have not changed with improvement in employment scenario (Table 5.44). In contrast to 6.7 per cent of the respondents in Uparla Thara, 23.4 per cent of the respondents in Dunera find no change or improvement in their lifestyle.

Table 5.44 : Effects of the Change on Lifestyle of People

Yes/No	*Name of Villages*					*Total*
	Gho	*Samanu*	*Uparla Thara*	*Basa*	*Dunera*	
Yes	—	—	56 (93.8)	—	36 (76.6)	92 (86.0)
No	—	—	4 (6.7)	—	11 (23.4)	15 (11.0)
Total	—	—	60 (56.1)	—	47 (43.9)	107 (35.7)

As compared to it, 86 per cent of all the respondents say that there has been a change in the lifestyle of the residents of the region. This group of respondents comprises of 93.8 per cent of the respondents from Uparla Thara and 76.6 per cent of respondents from Dunera.

Thus, most of the respondents find a change in lifestyle of the people but such change is more in Uparla Thara as compared to that in Dunera. The obvious reason is that Ranjit Sagar project in Uparla Thara area has provided jobs to people (in certain cases more than one member of the family has got jobs) who otherwise were largely unemployed and had low economic position as compared to Dunera. In Dunera, forest related activities do not provide regular work; it is either contractual or daily based; this may be the plausible reason for high number of respondents reporting no change in lifestyle.

If lifestyle has improved, then what are the visible features of such a change? One of the features of improvement of living standard is the increase in the number of vehicles as reported by 42.4 per cent of the respondents and another is renovation of houses (57.6 per cent, Table 5.45). Majority of the respondents from Uparla Thara have renovated their houses (55.4%); whereas those from Dunera have purchased vehicles (77.8%). In Uparla Thara, quite a good proportion of the respondents have purchased vehicles (44.6%) and they believe that owning a vehicle is the most crucial indicator of enhanced living standards.

Table 5.45 : Specify these Changes in Lifestyle

Changes	*Name of Villages*					*Total*
	Gho	*Samanu*	*Uparla Thara*	*Basa*	*Dunera*	
People have vehicles Scooter/car	—	—	25 (44.6)	—	28 (77.8)	53 (42.4)
Renovation of houses	—	—	31 (55.4)	—	8 (22.2)	39 (57.6)
Total	—	—	56 (60.9)	—	36 (39.1)	92 (30.7)

Another important dimension can be deduced from the above discussion is about the difference in economic scenario of the village. The village Dunera has been comparatively well off from that of the village Uparla Thara and so has been the structure of the houses. That may be the reason for the investment in renovation of the houses in Uparla Thara as compared to that in Dunera where people have invested more in the purchase of vehicles.

From the above discussion, it seems that only two villages of the study area have been able to improve their living standard as a result of development in their region. In other words, Kandi area is in dire need of development; economic; infrastructural and the like.

Rainfall

The amount and spell of precipitation is another crucial factor associated with forest areas. Studies show that deforestation leads to change in precipitation and temperature (Speth, 2004). Such changes ought to have its impact on cropping pattern, soil fertility, demand for water and even survival pattern of the people of those areas.

In this regard, a group constituting 54.3 per cent of the total respondents say that the quantity of precipitation is very less in the region (Table 5.46). The village-wise distribution of respondents in the selected villages shows that Gho, Samanu and Basa are finding a big change in the rainfall as compared to Uparla Thara and Dunera.

Table 5.46 : Rainfall in the Region

Rainfall	*Name of Villages*					*Total*
	Gho	*Samanu*	*Uparla Thara*	*Basa*	*Dunera*	
Very less	60 (100.0)	45 (75.0)	14 (23.3)	43 (71.7)	1 (1.7)	163 (54.3)
Decreased	—	15 (25.0)	18 (30.0)	17 (28.3)	3 (5.0)	53 (17.7)
Average	—	—	28 (46.7)	—	56 (93.3)	84 (28.0)
Total	60 (20.0)	60 (20.0)	60 (20.0)	60 (20.0)	60 (20.0)	300 (100.0)

The following response has been given 17.7 per cent of all the respondents out of the total sample. They say that precipitation quantity has decreased than that in the past. This group comprises of 25 per cent respondents from Samanu; 30 per cent from Uparla Thara; 28.3 per cent from Basa; and 5 per cent from Dunera. In this way, more respondents from Samanu, Uparla Thara and Basa find a decrease in rainfall than that from Dunera. Further, 28 per cent of the respondents say that the quantity of precipitation is average in the region and the view is held by a majority of respondents from Dunera (93.3%) and Uparla Thara (46.7%). Thus, respondents from Gho, Samanu and Basa are of the opinion that rainfall in their region is very less, and those from Uparla Thara and Dunera still have average rainfall in their region.

While moving on to the discussion about the frequency of rainfall, the majority (44.3 per cent of the respondents) says that the rainfall occurs only in specific months, those are from June-August (Table 5.47). Basa and Gho have the highest proportion of such respondents. However, being more specific, other 20 per cent of all the respondents say that it is only in the monsoon that the rainfall occurs. Majority of the respondents from Dunera (93.3%) constituting 18.7 per cent of the sample tell that the region experiences intermittent and heavy rainfalls. No other respondent from any other village under study gave a similar view.

Table 5.47 : Frequency of Rainfall in the Region

Frequency	*Name of Villages*					*Total*
	Gho	*Samanu*	*Uparla Thara*	*Basa*	*Dunera*	
Intermittent and heavy rainfalls	—	—	—	—	56 (93.3)	56 (18.7)
Rain with long spells	—	—	51 (85.0)	—	—	51 (17.0)
In Specific Months (June-August)	60 (100.0)	13 (21.7)	—	60 (100.0)	—	133 (44.3)
In Monsoon only	—	47 (78.3)	9 (15.0)	—	4 (6.7)	60 (20.0)
Total	60 (20.0)	60 (20.0)	60 (20.0)	60 (20.0)	60 (20.0)	300 (100.0)

The situation in Uparla Thara is not as good as that of the other villages under study. The respondents from the Uparla Thara say that the region experience rainfall with long spells and for many months together the region do not get rains. It is thus clear that precipitation is not taking place in adequate quantum except in Dunera.

Since rainfall is taking place in monsoon period and its frequency is less, it may have its impact on the cropping pattern. A majority of the respondents in the sample (58.0%) express that due to less of rainfall, the traditional crops are not available now (Table 5.48). Traditional crops of the region include Mash, Til, Kulth, and Chana. All those crops can be sown and grown only with adequate availability of water. View is held by Samanu and Basa besides 61.7 per cent from Uparla Thara. On the other hand, the majority of the respondents from Gho states that seasonal crops like Wheat, Rice; Maize has replaced the traditional pulses and oilseeds.

Table 5.48 : Impact of Rainfall Pattern on the Cropping Pattern

Impact	*Name of Villages*					*Total*
	Gho	*Samanu*	*Uparla Thara*	*Basa*	*Dunera*	
End of traditional crops	17 (28.3)	60 (100.0)	37 (61.7)	60 (100.0)	—	174 (58.8)
Seasonal Cropping has started	43 (71.7)	—	—	—	—	43 (14.3)
No Impact	—	—	23 (38.3)	—	60 (100.0)	83 (27.8)
Total	60 (20.0)	60 (20.0)	60 (20.0)	60 (20.0)	60 (20.0)	300 (100.0)

Those who state that seasonal crops are sown due to the changed rainfall pattern constitute 14.3 per cent of all the respondents. However, 28 per cent of all the respondents find no impact on the cropping pattern, with change, if any is, in rainfall. All the respondents from Dunera and 38.3 per cent from Uparla Thara support the above fact. Any other impact of the change in the rainfall is on the yield of different crops. A very high proportion

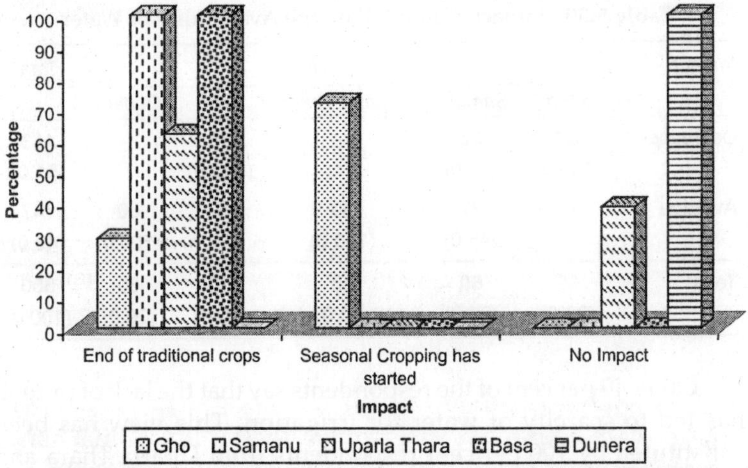

Figure 5.8 : Impact of Rainfall Pattern on the Cropping Pattern

of the respondents (82.0%) say that the yield of crops has decreased due to changed rainfall pattern (Table 5.49). All the respondents in Gho, Samanu, Uparla Thara, Basa have this belief. Only 10 per cent of he respondents from Dunera affirm this. Rest of them state that yield of crops has remained the same. It has neither decreased nor increased.

Table 5.49 : Impact of Rainfall Pattern on the Yield of Crops

Impact	*Name of Villages*					*Total*
	Gho	*Samanu*	*Uparla Thara*	*Basa*	*Dunera*	
Decreased	60 (100.0)	60 (100.0)	60 (100.0)	60 (100.0)	6 (10.0)	246 (82.0)
Remained same	—	—	—	—	54 (90.0)	54 (18.0)
Total	60 (20.0)	60 (20.0)	60 (20.0)	60 (20.0)	60 (20.0)	300 (100.0)

Adequacy or inadequacy of rainfall also affects the availability of drinking water to a large extent. There are 51 per cent of all the respondents who say that the drinking water availability has decreased (Table 5.50). All the respondents from Gho and Basa; and 55 per cent from Samanu are the votary of the above fact.

Table 5.50 : Impact of Rainfall on the Availability of Water

Impact	*Name of Villages*					*Total*
	Gho	*Samanu*	*Uparla Thara*	*Basa*	*Dunera*	
Decreased	60 (100.0)	33 (55.0)	—	60 (100.0)	—	153 (51.0)
Average	—	27 (45.0)	60 (100.0)	—	60 (100.0)	147 (49.0)
Total	60 (20.0)	60 (20.0)	60 (20.0)	60 (20.0)	60 (20.0)	300 (100.0)

Other 49 per cent of the respondents say that the lack of rainfall has led to scarcity of water for irrigation. This view has been constituted by 100 per cent respondents from Uparla Thara and Dunera; and 45 per cent from Samanu.

Besides availability of water, the temperature of the region has also been affected with change in rainfall pattern; which has been endorsed by 37.3 per cent of all the respondents. They say that the temperature has increased in both summers as well as winter (Table 5.51). Distribution of the respondents in the selected villages is 45 per cent in Gho; 28.3 per cent in Samanu; 58.3 per cent in Uparla Thara; 41.7 per cent in Basa; and 13.3 per cent in Dunera. In other words, except a small proportion of the respondents in Dunera, most of them find rise in temperature during summer and winter.

Another 33.7 per cent of all respondents hold a different view. According to them the temperature fluctuation has increased in summer as well as in winter. Earlier the summer temperature used to be bearable but now the temperature goes so high that it is difficult to come out in day time. On the other hand, the fall of temperature in winter is more than the earlier one. This view is endorsed by most of the respondents from Gho (55%); followed by those from Samanu (48.3%); and Basa (46.7%). Only some of the respondents from Uparla Thara have this opinion (18.3%). A very small group of respondents comprising of only 2.3 per cent of the total respondents (11.6 per cent from Basa) say that with change in rainfall pattern, the temperature remains higher in monsoon season now. Earlier in monsoons, the region received heavy rainfalls and, hence, the temperature used to remain cool.

Table 5.51 : Impact of Temperature on the Area

Impact	*Name of Villages*					*Total*
	Gho	*Samanu*	*Uparla Thara*	*Basa*	*Dunera*	
Temperature increases in both summer and winter	27 (45.0)	17 (28.3)	35 (58.3)	25 (41.7)	8 (13.3)	112 (37.3)
Fluctuation of temperature more in summer and winter	33 (55.0)	29 (48.3)	11 (18.3)	28 (46.7)	—	101 (33.7)
Temperature increase in monsoon is more as compared to the past	—	—	—	7 (11.6)	—	7 (2.3)
Abrupt fall in temperature in monsoons	—	14 (23.3)	14 (23.3)	—	—	28 (9.3)
Same as used to be	—	—	—	—	52 (86.7)	52 (17.3)
Total	60 (20.0)	60 (20.0)	60 (20.0)	60 (20.0)	60 (20.0)	300 (100.0)

But now, the monsoon temperature remains usually more than what it used to remain in the past. It is due to less rainfall. Some of the respondents state that there is an abrupt change in the temperature (9.3%). This view is held by many of the respondents from Samanu (23.3%) and from Uparla Thara (23.3%). According to them, the temperature falls abruptly with rainfall and immediately afterwards rises. However, 86.7 per cent of the respondents from Dunera find not much change in the temperature. This reason is that in Dunera, still there is a thick forest cover due to which the temperature of the region remains moderate as it was there in the past. Though the residents of Dunera also accept the fact that the rainfalls have decreased, but according to the group stated here, it has not affected the temperature of the region.

Further, the change in temperature has affected the community's health to a noticeable extent. About 84.2 per cent of the total respondents say that due to change in the temperature and rainfall pattern in the region, skin allergies, Asthma, High Blood Pressure and even in some cases paralysis due to high blood pressure are on the rise (Table 5.52). All the respondents in Gho and Basa; and majority (98.3%) in Samanu find rise in the incidence of above diseases. Some respondents (40.9%) from Uparla Thara too hold this view.

Table 5.52 : Effects of the Change in Temperature on the Health

Effects	*Name of Villages*					*Total*
	Gho	*Samanu*	*Uparla Thara*	*Basa*	*Dunera*	
Skin allergies, Asthma, Paralysis	60 (100.0)	59 (55.0)	18 (40.9)	60 (100.0)	—	197 (84.2)
Minor suffocation	—	1 (1.7)	26 (59.1)	—	10 (16.7)	37 (15.8)
Total	60 (25.6)	60 (25.6)	44 (18.8)	60 (25.6)	10 (4.3)	234 (78.0)

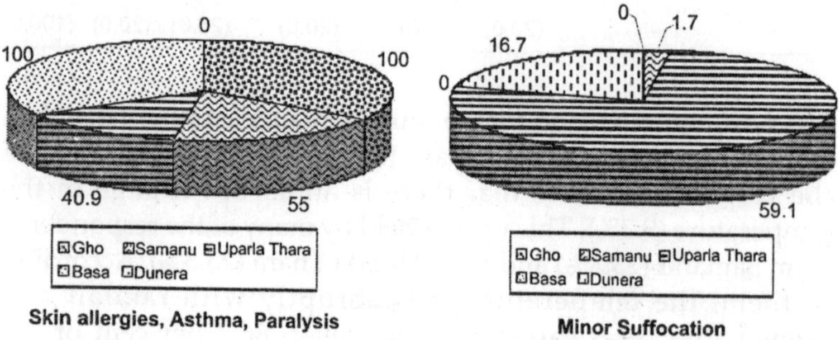

Figure 5.9 : Effects of the Change in Temperature on the Health

However, 15.8 per cent of all the respondents say that the change in temperature has resulted into minor suffocation problems, especially during rainy season when humidity level is high, but not any major health problems. Majority of the respondents in Uparla Thara (59.1%) support this view. This is also a problem as reported by 16.7 per cent of the respondents. So, the change in temperature and its fluctuation has a bearing on health of the people of Gho and Basa the most. Skin allergy, asthma and others are the main diseases which find association with the temperature change. People of Uparla Thara face health problems like suffocation, in raining seasons besides all the above diseases. Mohinder Pal Singh, Sarpanch of Mangani Panchayat in Gho,

Joginder Singh, a trader from Uparla Thara, Renu Bala an activist of the Mahila Mandal all support this notion that the climatic change consequent to deforestation has resulted into increase in spreading of diseases like asthma, skin allergies and high blood pressure. According to them these diseases have become very recurrent in the recent decade. People of Dunera do not face such health problems as temperature changes are not being observed in that area.

The respondents have been asked to enlist the changes in cropping pattern due to change in temperature. For 62.8 per cent of the respondents, the temperature fluctuation has resulted into a major change in the crops grown in the region (Table 5.53). Traditional pulses and oilseeds are no more grown in the region because fluctuation in temperature and rainfall has its impact on the maturity and the fruiting of the crop. The farmers do not get sufficient yield. Such a view is endorsed by all the respondents from Samanu and Basa, besides majority from Uparla Thara. Further, majority of respondents in Gho and Dunera find that people have shifted to cereal crops like Wheat, Maize, and Rice instead of traditional oilseeds, pulses and vegetables due to shifting rainfall and temperature. So, rainfall has changed the cropping pattern of the region.

Table 5.53 : Impact of Rainfall and Temperature on the Cropping Pattern

Impact	*Name of Villages*					*Total*
	Gho	*Samanu*	*Uparla Thara*	*Basa*	*Dunera*	
End of Traditional crops	17 (28.3)	60 (100.0)	37 (61.7)	60 (100.0)	—	174 (62.8)
Shift to foodgrains	43 (71.7)	—	—	—	60 (100.0)	103 (37.1)
Total	60 (21.7)	60 (21.7)	37 (13.4)	60 (21.7)	60 (21.7)	277 (92.3)

While stating other impacts of changing rainfall pattern, 45.3 per cent respondents say that their economic burden has increased (Table 5.54). This view has been forwarded by all the respondents from Basa; followed by Samanu (58.3%); Uparla Thara (38.3%);

Gho (21.7%) and Dunera (8.3%). As compared to the respondents from Dunera and Gho, economic burden of most of the respondents has increased. Other 8.3 per cent respondents say that their income has decreased to a significant extent as due to the fall in the agricultural productivity as a consequence of the change in rainfall pattern. The view is advanced by most of the respondents from Gho (36.7%); and a few in Uparla Thara (5.0%).

In the past, fruits like mango, guava were sown and produced on a large scale. The quantity of fruit produced was so sufficient that it was transferred to other areas for sale. From this, people used to earn good amounts. But with decreased rainfall, decline in soil fertility and change in temperature, the fruit production has decreased resulting in cutting of fruit trees.

Table 5.54 : Other Impact of Rainfall Pattern

Other Impact	*Name of Villages*					*Total*
	Gho	*Samanu*	*Uparla Thara*	*Basa*	*Dunera*	
Not Specific	35 (38.3)	17 (28.3)	–	–	37 (61.7)	89 (29.7)
Increased Economic Burden	13 (21.7)	35 (58.3)	23 (38.3)	60 (100.0)	5 (8.3)	136 (45.3)
Income has decreased due to lack of agricultural produce	22 (38.7)	–	3 (5.0)	–	-	25 (8.3)

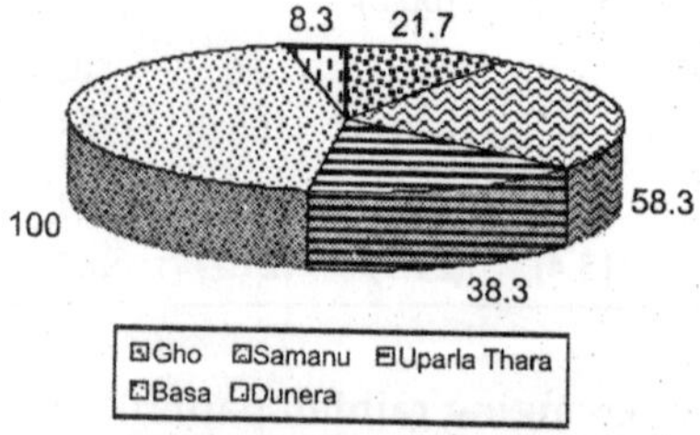

Increased Economic Burden

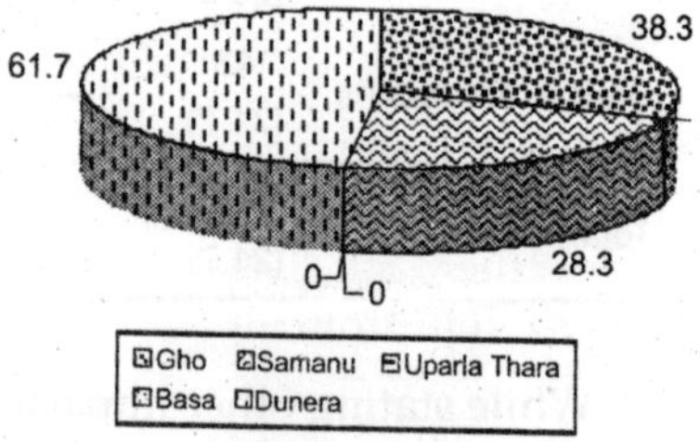

No Specific Impact

Figure 5.10 : Other Impact of Rainfall Pattern

Other 29.7 per cent of the respondents do not find any specific change in rainfall pattern. This view has been constituted by 61.7 per cent of the respondents from Dunera; followed by those from Gho (38.3%); and Samanu (28.3%). So, change in rainfall and temperature has increased the economic burden of the respondents particularly due to decreased production of marketable fruits and traditional crops of oilseeds, pulses, herbs, etc.

Women and Environment

Women have always had a very strong relationship with the environment; and have held a prominent place in ecological discourse. The evidence is Eco-feminism which explained Radical, Socialist and Liberal linkage between women and the environment. Out of theoretical framework, it is well realized that there is a strong linkage between environment and women's survival. Taking this content into consideration, a special stress has been given to women's livelihood pattern. An attempt has been made to explore various aspects of feminine life linked with the natural environment. A comparative analysis has been made on the basis of the pattern of living of women 10 years ago and in the present times. In all, 67 per cent of all the respondents tell that in addition to household chores, the women of the area are generally involved in works like household chores, collection of wood and in carpet weaving and embroidery works (Table 5.55). All the respondents in Gho; Samanu; and Basa have stated the above fact. Many of the respondents from Uparla Thara endorse it (35.0%).

According to other 20 per cent of the respondents, the women of the region are involved in household works and carpet weaving besides doing embroidery on shawls. Self-employment through cottage industry is found to be prominent in Dunera (58.3%) and Uparla Thara (41.7%). Forwarding another view, 13 per cent respondents say that women are involved in household works only and their percentage is low as compared to those engaged in one or the other task. The village-wise distribution of respondents is 23.3 per cent from Uparla Thara and 41.7 per cent from Dunera. The economic structure of these two villages reveals that many people are engaged in construction work at Ranjit Sagar Dam in Uparla Thara which provides consistent income and those in Dunera have a high economic status due to cottage industry

Table 5.55 : Types of Works the Women Do

Types	*Name of Villages*					*Total*
	Gho	*Samanu*	*Uparla Thara*	*Basa*	*Dunera*	
Household task/ collection of wood/ cottage industry	60 (100.0)	60 (100.0)	21 (35.0)	60 (100.0)	—	201 (67.0)
Self-employment through cottage industry	—	—	25 (41.7)	—	35 (58.3)	60 (20.0)
Household chores only	—	—	14 (23.3)	—	25 (41.7)	39 (13.0)
Total	60 (20.0)	60 (20.0)	60 (20.0)	60 (20.0)	60 (20.0)	300 (100.0)

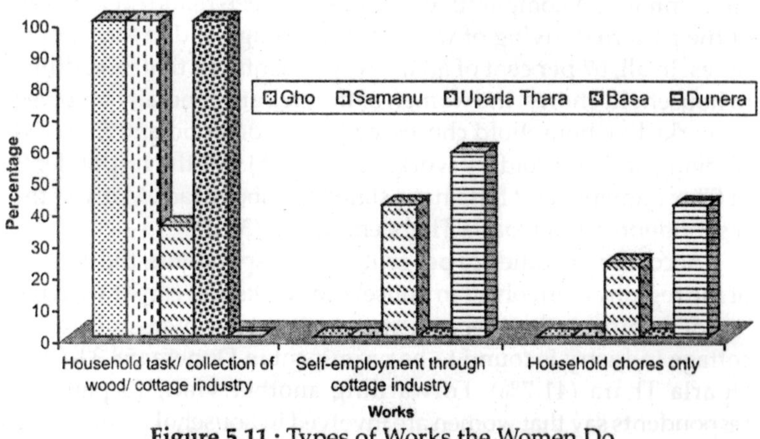

Figure 5.11 : Types of Works the Women Do

particularly preparing goods from the fruits of trees in the area. A study (Venkateshwaran, 1995) shows that women are replaced from outside work with rise in level of the family. This may be due to the reasons that women in Uparla Thara and Dunera are confined to household works only.

However, the pattern has not remained the same. According to 80 per cent of respondents, the work pattern and trend of the women in the area has drastically changed (Table 5.56). Leaving aside the respondents of Dunera, all the respondents in Gho, Samanu, Uparla Thara and Basa find a change in pattern of women's work. The respondents in Dunera state that all types of the works the women of the area used to do in the past are done now as well.

Table 5.56 : Change in Pattern of Women's Work

Change	*Name of Villages*					*Total*
	Gho	*Samanu*	*Uparla Thara*	*Basa*	*Dunera*	
Yes	60 (100.0	60 (100.0)	60 (100.0)	60 (100.0)	—	240 (80.0)
No	—	—	—	—	60 (100.0)	60 (20.0)
Total	60 (20.0)	60 (20.0)	60 (20.0)	60 (20.0)	60 (20.0)	300 (100.0)

To lay down a clear picture, the discussion now shifts to the works done by women in the past ten years. Earlier the women had been involved in agricultural tasks with the males of the household besides *pattal* making and collecting wood from the forest as reported by 77.1 per cent of he respondents (Table 5.57).

Table 5.57 : The Works Done by Women in the Past Ten Years

Works	*Name of Villages*					*Total*
	Gho	*Samanu*	*Uparla Thara*	*Basa*	*Dunera*	
Agricultural tasks; *pattal* making and wood collection	60 (100.0)	57 (95.0)	—	60 (100.0)	35 (100.0)	212 (77.1)
Agricultural Activities only	—	3 (5.0)	60 (100.0)	—	—	63 (22.9)
Total	60 (21.8)	60 (21.8)	60 (21.8)	60 (21.8)	35 (21.8)	275 (91.7)

Majority of the women in Gho, Samanu, and Dunera were involved in such task. On the other hand, majority of the women in Uparla Thara were engaged in agricultural activities like sowing and harvesting. About 23 per cent of the respondents keep this opinion. It is clear from the views derived that in the past ten years the majority of women have been involved in tasks like agricultural works, making dishes from the broad leaves of trees and collection of firewood. But in the present times, the main task done by the women includes household chores, carpet weaving and embroidery on shawls in addition to collection of firewood. Collection of firewood still remains a part of women's work life. They are largely replaced from the work in the fields to embroidery, etc., confined within the household; and on the other hand the important concern is *pattal* making.

In the past ten years women have been involved in making *pattals* and used it as an industry to earn good income, but now women do not spend much time on it. The discussion shall become clear in the following part, where time division for various works has been referred to. An analysis has been made in the context of how much time women devoted to a particular activity ten years ago and how much time they devote to the same activity in the present time. There are 61.9 per cent of the total respondents stating that women spend 10 to 15 hours on agricultural works (Table 5.58). In comparison to Gho and Basa, a large proportion of women in Samanu (85.4%) and Gho (73.3%) were spending time between 10-15 hours for agricultural work, *pattal* making, and collecting firewood and so on.

Table 5.58 : Time Spent by Women on Agriculture in the Past Ten (10) Years

Time (in hours)	*Name of Villages*					*Total*
	Gho	*Samanu*	*Uparla Thara*	*Basa*	*Dunera*	
5-10	19 (31.7)	7 (14.6)	16 (26.7)	23 (38.3)	35 (100.0)	100 (38.1)
10-15	41 (68.3)	41 (85.4)	44 (73.3)	37 (61.7)	—	163 (61.9)
Total	60 (22.8)	48 (18.2)	60 (22.8)	60 (22.8)	35 (13.3)	263 (87.7)

Further, 38.1 per cent of the respondents say that women used to spend 5 to 10 hours on agricultural work. This view is supported by a large proportion of respondents from Basa (38.3%) and Gho (31.7%). In this way, majority of the women in Samanu and Uparla Thara as compared to Gho and Basa spent more than 10 hours in different types of works. Only 58.3 per cent of the respondents from Dunera have given their response and all of them say that women used to spend 5-10 hours on different activities about 10 years ago.

The scenario has changed drastically in the present times as 40 per cent of all the respondents say that now women of the region spend 2 to 3 hours on agricultural works as compared to more than 5 hours in the past (Table 5.59). The percentage in the selected villages is 81.7 per cent in Gho; and 73.3 per cent in Basa and 45 per cent in Samanu.

Table 5.59 : Time Spent by Women on Agriculture at Present

Time (in hours)	*Name of Villages*					*Total*
	Gho	*Samanu*	*Uparla Thara*	*Basa*	*Dunera*	
2-3	49 (81.7)	27 (45.0)	—	44 (73.3)	—	120 (40.0)
3-4	11 (18.3)	4 (6.7)	—	26 (43.3)	—	41 (13.7)
No time given to agriculture now	—	29 (48.3)	60 (100)	—	—	89 (29.7)

Another 13.7 per cent of the total respondents express that women spend 3 to 4 hours on agricultural works in the present time. This response has been forwarded by 43.3 per cent respondent from Basa followed by 18.3 per cent from Gho; and 6.7 per cent from Samanu. Furthermore, 29.7 per cent of the total respondents say that now women do not give time to agricultural tasks. This is invariably true for all the women in Uparla Thara and nearly 50 per cent in Samanu. It may be inferred that women now spend less time on field job and many of them have withdrawn from such arduous tasks particularly in Uparla Thara.

So as to lay a comparison between the routine of women in the past time and that of the present, activity-wise analysis has been taken up. In case of *pattal* making, 77.1 per cent of all the respondents say that the women engaged in the activity about 10 years ago and now only 52.3 per cent have remained (Tables 5.60 and 5.61). Nearly 35 per cent of all the respondents say that about ten years ago, the women devoted 2 to 3 hours to this work. Whereas 42.9 per cent used to spend 3-4; and 21.7 per cent used to spend more than 4 hours a day.

Table 5.60 : Time Spent on *Pattal* Making in the Past Ten Years

Time (in hours)	*Name of Villages*					*Total*
	Gho	*Samanu*	*Uparla Thara*	*Basa*	*Dunera*	
2-3	12 (20.0)	30 (52.6)	—	27 (45.0)	6 (17.1)	75 (35.4)
3-4	36 (60.0)	14 (24.6)	—	21 (35.0)	20 (57.1)	91 (42.9)
4-5	12 (20.0)	13 (22.8)	—	12 (20.0)	9 (25.7)	46 (21.7)
Total	60 (28.3)	60 (28.3)	—	60 (28.3)	35 (16.5)	212 (70.7)

Table 5.61 : Time Spent by Women on *pattal* Making at Present

Time (in hours)	*Name of Villages*					*Total*
	Gho	*Samanu*	*Uparla Thara*	*Basa*	*Dunera*	
1-2	—	19 (31.7)	—	17 (28.3)	—	36 (22.9)
2-3	—	40 (66.7)	—	30 (50)	—	70 (44.6)
3-4	—	1 (1.7)	—	—	—	1 (0.6)
Intermittent after some days	37 (61.7)	—	—	13 (21.7)	—	50 (31.8)
Total	37 (23.6)	60 (38.2)	—	60 (38.2)	—	157 (52.3)

Most of the women in Samanu used to spend 2-3 hours a day on *pattal* making and the majority of the women from Gho and Dunera spent 3-4 hours for this work. In comparison, to other villages, many of the women in Dunera and Samanu were engaged in *pattals* making for this cottage industry based on forests ranging between 2-5 hours a day. This shows the demand that existed for *pattals* in the market about ten years ago.

The data in Table 5.62 reveals that there is a decrease in the demand as 52.3 per cent of the respondents have reported about the involvement of the women in *pattal* making. At present, the percentage of women engaged in the above activity has dropped to 61.7 per cent and the working women engage themselves in this activity whenever the demand for it comes out. In Samanu and Basa, majority of the women are taking up this activity for 2 to 3 hours a day as reported by 66.7 per cent and 50 per cent of the respondents respectively.

Another important chore which holds huge space in the life and routine of women of Kandi area is the collection of firewood. Before the adoption of stove and gas, firewood had been one of the tasks of women which consumed a lot of time of women. While talking about the period over ten years back, 60.2 per cent of the total respondents say that women took 1 to 3 hours to collect firewood from the forests (Table 5.62). The distribution of percentage in the selected villages is 71.7 per cent in Gho; 73.3 in Samanu and; 21.7 per cent in Basa. All the respondents from Uparla Thara used to take 1 to 3 hours to collect firewood.

Table 5.62 : Time Spent by Women on Collection of Wood in the Past Ten Years

Time (in hours)	*Name of Villages*					*Total*
	Gho	*Samanu*	*Uparla Thara*	*Basa*	*Dunera*	
1-3	43 (71.7)	44 (73.3)	21 (100.0)	13 (21.7)	—	121 (60.2)
3-4	14 (23.3)	15 (25.0)	—	28 (46.7)	—	57 (28.4)
4-5	3 (5.0)	1 (1.7)	—	19 (31.7)	—	23 (11.4)

Forwarding an addition to the discussion, 28.4 per cent of the total respondents say that for collection of wood, it took between 3 to 4 hours per day. This view is held by majority of respondents from Basa (46.7%) followed by those from Samanu (25.0%) and Gho (23.3%). For another 11.7 per cent of the respondents collecting firewood used to take 4 to 5 hours per day about ten years back. This category of respondents includes majority of respondents from Basa (31.7%) and a few from Gho (5.0%) and Samanu (1.7%).

With the passage of time, the time taken to collect firewood has significantly increased. As against 67 per cent of the respondents, 57.7 per cent of the respondents have given their views on the time consumed to fetch firewood now. Moreover none of the respondents from Uparla Thara and Dunera has recorded their views on this issue. According to 32.9 per cent of all the respondents say that women spend not less than 5 hours on collection of firewood (Table 5.63).

Table 5.63 : Time Spent by Women on Collection of Wood at Present

Time (in hours)	*Name of Villages*					*Total*
	Gho	*Samanu*	*Uparla Thara*	*Basa*	*Dunera*	
5-7	29 (48.3)	11 (20.7)	—	17 (28.3)	—	57 (32.9)
7-8	9 (15.0)	24 (45.3)	—	19 (31.7)	—	52 (30.1)
8 or more	22 (36.7)	18 (34.0)	—	24 (40.0)	—	64 (33.0)
Total	60 (34.7)	53 (30.6)	—	60 (30.6)	—	173 (57.7)

About 30 per cent of the total respondents say that it takes 7 to 8 hours to collect fuelwood now. According to them, women from Samanu (45.3%) and Basa (31.7%) take more time than those from Gho. Other than 37 per cent of the total respondents comprising of 40 per cent from Basa; 36.7 per cent from Gho and 34 per cent from Samanu say that women spend 8 to 10 hours a day for collection of wood in present time.

The analysis thus provides that women who usually spent one to five hours to fetch firewood earlier now have to spend five to ten hours a day. It means the time for collecting firewood has almost doubled. It is largely due to the deforestation that has taken place in the vicinity of the village for study.

In case of agricultural activities, the women used to give a lot of time about ten years ago, but now it is reduced to a negligible in some activities and even nil in other cases. Most of the women from Gho, Samanu, Uparla Thara, and Basa sailed in the same boat in the past and even in the present they have been affected similarly. In the past they used to devote good time to agricultural activities, pattal making and less time to collection of firewood; but now the time spent on agricultural activities has largely reduced and also it has reduced in case of *pattal* making. Whereas, now women spend more time on collecting firewood as the forests are denuded and pushed far away from their residential places.

Earlier the Kandi region had thick forest cover. Males were busy in agrarian tasks; so females took the responsibility on their shoulders of collecting wood. Due to geographical proximity of the forests to the dwelling places, the women of the area used to commute to the forests and come back home after collecting wood in few hours only. Along with this responsibility, they managed the task of household very well because the collection of wood did not consume more time. But now, with a huge scale of deforestation, the distance between the forests and the village has increased. Now the forests are not adjacent to the village boundaries, rather have gone kilometres far off from the boundaries. This has rather increased the work burden of women. And it has resulted both deterioration in their health as well as livelihood. Since the economic status of many of the women in the sample has been affected.

Analyzing the life routine of the women of Kandi area of Punjab, it can be said that though the working pattern has changed and the time devoted particularly to categories of works has altered drastically; women still remain a contribution to the economy and management of their respective households. Women manage many crucial tasks, without which the household cannot run smoothly. Though women now do not participate in agricultural work due to decline in agricultural profile of the region; but still the work burden of women has not decreased.

An exactly similar proportion of the sample adds a response in apposition to the just preceding discourse and express that the change in the women working pattern has affected the life of the girl child. The reason is that the girls are withdrawn from the schools and deprived of literacy when they are made to stay at homes to complete the pending household tasks.

A glance of bird's eye view throws light that, 60 per cent respondents comprising of 100 per cent respondents from Gho,

Samanu and Basa say that the major adverse effect of the change in women's working pattern on the life of the girl child is deprivation of literacy, which is really a serious concern for the region and the people too. Girls are enrolled in the primary or senior secondary schools, but they are conveniently withdrawn from the schools; simply because their help is needed in managing the household chores. Not only this, the health of the elderly women whose workload has increased also suffers from adversities. The studies conducted by Cranney (2001); Nanda and Ali (2006); and Dey (2006) also support the same findings.

The males were busy in agricultural tasks, and the women used to spend enough time on making *pattals* and earned sitting at homes. *Pattal* making served as a good income source for the women of the Kandi area. But, this industry has suffered from a jolt due to scientific and technological advancement. People prefer to buy plastic disposables easily available in the market on very low rates, instead of *Pattals* as a matter of hygiene, sophistication and also convenience. So, the business of *Pattal* making and selling has reduced in the region because now women do not fetch good price and the income is small in this task. In nutshell it could be concluded that all the women who ever earned by selling the *pattals* made by them, the passage of time and the technological advancement in the region have deprived them of the income once they used to earn about ten years ago.

The present study reveals a dimension of ecological bond between women and natural environment. The notions expressed by radical, socialist and liberal eco-feminism endorse the fact that there exists a super-organic relation between there two creators i.e. women and the natural environment.

The natural environment has been providing psychological contentment and a socialistic platform of earning to the women. And environment in the phase of degradation (especially in form of deforestation) has deteriorated the living standards of the women of Kandi areas. Firstly, the work burden of women has multiplied drastically leaving a negative effect on the health of the women. Secondly, the girl child is withdrawn from school to share the workload of the elderly women of the household, which directly affects the standard of women by depriving them of education.

6 Crisis Management

The ever increasing pressure on our scarce forest resources to meet the national, social and industrial needs is a cause of concern for everyone. The per capita forests have reduced from 0.11 hectare in 1983 to 0.74 hectare in 2001 (Forest Survey of India, 2001). According to the Wasteland Survey of India (2000) the total area of wastelands in the country is 6.38 lakh sq. km., which includes 1.4 lakh sq. km. of degraded notified forest lands. In such a situation management of the existing forests, along with preservation, post-protection or regeneration remains a major challenge for the governance. But the government, being an extract of the masses can be successful only if the masses adhere to, and complement to the policies and programmes made by it. A very practical method to cope with the biotic pressure and environmental loss is to involve the effected communities to protect the forest and the share the benefits therefrom. Joint Forest Management (JFM) is an outcome of this philosophy-participation of the community gives rise to the chances of success of any programme being undertaken by the administrative bodies. JFM has helped to mitigate the process of degradation of environment to a significant extent (Bhattacharya, 2007). Emile Durkheim's Theory of Development holds prominence in discourses related to development, growth and progress. The theory states that there are three stages of Development of a society. First stage is 'Hordes', second is 'Segments' and the third stage is 'Organisation'. Hordes are multitude of masses representing partly a nomadic characteristic. Then is segments which can be expressed or explained to be communistic. After it, comes the organization of the masses. An organized society is complex. Individuals are not like one another. Such a society is characterized by division of labour, differentiation of function, and a large number of occupation, specialisation of tasks, interdependence, effective communication, coordination, restitutive justice, as well as organic solidarity. This complexity develops on the platform of the simplicity engrossed in the earlier stages (Singh, 2006). While making an analogy it can be said that the governance is constitutive of the masses and thus the nature of the masses reflects through the governance. Governance is a name given to adequately organized groups of individuals possessing expertise of management and administration. Some- where or the other, it is difficult to separate the popularist strength from that of the governance as both constitute and complement each other amidst the contradiction forwarded mutually. In such a pretext to manage environment or to manage any other mass level issue, both the government and the masses need to be given equal participation. The third category here is the Non-State Actors i.e. Non-Governmental Organisations (NGOs). Hence, to combat issues like environmental degradation which encompass large section of masses, it is important to analyse and reallocate the roles of government, commoners and the Non-Governmental Organizations too. All these together constitute the society as a whole.

The contemporary approach to environmental management and protection suggests that concern for biological diversity requires a far more subtle appreciation of both human and natural influences. 'People exploit and degrade the natural environment' as a phrase dominates the phrase 'people can preserve and protect environment'. Earlier one being a dominant thought paradigm has now been questioned by the advocates of contemporary environmentalism. The contemporary environmentalism calls into question the separation of people from nature and support the view that people are part of nature. In most terrestrial and coastal environments, both the form and the degree of biological diversity result from a combination of cyclical ecological and climatic processes and post-human actions. Hence more importantly, conservation efforts may need to identify and promote those social processes which enable the local communities to conserve and enhance biodiversity as a part of their livelihood system. Indeed, the terms like 'People Participation' and 'Popular Participation' are now part of the regular language usage of many development agencies, including Non-Governmental Organizations (NGOs), government departments and also the Banks (Adman *et al.*, 1992 and Pretty, 1994).

Hence, ecological thinking realizes the importance of community participation in present times. There has been growing recognition that without local involvement, there is little chance of protecting wildlife and the forest also. Moreover, the cost of park and forest management goes very high in case the local communities are not involved (Ghimira and Michel, 2006). Considering the stated importance of community participation in environmental management, the present research work aims at exploring the stand of the communities in context of environmental management; factors which prompt them to participate in the environmental protection progress or to escape such efforts; mechanisms they think are more suitable and functional to retain or to recreate the green cover; role of the governmental or non-governmental agencies in environmental protection. In the following part of this chapter the theme of people's participation in environmental management is being explained multi-dimensionally. It is very crucial to know whether people of the Kandi belt understand the importance of their role in environmental management or not, along with understanding the importance of environment for their life and sustenance.

On being asked whether plants and trees are being planted in the region or not, 40 per cent of all the respondents say that the plants and trees are being planted (Table 6.1). The distribution of percentage in the selected villages is 100 per cent in Uparla Thara and Dunera. On the other hand, 60 per cent of the total respondents, comprising of all the respondents from Gho; Samanu; and Basa

Table 6.1 : Efforts being made to Plant Trees in the Region

Efforts	*Name of Villages*					*Total*
	Gho	*Samanu*	*Uparla Thara*	*Basa*	*Dunera*	
Yes	—	—	60 (100.0)	—	60 (100.0)	120 (40.0)
No	60 (100.0)	60 (100.0)	—	60 (100.0)	—	180 (60.0)
Total	60 (100.0)	60 (100.0)	60 (100.0)	60 (100.0)	60 (100.0)	300 (100.0)

strongly deny the recently quoted view and say that there have no efforts for plantations in their region.

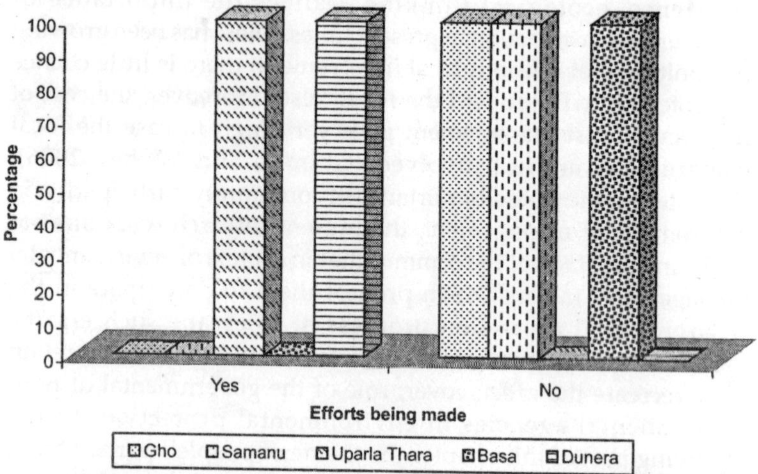

Figure 6.1: Efforts being made to Plant Trees in the Region

In apposition of the discussion, 47.3 per cent of all the respondents say that under the plantation schemes, generally the trees of Arzaan, Khair, Tahli and Kikar are planted. The percentage in the selected villages is 33.3 per cent in Uparla Thara and 56.7 per cent in Dunera (Table 6.2).

Table 6.2 : Types of Trees being planted in the Area under Afforestation Schemes

Types of Trees	*Name of Villages*					
	Gho	*Samanu*	*Uparla Thara*	*Basa*	*Dunera*	*Total*
Arzaan, Khair, Tahli, Kikar	—	—	20 (33.3)	—	34 (56.7)	54 (47.3)
Not known	—	—	60 (100.0)	—	—	60 (52.6)

Other 52.6 per cent out of the total respondents encompassed under this discussion (all such respondents from Uparla Thara) say that no doubt plants and trees are planted in the region by the

government, but varieties of those trees being planted are not known.

Making an addition to the discussion linked to the environmental morose of Kandi region, 64.3 per cent of the total respondents hold a grudge that the Government has never undertaken any Afforestation Programme in the region (Table 6.3). The percentage in the selected villages is 100 per cent in Gho, Samanu, and Basa, and 21.7 per cent in Uparla Thara.

Table 6.3 : Any Afforestation Programmes undertaken by the Government in their Villages

Yes/No	*Name of Villages*					
	Gho	*Samanu*	*Uparla Thara*	*Basa*	*Dunera*	*Total*
Yes	—	—	47 (78.3)	—	60 (100.0)	107 (35.7)
No	60 (100.0)	60 (100.0)	13 (21.7)	60 (100.0)	—	193 (64.3)
Total	60 (100.0)	60 (100.0)	60 (100.0)	60 (100.0)	60 (100.0)	300 (100.0)

It is only 35.7 per cent of all the respondents who hold a positive response stating that afforestation programmes have been undertaken by the government in this area. The village-wise distribution of such respondents is 78.3 per cent in Uparla Thara and 100 per cent in Dunera. The majority of the respondents inclusive of 64.3 per cent of the entire sample says that no afforestation programme has been undertaken by the government in their region. Table 6.1 aims at asking if any efforts have ever been made to plant trees or plants in the region or not; whereas Table 6.3 talks of the large scale plantation schemes for afforestation undertaken by the government. In both the contexts, the situation is not satisfactory. Neither small scale plantations nor any large scale afforestation programmes are being undertaken for the villages falling severe prey to deforestation, except in the villages Dunera and Uparla Thara, which is well reflected through the responses derived herein too.

People are not happy with response of government to other forms of environmental degradation other than deforestation. In this context, 80 per cent of the total respondents say that the government has not taken any step to improve the environment of the area (Table 6.4). All the respondents from the villages Gho; Samanu, Uparla Thara, and Basa fall under this category of response.

Table 6.4 : Steps taken by the Government/Panchayat to improve Environment of the Area

Steps	*Name of Villages*					
	Gho	*Samanu*	*Uparla Thara*	*Basa*	*Dunera*	*Total*
Yes	—	—	—	—	60 (100.0)	60 (20.0)
No	60 (100.0)	60 (100.0)	60 (100.0)	60 (100.0)	—	240 (80.0)
Total	60 (100.0)	60 (100.0)	60 (100.0)	60 (100.0)	60 (100.0)	300 (100.0)

Further, 20 per cent of all the respondents (all such respondents form Dunera), say that the government has taken steps to improve the environment of the region. It is only the respondents from Dunera who have notified the afforestation programmes undertaken by the Government.

Role of Local Governing Bodies

The political paradigm of the villages is featured with Panchayats and Mahila Mandals. These are the two local governing bodies which effect the social, economic, cultural and even environmental structures of the region.

The 73rd Constitutional Amendment Act, 1992 marked a new era in the democratic set-up of the nation as it created Panchayati Raj Institution (PRIs) of self-governance below the level of States in the federal set-up. It is also a landmark in the decentralized development as it encourages people's participation in the process of planning, decision-making, implementation, and delivery. These constitutional provisions provide for devolution of powers and responsibilities to different tiers of PRIs with respect to preparation of plans and programmes for economic development and social justice and their implementation in relation to 29 subjects listed in the Eleventh Schedule. So far, about 2,32,278 Panchayats at the village level, 6,022 Panchayats at the intermediate level and 535 Panchayats at the district level have been constructed in the country. The Panchayats are being manned by about 3 million elected representatives at all the levels, of which one-third are women. This is the broadest representative base that exists in any country in the world (Ram, 2007). Taking this fact into consideration, it becomes one of the most desired academic obligations of the researcher to explore the role of Panchayat and Mahila Mandal in the region. An attempt has been made to know what are the major functions performed by the Panchayat and Mahila Mandal of these villages and what is the people's assessment of the functioning of these governing bodies.

Even after having the world's strongest democratic set-up, the rural India thrives for environmental protection, amelioration of agricultural productivity and standards, water availability; sewage and sewerage adequacy, gender justice, and many more such issues. It implies that there are some lapses in the functioning of these local bodies, which need to be traced out with critical and analytical efficiency. Empirical research is the best method to extract the facts related to functioning of Panchayats. Mahila Mandals are a concrete evidence for the attempts made for political empowerment of rural women. But the way these Mahila Mandals are functioning, does not satisfy the rural dwellers and women. The following part of the chapter puts light on the function being performed by Mahila Mandals also. All the respondents expressed in common that no doubt, Mahila Mandals exist in their region; but the existence of Mahila Mandals does not cater to the needs of the women community and even the other residents.

There are 42 per cent of all the respondents who say that Mahila Mandal does not perform any crucial functions at all (Table 6.5). The percentage in the selected villages is 55 per cent in Gho; 55 in Samanu; 23.3 per cent in Uparla Thara; and 76.7 per cent in Basa.

Other 58 per cent of all the respondents say that Mahila Mandal performs minor function like giving donation on occasions of needs like marriages, etc., and even in case of deaths, emergencies, etc. The view has been constituted by 45 per cent respondents from Gho and Samanu; 76.7 per cent from Uparla Thara; 23.3 per cent from Basa; and all the respondents from Dunera. Other 42 per cent of all the respondents tell that these governmental bodies perform no task at all. This percentage comprises of 55 per cent

Table 6.5 : Functions of the Mahila Mandal

Functions	*Name of Villages*					*Total*
	Gho	*Samanu*	*Uparla Thara*	*Basa*	*Dunera*	
No work at all	33 (51.0)	33 (51.0)	14 (23.3)	46 (76.7)	–	126 (42.0)
Minor donation works	27 (45.0)	27 (45.0)	46 (76.7)	14 (23.3)	60 (100.0)	174 (58.0)
Total	60 (100.0)	60 (100.0)	60 (100.0)	60 (100.0)	60 (100.0)	300 (100.0)

respondents from Gho; 55 per cent respondents from Samanu; 23.3 per cent respondents from Uparla Thara; and 76.7 per cent respondents from Basa.

The importance and success of Mahila Mandal in the minds of the masses is a factor directly related to the functions performed by them in the villages. According to the people of Kandi area, the most important work in the region is to manage environment because environment is a crucial factor which is connected with many other factors like health, gender, economy, etc. All the respondents in common hold a grudge against the Mahila Mandals; as these Mandals does not even discuss the issues related to environmental degradation like deforestation, shortage of water, rainfall loss, etc. People say that redressal of environmental grievances is a far off thought for them as Mahila Mandal has never been seen having any discourse on environment or addressing environmental issues. In case of an absolute ignorance for environmental concern, no step has been taken till now to improve the environmental conditions; due to which the environment of the region is degrading consistently.

In the same context, the Panchayat officials give a defensive view. According to the views of Mohinder Pal Singh, the Sarpanch of Mangani Panchayat in Gho; Panchayats do not get enough funds to fulfil the obligation of environmental management. Village Gho has three Panchayat in all (i) Mangani Panchayat, (ii) Proper Gho, (iii) Khwana Panchayat According to his views, these three Panchayats get rupees 1,00,000 per month, out of which 20 per cent, i.e., rupees 20,000 comes in the share of Mangani Panchayat and rest gets divided among proper Gho Panchayat and Khwana

Panchayat. Mohinder Pal says that the amount received by his Panchayat is used on various welfare motives as desired by the villagers and Panchayat officials, and some of the amount is used to give payments which are due to the employees of the Panchayat for the works done in the past. Highly resembling statement has been given by Mahila Mandal official activist, Renu Bala. According to her, the money cannot be saved for environmental management when some people in the region are in dire need of help in case of health crises and in case of marriages of the daughters of poor parents.

It has been noticed that environment degradation has affected the livelihood and survival pattern of women of Kandi region. Their literacy, health, household pattern and even income have been affected with multiple environmental changes. Hence, it becomes a mandatory obligation of the Mahila Mandal to respond spontaneously to environmental degradation in order to help their community members too. But in fact these mandals have been a failure in this context as they have not justifiably responded to the environment related needs and requirements of the masses during the course of their interview.

People of Kandi area are though politically active and they participate in Panchayat's proceedings with interest; still they are not happy with the performance of the Panchayats in context of environmental management and protection. According to the respondents 'Environment' is the most neglected area of functioning as far as the Mahila Mandals and Panchayats are concerned. The responses derived and elaborated in this chapter clearly reflect discontentment which the masses hold about the local governing authorities and organizations. In case of partial or a complete failure of the government or governmental organization, the obligation of the ordinary masses and their leadership becomes a functional resort to rely upon. Ordinary people and Non-state actors like Non-Governmental Organisations (NGOs) are to undertake amelioration plans. Until and unless the ordinary people and the popularist power gets involved in the realm of improvement plans, success cannot be attained. The research undertaken in the selected villages forwards detailed information about people's participation and the existence of NGOs in the region. It is further helpful for effective policy making for environmental upgradation.

Community Participation

The status of people's participation in environmental management programmes and planning is not satisfactory rather disappointing. In all, only 95.3 per cent of the respondents contribute a response to this discussion; out of which 44.8 per cent believe that ordinary people should participate in programmes or activities for environmental management (Table 6.6). The percentage in the selected villages is 5.5 per cent in Gho; 55 per cent in Samanu; 68.3 per cent in Uparla Thara; 21.6 per cent in Tarhari Basa, and 66.7 per cent in Dunera. In other words, respondents in Uparla Thara, Dunera and Samanu have shown more interest in people as well in their participation in the environmental management as compared to those from Gho and Tarhari Basa. This reflects the awareness level and the government efforts towards afforestation in these villages.

Table 6.6 : Ordinary People's View about their Own Participation in Environment Upgradation Programmes

Should/ Should Not	*Name of Villages*					*Total*
	Gho	*Samanu*	*Uparla Thara*	*Basa*	*Dunera*	
Should Participate	3 (5.5)	33 (55.0)	41 (68.3)	11 (21.6)	40 (66.7)	128 (44.8)
Should Not	52 (94.5)	27 (45.0)	19 (31.7)	40 (78.4)	20 (33.3)	158 (55.2)
Total	55 (91.7)	60 (100.0)	60 (100.0)	51 (85.0)	60 (`100.0)	286 (95.3)

On the contrary, 55.2 per cent of all the respondents hold a contrary view that ordinary masses should not participate in these environmental management programmes. Such view is held by 94.5 per cent of the respondents in Gho; 78.4 per cent in Basa; 45 per cent in Samanu; 33.3 per cent in Dunera; and 31.7 per cent in Uparla Thara.

In continuation of the same context, 44.8 per cent of the total respondents who believe that the ordinary people should participate in such programmes; illustrate by saying that it is their civil responsibility for their own selves ana for other members of society too (Table 6.7). Such positive attitude for environmental management is largely held by respondents from Uparla Thara (68.3%), Dunera (66.7%), and Samanu (55.0%) as compared to those of Gho (5.5%) and Basa (21.6%).

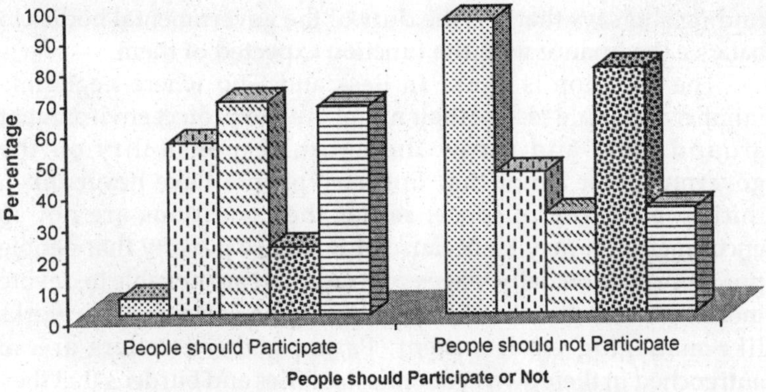

Figure 6.2 : Ordinary People's View about their Own Participation in Environment Upgradation Programmes

Table 6.7 : The Reasons behind the Community Participation

Reasons	*Name of Villages*					*Total*
	Gho	*Samanu*	*Uparla Thara*	*Basa*	*Dunera*	
Yes, because this is a civilian duty of masses to maintain environment around them	3 (5.5)	33 (55)	41 (68.3)	11 (21.6)	40 (66.6)	128 (44.8)
No, because it is the job of the government, not the ordinary masses	52 (94.5)	27 (45.0)	19 (31.7)	40 (78.4)	20 (33.3)	158 (55.2)
Total	55 (91.7)	60 (100.0)	60 (100.0)	51 (85.0)	60 (100.0)	286 (95.3)

On the contrary 55.2 per cent of all the respondents who do not support that the ordinary people's participation should participate in such programmes, hold that it is the responsibility of the government rather than that of the ordinary persons. This view is advocated mostly by the respondents in the village Cho (94.5%) and Basa (78.4%). The percentage of such respondents in other villages is comparatively low. Roy (1999) also concurs this finding and says that it is the duty of the governmental bodies to balance the finance with the function expected of them.

The situation is worse in Basa and Gho where negligible number of people realize their moral duty to protect environment around them and throw the entire responsibility on the government. It is not that ordinary people have never taken initiative for the purpose; rather the conditions are not so encouraging. It may be because of immense poverty that people put more time on daily wages contracts and are not able to devote more time and their hard earned money on social welfare works like managing environment. Perhaps, the dwellers are so entrenched in their own economic liabilities and burdens that they consider it least important to work or devote time for a general cause. The economic situation of these villages discussed in chapter 3 supports the above argument.

Further, only 27.2 per cent of all the respondents have participated in programmes for the upliftment of the environment (Table 6.8). Participatory contribution to environmental upgradation has been made by 58.3 per cent of the respondents from Dunera followed by 51.7 per cent from Uparla Thara; and 18.3 per cent from Basa. This again reflects the awareness level of the respondents in Uparla Thara and Dunera and their moral commitment to environment. Some participation from the respondents from Basa shows the emerging trend.

Table 6.8 : Your Participation in Such Community Participation Programmes

Participation	*Name of Villages*					*Total*
	Gho	*Samanu*	*Uparla Thara*	*Basa*	*Dunera*	
Yes	—	—	31 (51.7)	11 (18.3)	35 (58.3)	77 (27.2)
No	60 (100)	43 (71.7)	29 (48.3)	49 (81.7)	25 (41.7)	206 (72.8)
Total	60 (100.0)	43 (71.7)	60 (100.0)	60 (100.0)	60 (20.0)	283 (94.3)

On the contrary, 72.8 per cent of the total respondents admit that they have never participated in such a programme or an activity. The percentage in the selected villages is 100 per cent in Gho; 71.7 in Samanu; 48.3 in Uparla Thara; 81.7 in Basa; and 41.7 in Dunera. It shows that people from Gho and Samanu have never initiated any significant environment upliftment programme in their regions. Though the economic condition of the people of Gho; Samanu; and Basa are almost identical but still the people from Basa have participated in such activities, but this spirit has been found missing in Gho and Samanu. The participation rates in Uparla Thara and Dunera are in proximity to each other. It is evident from the discussion undertaken in the previous chapter that the economic status of the people of Uparla Thara and Dunera is far better than the people of other three villages. Economic stability in one's own life makes him motivated for social motives, due to which the residents of Uparla Thara and Dunera have been able to undertake such programmes. These programmes undertaken by the ordinary people are not of any large scale importance; but seem to be an optimum contribution to the efforts of environmental upgradation.

Out of the total sample, there are only 48.3 per cent respondents who say that they just undertook small level plantation in their own regions. The village-wise distribution of this percentage is 71.7 per cent in Samanu; 55.0 in Uparla Thara; 73.3 in Basa and 41.7 in Dunera.

People say that on some event of national holiday or of political importance, they get together and plant some trees in their village. These plants include trees of Mango, Kikar and other general trees used to get shadow for social settings in the future. According to the respondents, more than this is not possible because they have to spend money on buying plants for the purpose and they do not have spare funds for it. Their income is already inadequate and does not serve all the family needs and household requirements; hence they cannot afford to spend more amounts on such activities. It is clear that people of these villages show a negligible intention to participate in programmes related to improvement of environment; even after being the biggest victims of environmental degradation. The trauma becomes exaggerated since there is no agency to encourage them to do so. In modern times, media especially television is considered to be a source of knowledge as well as encouragement and awareness for rural people. But the situation in these villages under study is not satisfactory even in this context. All the respondents say that even Television does not play any role in encouraging people in participating in environmental upgradation programmes as they have never seen any programme through television which makes them aware of environmental conditions, etc.

The respondents say that they have never watched any programme on television which encouraged or guided them to undertake activities for environmental upgradation. They believe that if media takes initiative and that too specially television, it may catch attention of more people to save and protect their environment. This shows that the masses of these regions are largely ignorant about their moral duty towards the natural environment and cannot interpret the importance of their own role in the amelioration plans, and activities. In such a context it is important to make them guided and assisted. This task can be best performed by the Non-Governmental Organizations (NGOs) which have proved to be very functional and potential for the Indian social set-up. Many NGOs become increasingly aware during 1980s that the leadership needed to deal with the underlying causes of the human tragedy was not being provided by the government. Governments and international agencies themselves came to acknowledge the ability of NGOs to do what many governments have proven unable to do, i.e., to get range of essential goods and services to the poor (Chandra, 2007). NGOs strengthen the concept of democratic accountability also; which is very important for development of the masses, especially in the rural zones where ignorance instead of being a 'bliss' is a 'curse'. NGOs not only work themselves rather discover a voluntary aspect of the ordinary masses also. The masses are not volunteering to work for others. They lack volunteering. 'Volunteering' is wilful, spontaneous and purposeful participation in the welfare of the needy. It is purposeful because it is initiated towards acquiring definite ends, i.e., the welfare of the target groups (Shankar, 2004). Voluntary action in India is an integral part of our national character and history. It has been in existence through centuries. It explores new avenues for collective organized efforts (Awarchar, 2004). Even India's freedom is a consequence of people's participation and voluntary action of the masses.

This action is a prerequisite in environmental management also. A study made on tribal villages of Gujarat, namely 'Mahudi' and 'Mahunala' also states that in the management of the rural areas an attempt to bring about sustainable development there, the common property resources like forests have remained neglected in the process. This aspect comes out of the fact that a considerable number of households in Mahudi and Mahunala have remained away from the recent attempts made towards regeneration of the forests collectively (Shylendra and Ravi, 2005). Hence, it is well established fact that the communities need to participate in preservation and protection of environment and forests. But here, the role of NGOs becomes even more important and functional.

All the five villages studied under this research work consider and accept the importance of NGOs but all are not privileged in this context. Only 20 per cent respondents constituting of 100 per cent respondents from Dunera tell that there is an NGO working in their area (Table 6.9).

Table 6.9 : Any NGO Working in Your Area

Yes/No	*Name of Villages*					*Total*
	Gho	*Samanu*	*Uparla Thara*	*Basa*	*Dunera*	
Yes	—	—	—	—	60 (100.0)	60 (20.0)
No	60 (100.0)	60 (100.0)	60 (100.0)	60 (100.0)	—	240 (80.0)
Total	60 (100.0)	60 (100.0)	60 (100.0)	60 (100.0)	60 (100.0)	300 (100.0)

Rest of the 80 per cent of all the respondents show a state of disappointment by saying that no NGO functions in their areas. All the respondents from Gho; Samanu; Uparla Thara; and Basa formed this view. The responses derived herein state that the villages of Kandi areas are badly deprived of the social motivating force named NGOs. It is only Dunera out of the five villages studied, which has been a beneficiary of functioning of the NGO in the region. The residents of Dunera tell that the major functions performed by the NGO include infrastructural development, increase in literacy rates, and welfare of old aged people.

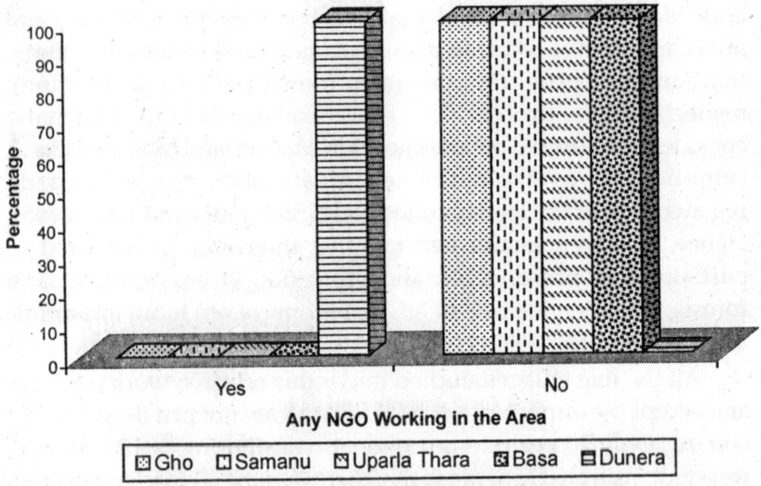

Figure 6.3 : Any NGO Working in Your Area

The development as stated by the residents if Dunera is not an experience of the other four villages, rather a 'dream far off' for them. The visit made to Dunera in the course of the field visits also depicted the successful functioning of the NGO there. In Dunera, the roads are well developed and well constructed, houses well built and white washed, no sewage issues were seen or heard of, properly functioning primary school can be seen, thick forest cover is still available, no sewage blockage is noticed and the market of the village is neat and clean.

According to the residents, all these features have been largely contributed by the NGO. The name of this NGO is Bhartiya Vikas Parishad. It works under financial auspices of a Canada based International NGO named 'Jindal Foundation'. Jindal Foundation adopted 'Dunera' in the year 2002 for development and progress. Since then, the condition of the village has immensely improved.

In the course of the field work it has been observed that though NGOs do not exist and perform in all the villages under study, but all the village communities realise the importance of NGOs. Residents of the four villages, namely, Gho, Samanu, Basa and Uparla Thara referred to *Dunera* as a fortunate village because of existence of an NGO there. According to the dwellers of these four villages, Dunera has developed to a significant extent and it has experienced least environmental losses because the NGO has been providing adequate welfare and maintenance services to the village. The notions get established after a few visits made to Dunera and after holding talk to the people living there.

The Case Study of the NGO proves the success achieved by it in Dunera. The local officials working for the NGO also endorse the fact that the advent of this NGO in their region has altogether altered the facets of survival of the residents of Dunera. Jindal Foundation is a Canadian NGO which has set an aim to work on Indian backward villages and make them an ideal place to live. Dr. Shiv Jindal (NRI from Canada) is the founding chairman of Jindal Foundation. Rajinder Pal Gupta, an Advocate functions as the Project Manager and Shri Amit Bhushan Gupta function as Convener of Jindal Foundation cell in Dunera. He is said to be the power of the region as he has worked for the aims and objectives of the NGO without any self-interest. Shri Surinder Kumar is the Secretary of the NGO in Dunera, who watches all the project being undertaken by the NGO and supervises them in detail. It can be said that Jindal Foundation provide financial and moral supervision and support. Along with this, the local members Bhartiya Vikas Parishad provide manpower to achieve the set aims. With the collaboration and active co-operation of Jindal Foundations, Canada and Bhartiya Vikas Parishad and under the governmental auspices of Vikas Yojna Programme initiated by the Jindal Foundations; five villages of India are being developed at par.

The five villages adopted by Jindal Foundation for development are: (i) Fazalpur (Sunder Nagar) in Uttar Pradesh, Dunera in Punjab, Khajjiar in Himachal Pradesh, Iklaspur in Andhra Pradesh and Mohabbatpur in Haryana. To attain success in the desired aims, Jindal Foundation, has made a strong liaison with all the branches of Bhartiya Vikas Parishad existing in these areas. Bhartiya Vikas Parishad is an already existing NGO in India, which is functioning in India for development and social welfare for such a long time. No doubt, Bhartiya Vikas Parishad was already working in Dunera also, but when Jindal Foundation extended ample financial support, the target became more achievable.

The residents of the Kandi region are the most concrete evidence of environmental degradation in the region, as the views they produced on the above discussed context reflected degradation of standards of living due to degradation of environment. In such a situation, the sufferers become the best source of workable suggestions. Because the one who suffers from a trauma knows better that which step to be taken would solve the issues on practical ground. An attempt was made to extract some workable suggestions from the residents of Kandi area of Pathankot tehsil, so that those could be made useful for the policy making in future.

On being asked about the suggestion to improve environment of the region, the residents forwarded multiple ideas. Majority of the respondents, that is 93 per cent of the total respondents say that to improve the environment of the region literacy rates need to be improved because it is through education only that people attain environmental awareness; and secondly, they suggested that maximum afforestation Programmes should be undertaken by the government and masses (Table 6.10). The percentage in the selected villages is 65 per cent in Gho; and 100 per cent in Samanu, Uparla Thara, Basa and Dunera. The respondents strongly hold that there is a need to construct the will for environmental protection in the masses, which can prove to be functional tool for amelioration. The same is supported by Risse (2007); Kaplan (2006); and Nagunjiri (2006) too.

Table 6.10 : Suggestions to improve Environment of Your Area

Suggestions	*Name of Villages*					*Total*
	Gho	*Samanu*	*Uparla Thara*	*Basa*	*Dunera*	
Literacy rates should be increased; environmental awareness should be increased	39 (65.0)	60 (100.0)	60 (100.0)	60 (100.0)	60 (100.0)	279 (93.0)
Vigilance of Panchayat and Forest Officials must be made stronger	21 (35.0)	49 (81.7)	34 (56.7)	—	32 (53.3)	136 (45.3)
More NGOs working in environmental domain should be invited and encouraged to the Kandi region	—	4 (6.7)	—	—	16 (26.7)	20 (6.7)

Most of the people believe that environmental awareness increases with education, hence literacy rates should be increased.

In apposition, it is important to state here that though Kandi area is a victim of illiteracy, but still the masses possess adequate knowledge about environment and environmental concepts. While expressing views about the factors behind deforestation in the region, Mohinder Pal Singh, Sarpanch of Mangani Panchayat in Gho also states that if literacy rates are improved resulting into an increase in awareness about the environmental importance; it will largely solve the issue and pave a way for environmental management. The reason is the immense dependence of the masses on environment and environmental sources for their sustenance. There are 45.3 per cent of all the respondents who shift the attention from education to the functioning of governance and forest departments.

The village-wise distribution of the given percentage is 35 per cent in Gho; 81.7 per cent in Samanu; 56.7 per cent in Uparla Thara and, 53.3 per cent in Dunera. According to these respondents the panchayat officials and members, and the forest department officials are not performing functions pertinent to environmental upgradation. People expressed a strong grudge by telling that the forest department officials are never seen in the region except in Dunera.

It is only in Dunera that forest department sends officials to check the status of the region's green cover and the forest guards are seen on duty. The notions get supported by the views given by the forests guard placed at Dunera. He says that they have been directed by the Forest Department of the region having its office placed at Shaupur Kandi region, that there must be a strict compliance with the duty hours. He also tells that the department sends officials to visit Dunera whenever some afforestation or any other forests related programmes are being undertaken.

Most of all the respondents say that the Panchayat has never taken steps to improve the environment of the region as stated in the earlier parts of the chapters also. They say that to improve the environmental condition in the region, there should be vigilance on the Panchayat's functioning and the forest department also. As far as the forest department is concerned, the officials are least bothered to forward requests for Afforestation programmes to the government.

Other 6.7 per cent of all the respondents say that the environmental conditions of the area can be improved only if NGOs start working in the region. This view has been forwarded by 6.7 per cent respondents from Samanu and 26.7 per cent from Dunera. These respondents believe that NGOs put efforts in improvement of environment and also motivate the ordinary people to participate in such programmes.

It has been evident in case of Dunera, where people have contributed significantly in management of environment. There is no NGO which functions in Gho, Samanu, Uparla Thara and Basa; but many of the residents of these villages admit that had there been an NGO in the region, the environmental conditions would not have been as worst as they are at present.

The residents of Kandi area owe the environmental management and protection in Dunera to the able functioning of 'Bhartiya Vikas Parishad' and 'Jindal Foundation' the NGOs functioning in the Dunera. Bhartiya Vikas Parishad, an NGO working under auspicious of a Canada based NGO named Jindal Foundation has efficiently been able to protect the environmental of Dunera with the help of services like sewerage maintenance and plantation programmes, etc. Due to the success of the NGO in Dunera, the residents of other villages believe that existence of a NGO is a strong instrument for the environment concerned motives of the area. They say that more NGOs are required to take interest in Kandi area, if the condition of Kandi area's environment is to be protected.

7 Summary and Conclusions

Environment, being one of the most important concerns of human life supports survival with the help of its units like water, air, forests, etc. In such a situation, environmental degradation poses serious threats to mankind in general, and many communities in specific. Degradation of environment is not an issue of a particular area; rather it has encapsulated the whole world into prey. It may be justifiably termed as a global issue. Many national as well as international organizations are working to prevent the devastating impacts of the global environmental threats, which become even more serious and alarming form in regional domains. In case of the areas and communities which have been dependent upon environment for decades, find their survival threatened if the environment around them gets attacked.

Environmental degradation occurs in many form; those may be water pollution, air pollution, noise pollution, and deforestation, etc. The conditions can be well imagined when environmental *pollution* is accompanied by resource related scarcity. This is well reflected through the haunting phenomenon of 'Deforestation', which is the cardinal concern of the present study too. Deforestation, not merely being cutting of trees in the vicinity of a particular region, can be better explained as an uncontrolled cutting of trees, due to an unhesitant and an unapologetic exploitation of the green resource. Many regions and communities have been dependent upon the forests for their survival as the forests have been a consistent source of many important goods and services needed for household chores, domestication of animals, health maintenance, and many more alike needs; for example fuelwood, fodder, ayurvedic herbs respectively. This role of the forests becomes even more crucial when for some communities only source of sustenance is forest and its produce.

In addition to these facilitations forwarded by the forests, there are other indispensable tasks performed by them. The green cover maintains the temperature, upholds climatic stability, acts as a carbon sink and produced fresh air for healthy survival. The forests have also been prominent for being inductive for rainfall; a source of employment generation; being a reflection of the religious sentiments of the masses by providing innumerable 'Totems' for worship. Analyzing these advantages of the forests, it becomes obvious that the loss of the green cover is exactly connoted to the loss of stable survival of the communities of the forests dependent areas in specific.

Mankind in the race of proceeding and developing on economic grounds has conveniently compromised the environmental onus; creating a non-sustained pattern of growth. When the concept of Environmental Degradation is being referred to, it transcends the natural geographical limits and be universalized in terms of effects and dimensions. The contemporary era of Globalization has given a genesis to an unlimited quest and focus for industrialization, urbanization, and technological development. The aim behind all these processes is economic growth, which easily compromise the environmental frontiers. All these processes require land and most of the cases forests become the target. Further, the population pressure puts even higher burden on the existing natural resources, forests being at the foremost target. The evidence is the infinitely expanding residential areas, which has also been noticed as one of the major causes behind cutting of forests. People do not use forests or other natural resource only for survival but also for sustenance. The difference between the two terms is just equivalent to the difference between the structure and the infrastructure. The loss of green cover can rightly be assumed to be a loss of survival convenience. There is a need to develop regional mechanisms to act as saviour against the ongoing deforestation, for which Research becomes a proficient tool of success taking prominence in such a situation. Environmental studies are the need of the hour because with an in-depth understanding of environment; firstly various facets and problems of survival are interpreted in authentic terms, and secondly, a strategic planning can be made.

Recently, Aiyar (2009) in *India Today*, while referring to the results of the National Survey for 'the State of States Awards' to the Best State of the Nation states that Punjab takes the lead for the seventh consecutive year. The State of Punjab is the best in Consumer Market, Infrastructure and Agriculture; takes second position in Macro Economy; and third in Investment Environment in the nation. Taking such a remarkable lead, Punjab as a State poses and reflects a remarkable potential for development and growth. Such a State with extreme capacity of development and growth ought to be saved from being a victim to mismanagement/ over-utilization/and underutilization of resources available in its own vicinity.

The results of the above-mentioned Survey also state that Punjab with its top most position in the nation stands challenged by Himachal Pradesh. The reason is that Himachal Pradesh is running excellently as the 'fastest developing State'; which may take over the position of the 'Best State' in the next annual Survey. In such a situation the concern has to be focused on management of the natural resources and the most identifiably the 'forests'. 'Deforestation' taking place in the Kandi area of Punjab is a challenge for the government and for the dwellers of the area too. The green cover is at a consistent threat, which further affects the socio-economic stability of the region very adversely. Forests lands of the Kandi regions are threatened further distorting the chances of sustainable growth of the region by encapsulating water availability, employment scenario, agricultural productivity, female literacy, social bonds, and availability of basic amenities of life into its prey. Hence, the consistently degrading scenario of the State's environment needs to be given an utmost consideration.

Speth (2004), through an environmental analysis, asserts that there are ten drivers of Environmental Deterioration. Those are: (1) population, (2) affluence, (3) technology, (4) poverty, (5) market failure, (6) policy and political failure, (7) the scale and rate of economic growth, (8) the nature of our economic system, (9) our culture and its values, and (10) the forces exerting upon the world by the globalization of the economy. All these forces lead to misuse and over-exploitation of the natural resources, which is a danger to preservation of the environment. These forces do not function in a similar way and intensity in all the regions. Rather, each zone of environmental degradation is dominated by specific reasons behind it. One of the objectives of the present study is to explore the causes behind deforestation of the Kandi region of Punjab.

This study aims at exploring the Impacts of Deforestation on Villages and Communities dwelling in Kandi Area of Punjab. This Sociological Study is broadly an inclusive of the discussion on the Role and Importance of Forests for the Village and the Communities; Factors behind Deforestation in the Kandi region; and Role of Community, State, Governmental and Non-Governmental Organizations in the Area. The sub-themes shall include discourses held on the Activities started after deforestation; Employment Scenario; Extinction of Species; Rainfall Pattern; Availability of Water and the Causes behind the fall in the Water table of the region, and the Role of Panchayat and the Government in Managing Water Crises; Impact of Deforestation on the Soil Fertility; Cropping Pattern; Use of Pesticides and Fertilizers; Change in the Lifestyles of the People; and Change in Temperature of the Region; Impacts of Environmental Changes on the Women's Life. Further, the discussions have been undertaken in context of Crisis Management including Efforts being undertaken for Afforestation and other Plantation Programmes; Community Participation; Role and Importance of Non-Governmental Organizations (NGOs); and the Suggestions to improve the environment of the region.

Methodology

The Research work encapsulates the Kandi Area of Punjab State. Punjab, as a State, covers an area of 50,362 sq. km. The northern boundaries of Punjab State include Himalayan sub-mountainous zone (locally called 'Kandi Area' of Punjab or Shivaliks). The geological characteristics of Shivalik region have been enumerated in the body of thesis under Chapter Two in details to make it appositional to understand the Role of the forests and the impacts of deforestation region. The Kandi Area covers an area of 4,600 sq. km., which constitutes nine per cent of the total area of the State. The area under research is distributed in districts of Gurdaspur (mainly in Tehsil Pathankot), Ropar and Hoshiarpur as depicted in the Northern part of the State.

In these areas maximum forests belong to village people under "*Mustarka Malka*". This term denotes common ownership over the available forests. The population of the Kandi Area is well aware of the fact that they had a common ownership over the natural green resource, i.e., forests due to which people had been making a multi-dimensional use of the forests.

From all the districts falling under Kandi areas, district Gurdaspur has been selected due to its proximity to the mountainous region having thick foliage cover as compared to other districts. Secondly, many rivulets pass through it that ends up in the river Ravi. There has been accelerated pace of soil erosion due to deforestation and this has affected the economy of the area. Easy accessibility is another reason for the selection of this district.

Gurdaspur district has 5 tehsils and 16 blocks whereas Hoshiarpur and Rupnagar districts have 4 tehsils each with 10 and 7 blocks respectively. This indicates that the area of Gurdaspur is larger as compared to other districts of Kandi area. Hence, if a study is conducted in a larger area, it automatically leads to authentic results because more people are given a chance to be involved in the process of data collection and maximum possible facts can be explored and used to explain the themes undertaken thereon.

From among the Five tehsils of Gurdaspur, Dharkalan and Pathankot tehsils fall under Kandi Area. As compared to Pathankot tehsil, the population of Dharkalan tehsil is totally rural (*Statistical Abstract of Punjab*, 2005; pp. 57). Therefore Dharkalan tehsil has been selected for the study. Further, from amongst the two blocks of Dharkalan tehsil, Dharkalan block has been selected using fish bowl method. Dharkalan tehsil has 28 villages. Out of these 28 villages, five villages have been selected on the basis of their respective population.

Selection of Villages

Tehsil Dharkalan includes 28 villages namely Darbahn, Dharkha Bangla, Sarti, Dukhnyali, Gho, Bharsudai, Dunera, Bharmlada, Nalloh, Phnagota, Dhar Khurd, Phagli Mama, Uparla Thara, Lanjera, Lohrun, Bhagatpur, Rohg, Bhanguri, Jalahar, Dhar Kalan, Hardo Saran, Chamrour, Thara Jhilkhla, Narainpur, Tarhari Basa, Kot Teeka Samanu, and Tureti. All these villages have variable sizes of population. These 28 villages have been categorized on the basis of their inhabited population. There are fourteen villages with population up to 1,000 persons. Only four villages have population of 4,000 or above. Realizing that many of the villages with population up to 1,000 have a small number of households, these villages have been excluded from the universe for drawing the sample. From the rest of the villages (number 14), five villages have been selected using the fish bowl method to maintain randomness.

The names of the selected villages is as follows; Kot Teeka Samanu, Tarhari Basa, Gho, Dunera and Uparla Thara. The population of the villages Gho and Dunera is 1625 and 2105 respectively. Rest of the villages has population above 4000. The exact size of population of Kot Teeka Samanu, Tarhari Basa and Uparla Thara is 5030, 6207 and 7362 respectively as per information provided by Patwari of the village.

Selection of the Respondents

Our knowledge, attitudes and actions are based to a large extent on samples. This is equally true in scientific research. Due to lack of resources at the disposal of the researcher, study of a fragment of the phenomenon might advance our knowledge and provide sourced conclusions from the results. For this, sampling method has been used to select the villages as well as the respondents. The selection of the respondents has also been made on random basis. The distribution of population and households in the selected villages has been depicted in Table 2.3 given in Chapter 2 of the book. The number of household in all the villages shows a significant difference. Village Gho has the smallest number and village Uparla Thara has the largest number followed by Basa.

From each of the selected villages, 60 respondents have been selected. This number has been fixed to each if the village in order to avoid bias. In order to avoid the over-representation/under-representation of certain villages in the sample, it was decided to give an equal weightage in terms of the number of the respondents to be selected for the study. Over-representation of a particular village may have the consequences on the generalization to be drawn for the study; particularly related to the environmental issues, which are not specific to the people but to the area itself. Likewise the under-representation may influence the conclusion drawn from the study.

Collection of Data

The villages being covered under the research work are the victims of widespread illiteracy; and the illiterate respondents can neither read the questions nor write the responses themselves. Keeping this phenomenon of Kandi areas in mind, it was decided to use 'Interview Schedule Method'. Interview schedule as compared to questionnaire method of course demands more efforts from the researcher but still the responses drawn after using interview method hold much more authentic and meaningful substance to substantiate the reliability of data. As experienced by the researcher, Interview Schedules were an absolutely successful research method, with reference to the concerned respondent sample. The interview schedule used in this research work included 85 questions dealing with multiple themes and sub-themes related to deforestation.

In addition to the information collected through Interview Schedule; data was also gathered from a few knowledgeable persons conversant with the area, its environment and the changes that have occurred over the years and the like. Certain Case Studies have been conducted to attain views from those persons/ institutions/organizations, which have not been covered as respondents but are conscious of the multi-dimensional angles of the problems.

The Case Studies are related to members of Mahila Mandal, Forest Guard, Sarpanch, Patwari, NGO and the activists of the NGO operating in the specified village of the Kandi area, and forest official appointed in the research area. Case Studies in the present research work were conducted by using 'Unstructured Interview' and the discussions undertaken with tne subjects of the cases forwarded a lot of information regarding the causes and the effects of deforestation. Fixed number and format of questions hinder the researcher to deviate from the main track of the research theme, which sometimes becomes a pre-condition to make a complete analysis of the facts.

Sometimes the responses are so diverse that it is difficult to enumerate using a structured interview method. This makes the researcher unable to discuss it, even if it is important. Hence, unstructured interview helps to extract a wider spectrum of responses from the cases being studied. Case study is an instrument to establish 'Authenticity' and 'Originality'; which are perhaps the most important credentials to make a research work a success.

Case Studies also help to attain views from those persons/ institutions/organizations; who/which had not been covered as respondents during the field work. Above all, the researcher while using Case Study method of research can analyze the research theme from a multi-dimensional angle; and incorporate various institutions/organizations/persons of immense importance in the research field to cross examine the views given by the respondents in the course of the field work and research. On the whole, the data from the 300 respondents, as the primary sources of information has been derived by using 'Interview Schedules' and supplement with some case studies.

Analysis of Data

The data collected was analyzed to understand the changes that have been experienced over the years. Data analysis involved various stages like preparation of Code Design, Code Sheets and Tabulation. After going through most of the interview a schedule, a code design was prepared that includes all the possible responses given by the respondents. Certain responses were categorized into a group keeping the nature of the response. The data from the interview schedule was then transferred to the code sheets using the code design.

On transferring all the data on the code sheets, single variable and double variable tables were prepared. Wherever it was necessitated multivariable tables were prepared. Percentages were calculated for the entire tables; where necessary median and correlations were also calculated. Further, bar diagrams and pie chart have been drawn to present the collected data and to highlight the comparative picture of the variation—Demographic and Environmental issues, the Role and Importance of Forests, Causes and Impacts of Deforestation, etc., as they absorb a great deal of information.

Objectives

The purpose of the study intends to achieve the following objectives :

1. To understand, what are the forces have led to deforestation in a particular area;
2. To understand the extent of deforestation and its impacts on economy and social life of people involved;
3. To understand the nature of the land-use patterns, in the region, where forest cover has been eroded;
4. To understand the role played by the communities of the area in environmental management; and
5. To understand the role of state and non-governmental organizations (NGOs) in Afforestation programmes and the rehabilitation of the affected people.

Research Questions

The purpose of the study intends to discuss the following Research Questions:

1. To understand linkage between environment and other aspects of survival of the people of this area.
2. To understand the categorical impacts of deforestation on village communities (men, women, children);
3. To understand intensity of extinction of species in the area;
4. To understand the extent of the potential of the people to relate the environmental local issues with that of the global issues;
5. To understand the extent of the affectivity of the policies and programmes formulated and enacted by the State or the national government; and
6. To understand the efficacy of forest department established in the area.

Findings of the Study

In spite of high illiteracy level, the people of this region possess a strong consciousness and analytical ability for the cause and effect relationship of various environmental and economical issues. Illiteracy in respondents is high, though facilities are available for education in the area under study. Though illiteracy is one of the major issues being faced by the people living in these regions; but it has not influenced the general social perception of the masses about environment specific or general social issues.

The socio-economic profile of the region points out the dominance of lower and backward castes respondents who are largely employed as agricultural and construction labour in the region. For this reason, the relationship between 'Caste' and 'Occupational Prestige' is found to be significant. Since most of the villages are employed in low prestige occupations, the income level of most of the respondents varies between Rs. 5,000 to Rs. 15,000. Respondents from Uparla Thara and Dunera have high income level as compared to the respondents from other villages. The study does not show a significant relationship between 'Income' and 'Occupation Prestige'. Similarly, there is no significant relationship between 'Income' and 'Caste' status. Of course, there is high proportion of the upper caste respondents in high income category, but its *vice versa* is not true.

Kandi area provides opportunities for establishment of forest based cottage industry. Interestingly, the cottage industry in the area is on a decline. Basa and Dunera to some level have cottage industry as compared to the other villages under study. The study further highlights the prominence of nuclear families as compared to the joint families.

The Kandi region has experienced a drastic loss of environmental wealth and natural resource. This environmental degradation has resulted into multiplicity of adverse repercussions too. There was a time when the area under research was popular for being rich in green cover; but as a matter of serious concern, now it is popular for being a victim to incessant deforestation. The environmental profile of the villages under study shows a bi-faceted scenario. The availability of the trees in the last ten years and that of the present depict clear differences in some villages under study, whereas, the situation in the rest of the villages is not that much affected.

Availability of Trees/Plants

Over the past ten years, trees of Pipal, Pla, Khair and Mango were available in ample. Out of all the respondents, 97 per cent hold the same view. However, a significant percentage (40.3%) expresses that the availability of fruit trees like Litchi, Guava and Jamun had also been ample. Natural herbs like Harar, Ber and Amla were also available according to the other 20 per cent of all the respondents. At present, trees like Pipal, Pla, Khair are available in abundance against the fruit trees which have been reduced. Only 9 per cent of all the respondents hold that these fruits are grown in the same quantum as they used to be earlier. Availability of Harar, Ber and Amla at present is again supported by the same percentage. All such respondents are from Dunera. Dunera is such a village under study, which has not experienced environmental degradation as has been in the other four villages under study. Unhesitant cutting of forests is the main cause of declining availability of trees/plants in the area. Decline in the availability of trees owes to change of temperature and population pressure (49.7%) and many of the respondents hold that soil erosion and decreased soil fertility are the other major causes behind the declined natural resource availability.

Effect of Changing Availability of Flora

While talking about the benefits of trees and plants to the communities and the consequences of this declining availability of the trees/plants, a significant proportion of the sample (61.7%) say that it has affected the availability of fodder in the region, income of various communities, the quantum and the nature of agricultural production, availability of natural herbs and work of making of *pattals* (disposable plates made with leaves of Pla tree), which earlier used to be a prominent source of earning for the women community. In the past, when trees/plants were available in adequate quantum, forests leaves and twigs were used as a source of fodder for the domesticated animals. Leaves, flowers, fruits, stem and roots were the source of herbal medicines for many minor ailments and diseases. They used to earn income by selling fruits, but now the *vice versa* situation has increased their economic burden. The availability of all these goods and services has reduced so much that people have to spend money to avail them from commercial places.

The impact of this phenomenon on village level has also been grave as it has aggravated the problem of poverty consequent to adversely affecting the fertility of soil also. In addition, the repercussions of this declined availability of goods/services on individual are as serious as that for villages. Majority of all the respondents (51.6%) express that this decline in the quantum of trees/plants followed by the decreased availability of goods/services has increased their economic burden.

Role and Importance of Forest

The importance of forests in the life of dwellers of Kandi region has been endorsed by all the respondents with variation in the responses. The most crucial role performed by forests for the villages as said by all the respondents is that forests control temperature of the region; maintain soil fertility; and help in bringing about economic stability by providing lots of amenities of life free of cost. Out of the total sample 20.3 per cent of the respondents add that wildlife protection is another important role played by the forests.

As far as the advantages of the forests for the people/communities of the villages under study are concerned, forests help to save money and maintain balance in economy by providing fodder for the domesticated animals; fuelwood for multiple household purposes; and along with these advantages, the forests also maintain the temperature and atmosphere of the area besides providing better and healthy living atmosphere. The most indispensable benefit of forests is its being a source of employment as stated by a significant proportion of the sample (90.7%) for whom generation of employment is one of the most cardinal advantages of the forests for the people living in the area under study.

Impacts of Deforestation

Deforestation certainly affects many of the activities of daily life. Same notion is reflected in the responses derived, hereby. All the respondents express that with rampant cutting of forests, soil fertility of the region has been adversely affected. Another group of the respondents forming a significant majority of the sample (80.0%) say that availability of fuelwood and fodder has drastically decreased due to deforestation. Other adverse impacts of deforestation have been noticed on religions activities and availability of medicinal plants.

The overall economic standard of the area has also been affected. The majority (80.0 per cent of all the respondents) express that the economic standard of the area has been affected. Only the respondents from Dunera (100.0%), constituting 20 per cent of the sample hold a contrary view and say that the economic standard of the area has not been affected. The profile of the villages too point out the same.

The reasons for such a diverse view given by the respondents from Dunera are evident from the discussion held in context of availability of forest in the region. Dunera has not experienced fall/loss of green wealth in the course of time as that of the other four villages under study have faced. Majority of the respondents endorsing the fall in the economic standards of the region say that their monthly expenditure has increased for the reason that now they have to spend money on those goods/services, which were earlier available due to thick forest in their region. Gho, Samanu, and Basa have experienced the maximum expenditure as compared to Uparla Thara and Dunera.

The findings of the study show that deforestation has affected most of the chores of the survival of the residents of the Kandi region. Deforestation took place in an uncontrolled manner. Incessant cutting of forests further have had a severe climatic impact on the region. This climatic change has captured uncountable zones of life into its prey such as, health, cultural settings, medicinal availability, water availability, employment scenario, agricultural activities, along with forwarding largely visible impacts on various communities and the general survival pattern. Various environmental studies (Aggarwal, 2002; Saxena, 1996; Speth, 2004) too concur the same finding.

The data analysis shows that the adversities emerged as consequence of deforestation do not seem to have an end; rather a vicious circle has been created in an encapsulation; in all deteriorating the economic standards of the villages and the dwellers of the region. This has been presented with the help of the following figure which depicts the vicious circle of the adverse impacts of deforestation (Figure 7.1).

The study highlights that depletion of thick cover of forests has affected the climatic conditions of the region. The rainfall pattern has changed. As stated by the respondents, rainfall in the Kandi area occurs heavily but its duration has changed. The region does not receive rainfall in the same quantum as it used to receive earlier. There is a change in the temperature of the region as well.

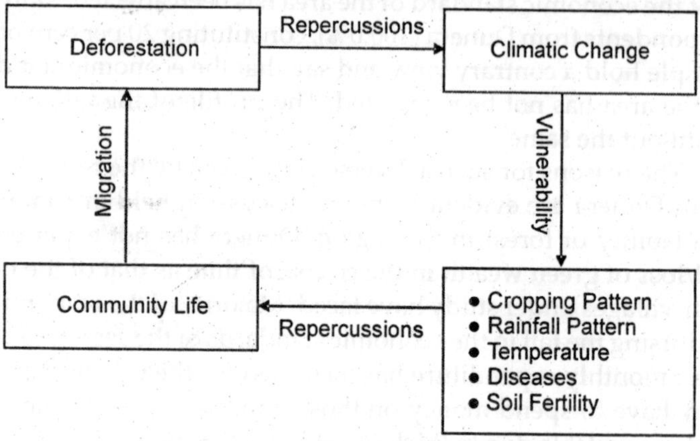

Figure 7.1 : The Vicious Circle

The study finds that the temperature remains moderate in an area, where forest cover is adequately spread; whereas it is not the same in deforested areas. Diverse views about the temperature of the area have been recorded. Majority of the respondents (37.3 per cent of all the respondents) tell that the temperature has increased both in summers as well as in winters. Respondents from Uparla Thara, Gho, Basa form a significant proportion of such respondents. Other view states that the increase in temperature is noticed more in monsoons, which earlier used to be cool but now are very humid and hot.

The data further shows that change in rainfall pattern associated with change in temperature have changed the cropping pattern from cultivation of horticulture crops to cereals crop. The study further highlights that the soil fertility too has decreased with deforestation. Such changes have its impacts on the lifestyle and food hobits of the people. Negi (1994), Aggarwal (2002) concur the same.

The extinction of species is another adverse repercussion of deforestation. Over the past ten years, distinct species like peacock, tiger, deer, neel gaye, tittar, snake and rabbit were the wealth of the region, but an uncontrolled cutting of forests has resulted into their extinction. The reason is that deforestation leads to displacement of these rare species, followed by the degradation of breeding conditions for these species due to which they start becoming extinct. These views have been held by most of the respondents in all the study villages. In spite of adverse consequences of deforestation and its realization, there are no afforestation programmes being undertaken in the region.

Factors behind Deforestation

In discussion of the factors behind deforestation, the majority of the respondents (40.7%) say that increased population and the consequent excessive exploitation of the natural resource are the main causes behind deforestation. In one of the villages, the major cause behind deforestation is the construction of Ranjit Sagar Dam in the region. The dam occupied a lot of geographical space of the region for which a large area of forests had to be cut. Other prominent cause is 'agricultural expansion', which has taken place after the fall of the agricultural profile of the region. People have expanded their agricultural lands in order to get a higher quantum of the agricultural produce; due to which the forests lands have been the ardent victims. Studies undertaken by Metz (2007) and Panda (2007) also support the same finding. Adding to the discourse of the reasons behind deforestation, some of the respondents opine that corruption is another cause behind the continuous destruction of forest cover. Consequent to these factors, except some (35.8%), most of the respondents find its adverse impacts on economy. In their opinion, these activities have rather resulted into further degradation of the economy of the region. Chattopadhayay (2004) also opines that environmental degradation has severe consequences on the economic well-being of the people along with other aspects of living.

Water

Nevertheless, Kandi region has scarcity of water but the problem has accentuated with deforestation and construction of Ranjit Sagar Dam. With deforestation, rainfall has reduced up to an appreciable extent and is insufficient to recharge the sources of water like ponds, wells, and *boulies,* which used to be the main source of water. The village profile clearly shows that the village had either ponds or wells or both that used to maintain the desired supply of water.

Many of those ponds available in these villages have dried up and turned to mud lands. Even if water is available in some ponds; the quality is so worse that, it cannot be consumed but still people use the same contaminated water. The reason behind this compromise is the absence of another better or lesser alarming alternative. The condition in Gho and Samanu is even more pathetic.

The ponds, from which the residents avail water for domestic purposes, are often visited by the stray animals like dogs, cows buffaloes, goats and sheep, such ponds are sources of water for human beings and animals alike. The villagers acknowledge that they are consuming polluted and contaminated water. The main reason for this situation is the changed pattern of rainfall largely due to deforestation. Nearly, 40 per cent of the total respondents attribute the scarcity of water to the variations in rainfall. In their opinion, due to shortage of rainfall and the duration of rainfall, the ponds and the wells do not get recharged thereby affecting the availability of water and subsequently decline in the water-table. This view is held by quite a large proportion of the respondents of the selected villages, including that where deforestation has not taken place on large scale. Since 83.3 per cent of the total respondents from Dunera too, states that water table is decreasing to some extent, show that the area lacks in water availability. Watkins (2006), Briscoe and Malik (2006), Tihillian (2008), and Saini (2008) provide a support to this finding through their studies.

Besides deforestation, population pressure has been found to be another reason for phenomenal increase in demand of water. Majority of the respondents from Uparla Thara assert population pressure as the main reason for the shortage of water. Residents from Basa and Samanu too find population pressure as one of the main reasons. The proportion of such respondents is smaller in Dunera as compared to the other selected villages. Moreover, lowering of watertable and the increasing demand of water therein has affected the life of the dwellers of the region adversely. Due to decreasing availability of water and the lowering of the watertable, people have to fetch water from the sources located away from the village and take more time to collect water than that of the past. The situation has drastically altered in the present resulting into a complete shift in the household management and the work-load of the communities to whom the task of collection of water is generally assigned to as per the social division of labour practiced in the region.

To cope with this situation, efforts have been made either by the government or NGOs to provide adequate water supply to the residents. A majority of the sample constituted by 58 per cent of all the respondents say that government supply points, along with the available wells and ponds in the region are the three main sources of water. Other 21.3 per cent of all the respondents who say that the main source of drinking water in the area is Government supply.

A few of them also have private water connections at their homes but those are very rare. The village Uparla Thara has the highest percentage of respondents owing to private water source (95.0%). Village profile as well as the profile of the respondents points out that the economic status of the residents of Dunera and Uparla Thara is better than that of the residents of Gho, Basa and Samanu. This has been found to be a reason behind lack of private water connections in the village Gho, Samanu and Basa. The people still depend upon ponds and wells, whether contaminated or not but still it serves crucial needs of the villagers.

According to the respondents of Uparla Thara, the private water connections do not supply drinking water regularly. Sometimes the gap between the last supply of water and the next one extends up to 24 hours, making the conditions pathetic for the villagers. Sometimes residents do not get water for household need and drinking purpose for full one day. People invariably, store water in buckets and other utensils for kitchen purpose. However, in Dunera people have not complained about scarcity or crisis of drinking water. So the respondents attribute the shortage of water to deforestation, change in rainfall pattern and population pressure. Though, deforestation as a main cause has not been reported but on probing, they, of course have pointed the relation between forests and rainfall.

The conditions related to availability of water for irrigation even do not depict any positive picture. It is as grave as that of the condition of water for drinking purpose. All the respondents say that the source of water for irrigation purpose is one that is 'rainfall'. There is no provision of wells for irrigation. The villagers have to depend upon the rainfalls for irrigation and it is due to this only, that the agricultural situation of the villages under study has not improved. Earlier the Kandi region received sufficient rainfalls to have one good crop but the situation is not the same as before. Even, the village Dunera though has sufficient coverage but attribute this change (lack of rainfall) to the overall climatic changes in the region.

The Kandi region suffers from a severe water crisis. Paucity of water affect all the dimensions of survival of the people. Figure 7.2 depicts the scenario clearly.

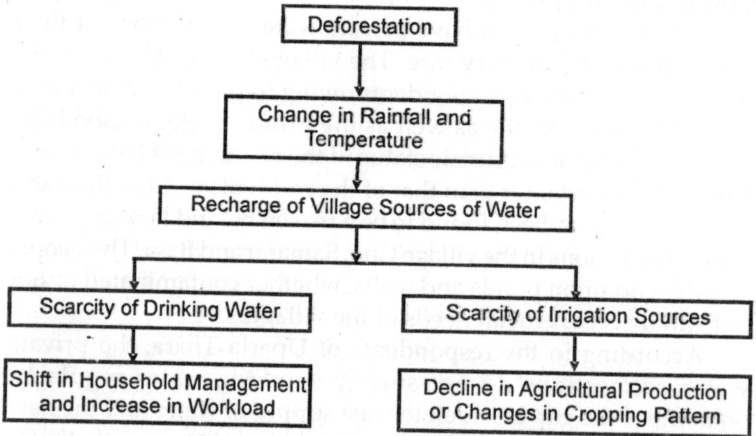

Figure 7.2 : Deforestation and Water

All the respondents from the villages Gho, Samanu, Uparla Thara and Basa say that the water level in the area has decreased. The above fact is further corroborated because all the respondents except of Dunera hold the view that the groundwater level of the region was not as low in the past as it is now. They say that the major reason behind this fall in water level is lack of rainfalls, excessive population pressure, and construction of dam and diversion of water.

According to the people, after the construction of Ranjit Sagar Dam in the region, the economic status of the villagers of Uparla Thara has enhanced largely due to the provision of part-time/contractual/permanent jobs; but it has also caused some adverse consequences out of which, decreased availability of water is the most serious one. As explained and accepted by the people of Uparla Thara, deforestation has not affected their lives as adversely as the reduced availability of water has done. The reason is that if forests are now not available and the people do not avail goods and services from them; but people earn good salaries and income from the jobs at the construction site and, hence, can afford to buy all those goods and services from the market. But the decreased availability of water has to a large extent affected their life and pattern of survival. On the other hand, the respondents from Samanu accept that the construction of dam is one of the causes behind falling of water level. But unlike the residents of Uparla Thara, the construction of dam has not benefited the life of the residents of Samanu.

In addition, people hold that lack of rainfall has affected the agricultural production and since people of these villages are economically poor, cannot afford to install or buy any technological provision for extracting groundwater. Due to all this they depend entirely upon rainfalls. Over the past two decades, the rainfall has reduced, hence, the issue of water scarcity has aggravated.

People do not have any strong defense mechanism against the shortage of water. There are 93 per cent of all the respondents who have contributed a response in this very discussion. A group comprising of 35.8 per cent of all the respondents say that they fetch water from ponds and wells to fulfil their individual and household related needs of water. Majority of the respondents from Gho and Basa (70.0%) rely on ponds and wells for their water related needs irrespective of water quality.

Another way to meet such eventuality is to wait for supply by the government installed submersible pumps in their villages (63.4%). Some of the respondents have stated that there is no solution to this problem. It is clear that the conditions related to water availability in the region is deplorable and efforts have to be undertaken to solve it.

The administration does not seem seriously working for the major concern of the region. In view of 66.3 per cent of the total respondents, the government/panchayat has played no role to improve or solve the existing water crisis in the area. A very few respondents who hold that government/panchayat has put efforts to help the water crisis but they have not done anything else than installing some tubewells and submersible pumps to meet the water needs of the people; which have really not helped the masses as such. They neither endorse nor even deny the efforts of government or panchayat people want the panchayats/government to play a significant role to mitigate water crisis.

In short, the region had for long been facing immense shortage of water for drinking and for irrigation, but the problem has got aggravated with an increase in temperature, reduced rainfall, population pressure and construction of dam and deforestation. This has jeopardized the communities and the villages in the Kandi region. The poor economic conditions with changes in agriculture associated with the rainfall and temperature has affected the economy of the villages. Due to poor economic conditions, the people are unable to install water connections or perhaps to draw water for irrigation.

Rainfall

The amount and spell of precipitation is another crucial factor associated with forest cover areas. Such changes ought to have its impact on cropping pattern, soil fertility, demand for water and even survival pattern of the people of those areas. The adversities do not only remain limited to households but extend to communities as well. The scarcity of rainfall besides affecting the adequacy of drinking water, affects the irrigation scenario also. All this hinders the agricultural productivity of the region. The agrarian profile of Kandi area has also suffered from a jolt due to reduced rainfall; change in temperature; and climatic change, creating immense shortage of water for irrigation. The quantity of precipitation has decreased over the years and now, it is very less in the region (54.3 per cent of all the respondents).

The respondents from Samanu, Uparla Thara and Basa find a decrease in rainfall than that from Dunera. A few of the respondents have also said that the quantity of precipitation is average in the region and the view is held by a majority of respondents from Dunera (93.3 per cent). Thus, respondents from Gho, Samanu and Basa are of the opinion that rainfall in their region is very less whereas those from Uparla Thara and Dunera find average rainfall in their region. The study thus infers that quantity of precipitation in Kandi region has decreased over the years.

Since rainfall is taking place in monsoon period and its

frequency is less, it again has a serious impact on the cropping pattern. The study points out that due to less rainfall, the traditional crops are not sown now. Traditional crops of the region include *Mash, Til, Kulth,* and *Chana.* These crops have been replaced by wheat, maize (cereals). This view is held by all the respondents from Samanu and Basa and majority of the respondents from Uparla Thara. So, change in rainfall has its impact on the type of crop grown in the region though this change is limited to certain areas of the Kandi region.

Change in the quantity of precipitation has not only affected a change in cropping pattern, but it has also its impacts on availability of drinking water to a large extent as reported by 51 per cent of all the respondents including those from Gho, Basa and Samanu. This has also been responsible for scarcity of water for irrigation.

Another important impact of this change in rainfall pattern is on the temperature of the region, which is endorsed by most of the respondents from different villages. Further, the change in temperature has affected the community's health to a noticeable extent. About 84.2 per cent of the total respondents say that due to change in the temperature and rainfall pattern in the region, skin allergies, Asthma, High Blood Pressure and even in some cases paralysis (due to high blood pressure) are on the rise. However, 15.8 per cent of all the respondents say that the change in temperature has resulted into minor respiratory problems, especially during rainy season when humidity level is high, but not any major health problems.

So, the change in temperature and its fluctuation has a bearing on health of the people of Gho and Basa the most. Skin allergy, asthma and others are the main diseases which find in association with the temperature change. People of Uparla Thara face health problems like suffocation especially in the rainy seasons besides all the above diseases. This finding is further supported by Mohinder Pal Singh, Sarpanch of Mangani Panchayat in Gho, Joginder Singh, a trader from Uparla Thara and Renu Bala an activist of the Mahila Mandal who hold that the climatic change consequent to deforestation has resulted in an increase in the incidents of diseases like asthma, skin allergies and high blood pressure. According to them these diseases have become very recurrent in the recent decade. On the contrary, the respondents from Dunera have not reported such health problems. From this, it may be inferred that climatic change along with deforestation and the incidence of morbidity are interrelated.

Impacts on Agricultural Productivity

The discussion about rainfall pattern and the availability of water for irrigation purpose is dominantly related to the discourse on agricultural production because the quantum of water directly effects the conditions for germination and growth of crop; thereby affecting the agricultural productivity. Productivity of agriculture is also related to the fertility of soil. Respondents constituting 78.7 per cent of all, agree with the notion that soil fertility in their area has decreased. They have attributed this to deforestation.

Further exploring the reasons behind declining social fertility, 81.3 per cent of the respondents say that the main factors behind decreasing soil fertility are decreased rainfalls, deforestation and soil erosion. Some of the respondents from Dunera attribute change in temperature for declining fertility in the region but this view is strongly held by a majority of the respondents from Uparla Thara.

The villages in Kandi areas are largely dependent upon forests and agriculture. The forests provide them multiple facilities/goods/services and the agriculture acts as a main source of income for the people of the area. The economy of these villages has largely been structured and supported by agriculture (quite evident from the profile of the village), hence any degradation in the soil fertility leads to degradation in the overall village economic life thereby directly affecting the economy of the region. The change in level of soil fertility has a direct implication on cropping pattern of any region. Majority of the respondents constituting 80 per cent of the total sample comprising of all the respondents from the villages Gho, Samanu, Uparla Thara and Basa support this view. On the contrary, other 20 per cent of the total respondents (all such respondents from Dunera) say that they still grow the crops which they used to grow in the past but the production per unit has declined. Environmental degradation resulting into adverse impacts on the fertility of soil has serious repercussions on the agricultural productivity, which needs to be taken ardently serious

(GoI, 2000; Athavala, 2003; Vyas, 2003; Nath, 2004; Anant, 2006; Sarkar, 2007; and Mamoria, 2007).

The yield of crops has decreased; which is certainly a matter of concern for them, as agriculture is one of the main sources of livelihood. In such circumstances, the use of the agro chemicals increases. Though the use of agro chemicals is more in Uparla Thara than that of the other villages; the use of fertilizer/pesticide is not so prominent and rather even not convenient in Kandi area because people are immense victims of poverty in most of the cases and cannot afford to spend money on buying fertilizers.

The study shows that all the villages under study except Dunera, have experienced loss of the agrarian produce. Another fact is that this decline in the agricultural production has not affected all the study villages equally. In case of the villages Gho, Samanu and Basa, the fall in the agricultural produce has resulted into serious economic consequences because the residents of these villages earlier largely depended upon the horticulture and agriculture produce to earn after making a commercial use of them; but now with decrease in agricultural productivity the economic standing of the villages has suffered a serious loss.

The condition is not that serious in Uparla Thara and Dunera. The people of Dunera are still producing an ample amount of agricultural produce and still are earning good from it. On the other hand the people of Uparla Thara are now least dependent upon agriculture as a source of sustenance because the improvement in the employment scenario due to the generation of employment by the Ranjit Sagar Dam. The most miserable victims of the decline in the agricultural productivity are the villages Gho, Basa, and Samanu.

From this, it may be concluded that shortage or change of rainfall has affected the productivity of the region with its consequence on economy. Parry (2007) too, has concluded that rainfall pattern affected by deforestation results in decline of soil fertility, agricultural production leading to immense degradation of economic standards of the villages and the communities.

Employment Scenario

The economic status of the regions under study and the standard of living of the people thereby, ought to be a serious concern for the administration. The target of the government needs to be shifted to employment paradigm and such efforts should be made that are helpful to upgrade the economy of the region and economic standards of the masses. But in the Kandi areas no attempts have been made to compensate the losses occurring due to deforestation or agricultural degradation. The position of the masses dwelling in the Kandi area of Punjab, along with their living standards is being worsened due to absence of any constructive step being taken by the government to combat with the economic turmoil existent in the region.

Instead of cutting forests for economic development; forests could have been used for the purpose of generating employment; the purpose of which would again have been the same. Forest based industry can strengthen the economy of the region but no forest based industry has been established till now. No efforts have been contributed to the zone which possesses the potential to ameliorate the employment related circumstances. There are only 33.3 per cent of all the respondents (all from Uparla Thara and 65 per cent from Dunera) who assert that the employment in the region has changed and improved. Except these respondents all the rest say that there has been no improvement in the employment scenario of the region.

It becomes quite evident that the residents of Uparla Thara and Dunera only have realized improvement in the employment scenario. The residents of Uparla Thara have got benefited in context of job opportunities generated out of the construction of Ranjit Sagar Dam as reported by all respondents from Uparla Thara. On the other hand, the people of Dunera have been benefited to some extent with the efforts made by the Canada Based NGO, named 'Jindal Foundation'. This NGO has improved the infrastructure in the village and to maintain services like sewage, sewerage, solid waste management, roads and streets, school, Computer Lab, etc. This has provided many a resident of the village work on regular bases.

As far as Dunera is concerned, it still has forests and a thick green cover in the region. According to the people of Dunera, they have not experienced any prominent environmental loss or degradation. Rather the government has undertaken many afforestation programmes in this area, which has further given many employment opportunities to the residents of Dunera.

Nearly, 65 per cent of the respondents from Dunera say that it is due to the maintenance, preservation and the regulated use of the forest cover that has sustained employment opportunities. People from Dunera say that forests give them a lot of chances to earn through part-time/daily wage basis/seasonal and *ad hoc* jobs. Government undertakes many projects pertaining to forests and other natural resources, for example. Afforestation programmes, cutting of trees for commercial purposes, 10 years felling programmes, etc. People are employed for works like cutting trees, digging pits and the like. A study conducted by Vyas (2001) also supports the finding that if forests are maintained, they can be a source of generating employment for the people and thereby can make people economically sound and strong.

Hence, for the residents of Dunera, cutting of the forests by the government for commercial forest products and the afforestation programmes, both serve as sources of earning for them. Hence it is clear that the employment conditions of Uparla Thara and Dunera have improved. In all, the most disadvantaged villages have been Gho, Basa and Samanu in all the study villages. In other words, there has been no amelioration in the condition of employment in Gho, Samanu, and Basa.

The study thus infers that employment scene has improved only in two villages out of the five under research, i.e., Dunera and Uparla Thara. Further, the change in employment scenario as stated by people of Dunera and Uparla Thara has not affected all the people equally. Young and old are largely employed as compared to others under afforestation schemes. So, there are some communities or groups which have been benefited more than the rest. Improved employment scenario is reflected in the lifestyles of the people which include owning a personal vehicle like car or scooter; or renovation of the houses, etc.

Women and Environment

A majority of all the respondents tell that in addition to household chores, the women of the area are generally involved in works like collection of wood, in carpet weaving and embroidery works. All the respondents from Gho, Samanu, and Basa and many of the respondents from Uparla Thara endorse this fact. According to other 20 per cent of all the respondents, the women of the region are involved in household works and carpet weaving besides doing embroidery on shawls. However, self-employment through cottage industry is found to be prominent in Dunera (58.3 per cent of the respondents) and Uparla Thara (41.7 per cent of the respondents).

The pattern of women working has not remained the same. According to 80 per cent of respondents, the women's working pattern has altered drastically as compared to the women working pattern of the past ten years. Leaving aside the respondents of Dunera, all the respondents in Gho, Samanu, Uparla Thara and Basa find a change in pattern of women's work. The respondents in Dunera state that all types of the works the women of the area used to do in the past are done presently as well.

There are 13 per cent of all the respondents who hold that women are involved exclusively in household works only. The economic structure of these two villages reveals that many people from Uparla Thara are engaged in jobs offered after the construction of Ranjit Sagar Dam which provides consistent income; and those in Dunera have a high economic status due to cottage industry particularly preparing goods from the fruits, for example preparing and selling mango pulp (*aampapad*). This finding goes along with that of Venkateshwaran (Venkateshwaran, 1995) that shows that women are replaced from outside work with rise in level of the family. This is largely true of the women in Uparla Thara and Dunera are confined to household works only.

This discourse has been taken in the context of chores like collection of fuelwood from the forests; making *pattals*, and undertaking of the agricultural activities. The pattern of working of women has been explored in these three domains and the analysis shows that there is a huge difference between the trends of women's working in the past and in the present times. The tasks they used to perform in the past ten years are not done with the same intensity; neither the same amount of time is given to the relative tasks as it used to be given in the past.

Majority of the women in Gho, Samanu, and Dunera were involved in tasks like making *pattals*, doing embroidery works on shawls, weaving carpets; whereas, on the other hand majority of the women in Uparla Thara were engaged in agricultural activities like sowing and harvesting. Now, the women from Uparla Thara do not devote that much time and efforts in agricultural activities because the jobs availed by their household members at Ranjit

Sagar Dam site have made it optional for them to undertake agriculture as a mandatory activity. The stable income earned by the members of the family easily makes them quit such a labourious task.

The most affected economic activity is *pattal* making. In the past ten years women have been involved in making *pattals* and used it as an industry to earn good income, but now women do not spend much time on it due to change in demand and also the cutting of broad leave trees. This cottage industry has suffered from a jolt due to scientific and technological advancement. People prefer to buy plastic disposables easily available in the market on very low rates, instead of *pattals* as a matter of hygiene, sophistication and also convenience. So, the business of *pattal* making and selling has reduced in the region because now women do not fetch good sale and income with this task. In all it can be said for all those women who ever earned by selling the *pattals* made by them, the move of time and the technological advancement in the region have deprived them of the income they used to earn about ten years ago.

Further, most of the women in Samanu used to spend 2-3 hours a day on *pattal* making and the majority of the women from Gho and Dunera spent 3-4 hours for this work. In comparison, to other villages, many of the women in Dunera and Samanu were engaged in *pattals* making and were spending time ranging between 2-5 hours a day for this activity. This was because of the demand that existed for *pattals* in the market about ten years ago.

Another important chore which holds huge space in the life and routine of women of Kandi area is the collection of firewood. Collection of fire/fuelwood still remains a part of women's work life. They are largely replaced from the works in the fields to embroidery, etc., which can be undertaken within the household itself. Before the use of stove and gas, fetching of firewood from the jungle had been one of the tasks of women which consumed a lot of time of women. While talking about the period over ten years back, 60.2 per cent of all the total respondents say that women took 1 to 3 hours to collect firewood from the forests. Further, while rendering an addition to the discussion, 28.4 per cent of all the total respondents say that for collection of wood, it took between 3 to 4 hours per day.

With the passage of time, the time taken to collect firewood has significantly increased. As against 67 per cent of all the respondents, only 57.7 per cent of the respondents have given their views on the time consumed to fetch firewood now. Moreover, none of the respondents from Uparla Thara and Dunera has recorded their views on this issue. According to 32.9 per cent of all the respondents say that women spend not less than 5 hours. on collection of firewood. About 30 per cent of the total respondents say that it takes 7 to 8 hours to collect fuelwood now. According to them, women from Samanu and Basa take more time than those from Gho. Other 33 per cent of all the total respondents (comprising of 40 per cent from Basa; 36.7 per cent from Gho and 34 per cent from Samanu) say that women spend 8 to 10 hours a day for collection of wood in present times. The analysis thus provides that women who usually spent one to five hours to fetch firewood earlier now have to spend five to ten hours a day. It means the time for collecting firewood has almost doubled. It is largely due to the deforestation that has taken place in the vicinity of the villages for study. Boserup (1970), Venkateshwaran (1995), and Cranney (2001) too support the above findings.

A serious connotation is forwarded by 60 per cent of all the respondents comprising of 100 per cent respondents from Gho, Samanu and Basa say that the major adverse effect of the changed women's working pattern on the life of the girl child is deprivation of literacy, which is really a serious concern for the region and the people too. Girls are enrolled in the primary or senior secondary schools, but they are conveniently withdrawn from the schools; simply because their help is needed in managing the household works. Cranney (2001) too has found the same in her study conducted in Himachal Pradesh.

The study also finds a change in the pattern of work of women. The women of the region used to spend lot of time for agricultural activities about ten years ago, but now it is reduced to negligible in some activities and even nil in other cases. Most of the women from Gho, Samanu, Uparla Thara, and Basa used to devote good time to agricultural activities, *pattal* making and less time to collection of firewood; but now the time spent on agricultural activities has largely reduced and also it has reduced in case of *pattal* making. Whereas, now women spend more time on collecting firewood as the forests after being cut have become distant from their residential places. This reflects the change of domain of women activity in the region. This very change in the women working pattern has affected the life of the girl child. The reason is that the girls are withdrawn from the schools and deprived of literacy when they are made to stay at homes to complete the pending household tasks.

Nevertheless, the work burden of women has multiplied drastically leaving a negative effect on the health of the women. Secondly, the girl child is withdrawn from school to share the work-load of the elderly women of the household; which directly affects the standard of women by depriving them of education. The above discourse held on the impacts of the deforestation on the women of Kandi area and their life does not refute that the men and their life standards have not been affected. Both the communities (men and women) have been affected, though with varying intensity.

The study thus infers that population pressure and developmental activities are the main forces leading to deforestation. With deforestation, changes in the climate, rainfall and water availability have taken place, which are responsible for the change in the cropping pattern of the region. Leguminous and oilseeds, horticulture and herbal plants cultivation is replaced with the cultivation of cereals crops but it has not improved the economic standing of the people of the region. Further, with deforestation, soil fertility and crop yield has declined; certainly where deforestation has not been rampant, these effects are not so pronounced. For this, the consequences of deforestation vary from village to village. The study further infers that the efforts of the government and certain NGO's have improved the infrastructure and employment scenario of the region.

People though have little faith in Panchayat, Mahila Mandal and Forest Department for improving environmental conditions, they hold that besides education if NGOs start working in the region, the environmental conditions of the area can be improved. These respondents believe that NGOs put efforts in improvement of environment and also motivate the ordinary people to participate in such programmes. It has been evident in case of Dunera, where people have contributed significantly in management of environment. There is no NGO which functions in Gho, Samanu, Uparla Thara and Basa; but many of the residents of these villages admit that had there been an NGO in the region, the environmental condition would not have been as worse as it is at present. This finding has also been concurred by Rao (2001), Hazra (2001), Hanningam (1997), Moosvi (2001), Rajagopalan (2005), Pallavi, (2009). The responses extracted from the respondents reflect lack of 'civic will' for maintenance and sustenance of forests and environment in the region.

In all there exists some ocular similarities between the socio-economic standings of the villages Gho, Samanu and Basa; whereas, Dunera and Uparla Thara hold distinct characterizations. Gho, Basa and Samanu are victims of poverty, which further got aggravated due to incessant cutting of forests. Cutting of forests has directly had an adverse impact on earning of women and availability of many basic amenities for sustenance; which gets largely affected with deforestation. No doubt deforestation took place in Dunera and Uparla Thara too, but the adversities did not affect the living standards as worse as it happened in Gho, Samanu and Basa. The residents of Uparla Thara are the biggest beneficiaries of the developmental project undertaken in their region. Employment conditions improved after the construction of Ranjit Sagar Dam; which has raised the standard of living of the people. Since construction of the site of the dam was the main reason behind deforestation in the vicinity of Uparla Thara, people do not attribute any economic downfall to the cutting of trees. On the other hand, Dunera did not experience as severe deforestation as that of Gho, Samanu and Basa; that is why the climatic conditions of the area did not alter that much that it could affect the agricultural productivity. Dunera still has better agricultural conditions as compared to other villages under study.

In nutshell, various rubrics of social and economic life are interrelated with the environmental conditions of the Kandi area. Deforestation is one of the elements that have multiple repercussions in terms of changing temperature, rainfall, water availability, cropping pattern, and the types of plants grown in an area. These changes further affect the economic status of the inhabitants of the area. For this reason, the emphasis is laid in 'System Theory', rather than that of 'Shallow or Reformist Ecological Perspective' and 'Deep Ecological Perspective'. Various elements of nature and various aspects of human life are so interwoven that any change in the one effects the development and growth of the other. In other words, for formulating a strong environment oriented policy, people and the environment in which they are inhabited and over which their sustenance depends should not be taken as a 'part' rather a 'whole'.

Suggestions for Amelioration of the Environmental Standards of the Region given by the Respondents :

(a) The literacy rates in the region should be improved because the people of the area hold a strong view that education will make people trained to make rational use of the environmental resources and will make the masses more inductive to sustainability. For this very suggestion the respondents think that the best action plan is to add environmental education in the curriculum of the education up to middle class. The general environmental awareness shall make the people realize the relevance of the non-renewable natural resources. This can further help to make the masses conscious of the use of natural resources like trees and water.

(b) The political organizations like Panchayats and Mahila Mandal functioning in the regions need to be vigil for environmental protection and maintenance. These bodies are suggested to incorporate environmental management and protection as a target of their political governance. Tili now the people have not witnessed these bodies functioning for environment or the related issues. Not only this, there has been no formal or informal discussions undertaken by them in context of environment or the related issues. According to the people of the Kandi region, if these units of governance discuss these issues with the masses, or if the masses watch them being cautious for the environmental concerns; further degradation or exploitation of the environment can be inhibited.

(c) The forest department in the region also needs to take up radical vigil over use of the natural resources in the vicinity of the region. Each village should have its own forest official who resides in the vicinity of the village and who is able to watch the forests cover denudation in the region and inform the department in case any threat to forests is noticed, so that the needed steps can be taken at the earliest.

(d) More and more afforestation programmes should be

undertaken. This goes in the domain of the panchayats and also the forest departments functioning in the respective regions. Even if after an afforestation programme has been undertaken, the government should have a vigil over the type of the plants/trees ordered to be and the type of the trees/plants afforested in fact. These are such disparities, which needs to be checked strictly by the departments monitoring the environmental scenario in a particular region.

(e) Another suggestion put forth by the people is that more and more Non-Governmental Organizations (NGOs) should be encouraged to come to Kandi region and adopt the villages therein for the purpose of environmental up-gradation and maintenance. This suggestion finds its roots in the remarkable success of the Canada based NGO working in the village Dunera, which has proved its mark in infrastructural amelioration of the living styles of the region and has also taken a lead in upgrading the educational and professional domains of the region. The successful functioning of this body has proved that NGOs can act as an instrument of socio-economic reconstruction of the region and moral rebuilding of the masses dwelling in those regions.

(f) Other suggestion goes for media and its programmes and networking. The people of the region have told that there are no Television programmes which make people aware of the environmental conditions. Rather, media in contemporary times takes up all such issues and explores them through various channels and programmes. The government is advised to recheck the networking of such channels/programmes in these deprived areas. If it is done it can be a strong means of functional literacy of the masses, which shall function in a positive connotation to protection, preservation and maintenance of the environment of the area.

(g) The government and the non-governmental organizations working in the region must adopt techniques and methods of Water Harvesting in the region. This can solve the water crises to a significant extent and can at least be helpful to afford water in the periods of excessive scarcity of water.

(h) Forest based industry needs to be encouraged in the Kandi region. *Pattal* making used to fetch a good income in the past but with cutting of the broad leaveses trees, this cottage industry has suffered, thereby affecting the economic standing of the region. Such cottage industry or other forest based industry should be encouraged. This shall not only improve the environmental scene of the region but also help to revive the cottage industry and generate employment opportunities for the people of the region (the dream of Gandhi).

Any judicious analysis being made in context of environmental issues cannot ignore the importance of participation of common masses in improvement paradigm. Human beings themselves become the causation factor of environmental degradation leading to their own victimization in forthcoming times. Solutions emerge and even succeed at mass level only. Sustainable development is possible if common people develop a sense of environmental democracy under an objective rule of conduct posing a neutral concern for economy as well as for environment too.

People must be given more powers if they are expected to operationalize any mass movement for environmental protection. The rhetoric of people's participation needs to be zealously implemented in environmental management in the research area. People must internalize an attitude which undertakes just one notion that nature has blessed us with potential resources, the protection, preservation and management of which is our responsibility.

To make the present generations contended along with securing the interests of the future generations the goals of 'Sustainable Development' need to be invested in. For this purpose, the common masses and the government need to pool efforts and concern simultaneously.

Bibliography

Adman, S. *et al.* 1992. *People's Participation : NGOs and the Flood Action Plan*, Dhaka, Research and Advisory Services.

Agarwal, Arun. 2001. 'Common Property, Forest Management and Indian Himalaya', *Contribution to Indian Sociology*, 181-183. Vol. 35, No. 2, New Delhi, Sage Publications.

Agarwal, Arvind. 2007. 'Globalization, Development and Environmental Degradation: A Human Rights Perspective' in Satish, C. Shastri, *Human Rights, Development and Environmental Law—An Anthology*. Jaipur. Bharat Law Publications.

Aggarwal, Anil and Sunita Narain. 1996. *The First Citizen's Report 1982*, pp. 57-59. New Delhi. Centre for Science and Environment.

Aggarwal, S.K. and P.S. Dubey. 2002. *Environmental Controversies*, New Delhi, APH Publishing Corporations, pp. 293-305.

Aiyar, Shankar, 2009. 'India's Best and Worst States'. pp. 20-31. *India Today*. September, 22-28. Vol. XXXIV. No. 39.

Anandrajkumara, P. 1995. "Voluntary Organizations in Rural Development: A Constructive Approach", Vol. 43. *Kurukshetra*. pp. 14-16.

Anant, T.C.A. 2006. 'Institutional Reforms for Agricultural Growth', pp. 97-111, in N.A. Majumdar and Uma Kapila, *India's Agriculture in the New Millennium*, New Delhi. Academic Foundation.

Anderson, E. Ralph. *et al.* 2009. *Human Behaviour in the Social Environment: A Social System Approach*. Transaction Publishers. New Jersy.

Anil Arvind and Sunita Narain. 1985. *Women and Natural Resources, Social Action*, October-November. pp. 301-335.

Athavala, R.N. 2003. *Water Harvesting and Sustainable Supply in India*, Centre for Environmental Education, New Delhi, Rawat Publications.

Avard,. 1991. *Role of NGOs in Development : A Study of Situation in India*, New Delhi. AVARD.

Bansil, P.C. 2004. *Water Management in India*. New Delhi, Concept Publishing Company Pvt. Ltd.

Barbara, Hertz, K. Subbarao and Masooma, Kabib *et al.* 1991. *Letting Girls Learn: Promising Approaches in Primary and Secondary Education*. Washington, D.C., World Bank.

Baviskar, Amita. 2007. *Waterscape: The Cultural Politics of Natural Resource*, New Delhi. Permanent Black.

Bebarta, Kailash, Chandra. 2007. *Forest Planning at Landscape Level*. New Delhi, Concept Publishing Company Pvt. Ltd., New Delhi.

Beneria, Lourdes and Roldan Martha. 1997. *The Cross Roads of Class and Genders*. London. The University of Chicago Press.

Berman, Tzeporah. 1993. *Towards an Integrative Ecofeminist Praxis*, Canada, Canadian Women Studies.

Bettille, Andre. 1969. *Caste, Class and Power*. Bombay, Oxford University Press.

Bhalla, G.S. 2006. *Condition of Indian Peasantry*, New Delhi, National Book Trust of India.

Bhargava, Gopal. 2004. 'Environmental Challenges and Sustainable Future' 40, *Employment News Weekly*, New Delhi, Vol. XXVIII. No. 51.

Bhatacharya, B. 2000. 'Environment and Trade: Some Issues', Rao P. Sasi Bhushana and Rao R. Mohana. *Environmental Management and Audit*, New Delhi, Deep & Deep Publications Pvt. Ltd.

Bhattacharya, A.K. 2007. *Public People Private Partnership for Sustainable Forest Development*, New Delhi. Concept Publishing Company Pvt. Ltd., New Delhi.

Bhoria, K.S. (ed.). 1984. *Gazetteers of India: Haryana*—Ambala *(Haryana)*. Gazetteers Organisation. Chandigarh. Revenue Department. Extracted from http//gbpihed.gov.in/envis/HTML/ Vol. 92/yadwidersingh.html.

Biswajit, Chatterji and Dilip Kumar Ghosh. 2003. Globalization and Decentralized Governance; Reflections on Panchayat in India, *The Indian Journal of Public Administration*, April-June. Vol. XLIL, No. 2, p. 130.

Biswas, K. Asit and Cacilla Tortajada. 2005. *Appraising Sustainable Development: Water Management and Environmental Challenges*, New Delhi, Oxford University Press.

Black, Maggie and Rupert Talbot. 2005. *Water—A Matter of Life and Health,* New Delhi, Oxford University Press.

Boserup, E. 1970. *Women's Role in Economic Development,* Great Britain, Gower Publishing Company Ltd.

Briscoe, John and R.P.S. Malik. 2006. 'Principled Pragmatism and Rules for Reformers in India', in *India's Water Economy: Bracing for the Turbulent Future,* The World Bank Publication, New Delhi. Oxford University Press.

Brown, R. Lester and Orient Longman. 2002. 'Ecology over Economics', p. 56. *Down to Earth,* Vol. 10, No. 23, April 30.

Burgess, E.W. 1926. *The Urban Community.* Chicago.

Capra Fritjof. 1985. 'Bootstrap Physics: A Conversation with Geoffrey Chew's'. *A Passion for Physics: Essays in Honour of Geoffrey Chew,* Philadelphia. Finkelstein and Chung-I Tang.

Castaneda, Carlos. 1971. *A Separate Reality,* New York, Simon and Schuster.

Ch. Balarumumulu. 2002. Participatory Development: The Experience of Andhra Pradesh. 667, *The Indian Journal of Public Administration,* October-December. Vol. XLVIII. No. 4.

Chahal, S.K. 1994. *Environment and World Life: Towards a New Paradigm,* New Delhi, Ashish Publishing House.

Chandra, Snehlata. 2007. *Non-Governmental Organizations: Structure Relevance and Functions,* New Delhi, Kanishka Publishers.

Chattopadhayay, Sri Kumar. 2004. *Regional Dimensions of Rural Poverty in India,* Jaipur. Rawat Publications, pp. 377-396.

Chauhan, I.S. and Arun Chauhan. 1998. *Environmental Degradation: Socio-Economic Consequences,* New Delhi, Rawat Publications.

Chopra, J.K. 2007. *Unique Quintessence of Sociology,* 447, New Delhi, Unique Publishers.

Clayton, M.H. Anthony and Radcliff Nendals. 1996. *Sustainability: A System Approach,* London, Earth Scan Publication Ltd.

Cranney, Brenda, 2001. *Livelihood and Environment—Local Environment and Lived Experience—The Mountain Women of Himachal Pradesh,* New Delhi, Sage Publications.

Das Gupta, Partha *et al.,* 1994. 'The Environmental Resource Base and Human Welfare' Ersling Kersten Lindell and Landberg Hans, Das Gupta, *Population Economic Development and the Environment: The Making of Our Common Future,* London. Oxford University Press.

Debroy, Bibek, and Laveesh, Bhandari. 2009. 'How the states were ranked'. *India Today*, p. 32, Vol. XXXIV, No. 39, September 22-28.

Desai, A.R. 1948. *Social Background of Indian Nationalism*. Bombay, Popular Prakashan.

Devall, Bill. 1996. 'The Deep Ecological Movement' in Clayton Merchant. *Ecology*, New Delhi, Rawat Publication, pp. 125-140.

Deolalikar, B. Anil. 2005. 'Gender Disparity in Schooling', in *Attaining Millennium Development Goals*, New Delhi, Oxford University Press.

Dey, Chandra. 2006. 'Women, Forest Products and the Protected Areas: A Case Study of Jaldapara Wildlife Sanctuary in West Bengal, India', in Krishna, B. Ghimira and Michael, P. Pimbart, *Social Change and Conservation*, London, Earthscan.

Dhaliwal, G.S. 1998. *Fundamentals of Environmental Sciences*, New Delhi, Kalyani Publishers.

Dryze, K. John S. and David Schlosbeeg. 1998. *Debating the Earth—The Environmentalism Politics Reader*, New York, Oxford University Press. 356-358.

Eckersley, Robyn. 1995. *Market, The State and the Environment: Towards Integration*. Melbourn. Macmillan Press.

Einstein, Albert. 1949. *Philosopher-Scientists*. Evanston, Library of Living Philosopher.

Faizi, S. 2001. 'A Diverse Bill', pp. 50-52. *Down to Earth*. Vol. 9, No. 24, May 15.

Fisher, Robert and Joseph, Kling. (Eds.) 1993. *Mobilizing the Community : Local Politics in the Era of the Global City*, Newbury Park.

Forest Survey of India (FSI). 2001. *State of Forest Report 2001*, Dehradun. MoEF.

Francis, C. 1993. Rural Development: People's Participation and the Role of NGOs. 12, *Journal of Rural Development*, pp. 205-210.

Futehally, Laeeq. 1988. *Our Environment*, New Delhi, National Book Trust.

Ghazala, Shahabbudin. 2001. 'Forest Fragmentation, That's What is Causing Bio-Diversity Losses', pp. 24-25. *Down to Earth*, Vol. 9, No. 16, 15 January.

Ghimira, B. Krishna and Michel, P. Pimbeet. 2006. "Social Change and Conservation". *Earthscan*, London. pp. 297-309.

Ghosh, Sancheeta. 2007. 'Concern for Environmental Degradation in India's Planning: A Review', *in* C.P. Prakasan and R.B. Bhagat. *Population and Announcement Linkages*. Jaipur. Rawat Publications.

Ghurey, G.S. 1950. *Caste and Class in India*, Bombay, Popular Book Depot.

Gibbon, David *et al.* 1995. 'Sustainable Development : A Challenge for Agriculture', in Morse Stephen and Stocking Michael, *People and Environment*, London, UCL Press.

Gill, M.S. 1991. *Spatial Pattern—A Socio-Ecological Analysis*. New Delhi. Natural Book Organization.

Government of India (GoI). 1999. *Economic Survey 1989-99'*. Delhi, Ministry of Finance. Economic Division.

Government of India (GoI). 2000. *National Agriculture Policy*, New Delhi, Ministry of Agriculture.

Guha, Ramachandra 1996. Radical Environmentalism: A Third-World Critique, in Clayton Merchant. *Ecology*. New Delhi, Rawat Publications.

Gulati, S.C. and Suresh Sharma. 2008. Population Pressure and Deforestation in India. http://jegindia.org.visited on 26th July, 2009. at 4:00 pm.

Gupta, S.P. 2007. 'Environment, Sustainable Development and Tradition', in V.S. Phadke and Swapna Banerjee Guha. *Urbanization Development and Environment*, New Delhi, Rawat Publications, p. 18.

Gupta, Sunita. 2000. *Global Environment*, New Delhi, Sarup & Sons Publications.

Hanningam, A. Johan. 1997. *Environmental Sociology—A Social Constructional Perspective*, London. Routledge Publishers. pp. 146-162.

Hazra, Anupam. 2009. 'Gender Disparity in Education', *Yojana*. September, 53, p. 32.

Hazra, Arnab, Kumar. 2001. 'Community Based Forest Management (Review)'. *Down to Earth*, Vol. 10, No. 3.

Heisenberg, Werner. 1970. *Der Teil Und Ganze*, New York. Harper & Row.

—, 1971. *Physics and Philosophy*, New York. Harper & Row.

Iyer, G. 1996. *Sustainable Development—Ecological and Socio-Culture Dimensions*, New Delhi, Kay Kay Printers.

Iyer, R. Ramaswamy. 2007, *Towards Water Wisdom: Limits, Justice, Harmony*, New Delhi, Sage Publications.

Kadikoli, Gopal and Rabindra Nath. 1996. 'Forestry as Carbon Sink in India' Rathore M.S. *Environment and Development*, New Delhi, Rawat Publications.

Kaplan, Allan. 2006. 'Capacity Building; Shifting a Paradigm of Practice', in Elind Nagunjiri. *Participatory Methodology in Rowland Development Methods and Approach: Critical Reflections*. Rawat Publications, New Delhi. pp. 60-73.

Karkara, G.S. 2000. *Environmental Law*. Allahabad, Central Law Publication.

Kaur, R. 2007. 'Waste Material'. *Down to Earth*, Vol. 16, No. 15.

Kaur, R. 2008. 'Toxic in Your Backyard'. *Down to Earth*. Volume 16, No. 16.

Kayasthas, S.L. 1992. 'Environment and Development—Emerging Perspectives and Imperatives', in *Development and Sociology—Essays in Honour of Prof. Mohammad Shafi*, Jaipur. Rawat Publications.

Kelkar, G. and Nathan D. 1991. *Gender and Tribe, Kali for Women*. New Delhi.

Kellywich and Gravich Sarah. 1995. 'Global Warming and Development'. Morse Stephen and Stocking Michael. *People and Environment* England. UCL Press, King's Lynn and Guilford Press.

Khanna, P. and Babu Ram. 2000. 'Environmental Education of Economic Growth' in P. Rao Sasi Bhushana and Rao P. Mohana. *Environmental Management and Audit*. New Delhi. Deep & Deep Publications.

Kothari, Ashish. 2000. 'India's Bio-Diversity Bill Comes Under Security'. p. 24. *Down to Earth*, Vol. 9, No. 13.

Kuhn, Thomas. 1970. *The Structure of Scientific Revolution*. Chicago. Chicago Press.

Kulsreshtha, A.C. and Singh Gulab. 2000. 'System of National Accounts and Environmental Accounting', in Rao P. Sasi Bhushana and Rao P. Mohana. *Environmental Management and Audit*, New Delhi. Deep & Deep Publications.

Kumar, Arvind. 2002. *Environmental Pollution and Agriculture*. New Delhi. Efficient Offset Printer, p. 477.

Larson, Ross. *et al.*, 2005. 'Agriculture and Rural Development in India: Sustaining Reforms, Reducing Poverty. *The World Bank Development Policy Review*, New Delhi, Oxford University Press.

Lee, A. James. 1985. *The Environment, Public Health and Human Ecology: Considerations for Economic Development*. London, The John Hopkins University Press.

Lodha, R.M. 1996. *Environment and Industry—An Alarm.* Udaipur. Shiva Publishers.

Majid, Hussain, Sajit Hussain Sayed Zaidi. 1996. *Environmental Management in India.* New Delhi. Manak Publication, pp. 75-94.

Mamoria, C.B. and Badri Tripathi. 2007. 'Problem of Soil Erosion', in *Agricultural Problems of India,* New Delhi, Kitab Mahal.

— —, 2007. 'Agriculture and Productivity Trends, in Problem of Soil Erosion', in *Agricultural Problems of India,* New Delhi, Kitab Mahal.

Martell, Luke. 1994. *Ecology and Society—An Introduction,* 23, Great Britain, Polity Press.

Martinez, John. 2007. "Oil and Climate Change: Voices from the South", in *Economic Political Weekly,* Vol. XLII, No. 50, December 5.

Mehrotra, A. and R.K. Suri. 1994. *Remote Sensing for Environment and Forest Management,* 94, New Delhi, Indus Publishing Company.

Metz, Bert. 2007. Climate Change: 2007. *Mitigation of Climate Change.* Fourth Assessment Report of the Intergovernmental Panel on Climate Change. Summary for the Policy Makers and Technical Survey, United Nations Environment Programme (UNEP).

Merchant. 1996. *Ecology,* 120-281. New Delhi, Rawat Publications.

Milton, Kay. 1993. *Environmentalism—The View from Anthropology.* London. Routledge Publishers, pp. 178-180.

Mishra, R.P. 1995. *Environmental Ethics—A Dialogue of Cultures,* New Delhi. Concept Publishing Company Pvt. Ltd., New Delhi.

Mitra, Amit. 2000. 'Joint Forest Management: Case Study' Rao P. Sasi Bhushana and Rao P. Mohana. *Environment and Audit.* 102. New Delhi. Deep & Deep Publications Pvt. Ltd.

Mittal, Kapil, 2006. *Research Methodology in Social Sciences.* New Delhi, Vista International Publishing House.

Mohanty, Narayan Rabi. 1998. 'Environment and Development Search for an Alternative Paradigm' Pawar and Patis, *Sociology of Environment* by 76-88, New Delhi, Rawat Publications.

Moosvi, Ali Raza. 2000. 'Rural Development through Joint Forest Management—A Case Study', pp. 286-289. Mishra G.P. and Bajpai B.K. *Community Participation in Natural Resource Management,* Jaipur. Rawat Publications.

Mukherji, Ramkrishan. 1957. *The Dynamics of Rural Society*. Berlin, Academic Verlag.

Naess, Arne. 1989. *Ecology, Community and Life Style*, Cambridge, Cambridge University Press.

Nagunjiri, Elind. 2006. *Participatory Methodology in Rowland Development Methods and Approach: Critical Reflections*, Rawat Publications, New Delhi. pp. 227-234.

Nanda, A.R. and Almas Ali. 2006. 'Health Sector: Issues and Challenges, in *India's Social Development Report*, Council for Social Development, New Delhi, Oxford University Press.

Nath, V. 2004. *Regional Dimensions of Rural Poverty in India*, Jaipur. Rawat Publications, pp 319-329.

Negi, S.S. 1994. *India's Forests, Forestry and Wildlife*, New Delhi, Indus Publishing Company.

Orustein, Robert. 1976. *The Mind Field*. New York. Octagon Press.

Pallavi, Aparna and Sumana, Narayana, 2009. 'Two Tribal Villages get 2,349 hectares', p. 17. *Down to Earth*, Vol. 18, No. 8, September 1-15.

Panda, Manoj. 2007. Agriculture and Poverty Reduction, in Shovan Roy. *Handbook of Agriculture*, New Delhi. Oxford University Press.

Parry, Martin *et al.* 2007. 'Climatic Change 2007'. *Impact, Adaptation and Vulnerability. Fourth Assessment Report of the Intergovernmental Panel on Climatic Change, UNEP*, Bjorn Svenson, Science Photo Library.

Patanaik, Naba Kumar and Rao Bhushana P. Sasi. 2000. 'Environmental Education for 21st Century', *in* Rao P. Sasi Bhushana and Rao P. Mohana. *Environment, Management and Audit*. New Delhi. Deep and Deep Publications Pvt. Ltd.

Pepper, David,/1996. *Modern Environmentalism: A Introduction*. New York, Routledge Publishers.

Peter and Calvert, Susan. 1999. *The South, the North and the Environment*, London, Biddles Ltd. Guilford and King's Lynn Printers.

Pojman, Louis P. 2000. *Global Environmental Ethics*, 176-186, London. Mayfield Publishing Company.

Prasad, NLNS. 2000. 'Role of NGOs in Environmental Conservation', in Rao Bhushana P. Sasi Bhushana and Rao P. Mohana. *Environmental Management and Audit*, New Delhi, Deep & Deep Publications.

Pretty, J.N. 1994. *Alternative Systems of Inquiry for Sustainable Agriculture*, IDs Bulletin, Vol. 25, No. 2, pp. 37-48.

Punalikar, S.P. 2000. 'Inferences Between Development and Environment: A Micro Narrative on Tribal Society in Gujarat', *in B.C.* Barik *Resource Management and Contours of Development*. New Delhi, Rawat Publications, pp. 70-72.

Puri, G.S. 1949. *The Problem of Land Erosion and Land Slides in Hoshiarpur Siwalik*, Indian Forester, pp. 45-51.

Rajagopalan, R. 2005. *Environmental Studies*, New Delhi, Oxford University Press.

Raju, A. Jagganath. 2000. 'Sustainable Development CCD'. Rao P. Sasi Bhushana and Rao Mohana. *Environmental Management and Audit*, New Delhi, Deep & Deep Publications & Pvt. Ltd.

Ram, Sundar. 2007. *Panchayati Raj and Empowering People: New Agenda for Rural India*, New Delhi, Kanishka Publishers.

Raghunandan, T.R. 2007. 'Rural Infrastructure, Panchayati Raj and Governance' in *Human Development Report 2006*, Published for United Nations Development Programme (UNDP), New Delhi. Oxford University Press.

Rao, P.K. 2001. *Sustainable Development—Economics and Policy* U.S.A. Blackwell Publishers. pp. 43-45.

Rathore, M.S. 1996. 'Environment and Development Areas of Conflict and Convergence', in M.S. Rathore. *Environmental Development*, Jaipur Rawat Publications, pp. 15-45.

Reddy, Narayan. 2002. *Building Capacities for Sustainable Development*, Kanishka Publishers and Distributors, New Delhi.

Reddy, V. Ratna and S. Mahendra, Dev. 2006. *Managing Water Resources—Policies, Institution, and Technologies*, New Delhi, Oxford University Press.

Reddy, Narsimha and Srijit Mishra. 2008. 'Crises in Agriculture and Rural Distress in Post Reform India', pp. 40-50, in R. Radhakrishanan. *India's, Development Report 2008*, New Delhi, Oxford University Press.

Relan, M. Arora. 2007. 'People, Parks and Wildlife: Towards Co-existence', in Satish, C. Shastri. *Human Rights, Development and Environmental Law—An Anthology*, Jaipur, Bharat Law Publication.

Risse, Thomas. 2002. 'Social Constructivism Meets Globalization', pp. 126-148, in Danial Hald and Anthony McGraw. *Globalization Theory: Approaches and Controversies*, Malden, Polity.

Robertson, R. 1992. *Globalization: Social Theory and Global Culture*, London, Sage Publishers.

Rogers, Barbare. 1981. *The Domestication of Woman*. London. Tavistock Press.

Roy Burman, B.K. 1995. 'People's Perception of Nature' Mishra', in R.P. Misra. *Environmental Ethics—A Dialogue of Cultures*, New Delhi, Concept Publishing Company Pvt. Ltd.

Rubin, G. 1975. 'Traffic in Women', in *Toward an Anthropology of Women*, New York. Monthly Review Press.

Sahoo, Basudev. 1996. *Environment and Economic Development*. New Delhi, APH Publishing Corporation.

Saini, S.S. 'Rain Water Harvesting in Punjab—An Experience'. Extracted from http://dswcpunjab.gov.in/contents/data_folder/SSSaini_Paper.htm, accessed on 6th October, 2009.

Salgara, S.A. and Iyer M.P. 1993. *'Environmental Chaos'*. Lodha R.M. *Environmental Ruin, The Crisis of Survival*, New Delhi, Indus Publishing Company.

Sarkar, Jayanata. 2007. *The Indian Economy*, New Delhi, Pearsons Longman.

Saxena, H.M. 2006. *Environmental Studies*. New Delhi, Rawat Publishers.

Saxena, N.C. 1996. 'Policy and Issues in Forestry'. M.S. Rathore. *Environment and Development*, New Delhi. Rawat Publications. 88-116.

Scherr, J. Sara and Jeffery, A. McLey. 2007. *Farming with Nature: The Science and Practice of Ecoagriculture*. Washington, Island Press.

Shafi, Mohammad and Mehndi Raza. 1992. *Forestry Ecosystems of the World*, New Delhi. Nice Printers.

Shankar, R. 2004. 'Voluntary Organizations: Social Change Initiators', *in* S.N. Pawar: *et al. NGOs and Development The Indian Scenario*, New Delhi, Rawat Publications.

Sharma, K.L. 1982. 'Caste and Class in India: Some Conceptual Problems'. A Paper read out at XVI All India Sociological Conference. Mimeo.

Sharma, B.R. (ed.) 1987. *Gazetteers of India: Punjab, Rupnagar*, Chandigarh. Revenue Department.

Sharma, S.L. 1996. 'Sustainable Development: Socio-cultural Imperatives', in Iyer. *Sustainable Development*, New Delhi. Vikas Publishing House.

Shastri, Madhu and Rajesh, Gaur 2007. 'Environmental Priorities in India', in Satish, C. Shastri, *Human Rights, Development and Environmental Law—An Anthology*. Jaipur. Bharat Law Publication.

Sheth, Pravin. 1997. *Environmentalism—Politics, Ecology of Development*, New Delhi, Rawat Publications. 55.

Shiva, Vandana. 1991. *Ecology and the Politics of Survival*, New Delhi, Sage Publications.

Shylandra, H.S. and Uma Ravi. 2005. *Diversification and Sustainable Rural Livelihood*, New Delhi, Concept Publishing Company Pvt. Ltd.

Singh, Yogendra. 1974. 'Sociology of Social Stratification', in *A Survey of Research in Sociology and Social Anthropology*, Vol. 1, ICSSR. Bombay, Popular Prakashan.

—, 1981. 'Sociology of Social Stratification-II', in *A Survey of Research in Sociology and Social Anthropology*, Vol. 1, ICSSR, Bombay, Popular Prakashan.

Singh, Y. 1990. *Landform Features in the Chandigarh Siwalik Hills*. (1-4):. Res. Bull. (Sci.) 41, Panjab University, pp. 33-34.

Singh, R.B. 2002. *Human Dimensions of Sustainable Development*, New Delhi. Rawat Publications.

Singh, Uma Shankar. 2003. '*Fighting Forest Fires*', in Rao P. Sasi Bhushana and Rao P. Mohana. *Environment, Management and Audit*, New Delhi. Deep & Deep Publications Pvt. Ltd.

Singh, Jaspal. 2005. *Methodology and Techniques of Social Research*. New Delhi. Kanishka Publishers.

Singh, Jaspal. 2006. *Sociology of Organisation: Strategy for Removing Poverty*, New Delhi, Kanishka Publishers.

Sinha. 1997. *Human Health and Environment*, New Delhi, A.P.H. Publishers.

Smil, Vandev. 1933. *Global Ecology—Environmental Change and Social Flexibility*, New York, Routledge Press.

Smith, Keith. 1996. *Environmental Hazards*. 2nd Edition, New York. Routledge.

Speth, Gustave, James. 2004. *Global Environmental Challenges—Transitions to a Sustainable World*, New Delhi, Orient Longman.

Statistical Abstract of Punjab. 2005.

Tihillian, RH. 2008. 'Foreword', for S.K. Agarwal's, *Towards Improving Governance*, New Delhi, Academic Foundation.

Tripathi, Satyendra. 1987. *Development for Rural Poor*, Jaipur, Rawat Publications.

Vaus, De, D.A. 2003. *Surveys in Social Research*, Delhi, Rawat Publications.

Venkateshwaran, Reddy. 1995. *Environment Development and the Gender Gap*, London. Sage Publications, pp. 54-80.

Verma, J.S. 2006. *The New Universe of Human Rights*. New Delhi. Universal Law Publishing Co. Pvt. Ltd.

Vyas, S. Vijay. 1996. 'Environmental Policies and Policy Implementation in India'. M.S. Rathore, *Environment and Development*, Jaipur. Rawat Publications.

—, Hot Conversions'. 47-48. *Down to Earth*, Volume 10, No. 4, July 15.

—, 2000. 'Power to the People'. *Down to Earth*, 16. Volume 9, No. 13, November 30.

—, 2003. *India's Agrarian Structure: Economic Policies and Sustainable Development, Variation on the Theme*, New Delhi, Academic Foundation.

Wadia, D.N. 1949. *Geology of India*, London. Macmillan Co. Ltd.

Watkins, Kevin. 2006. 'Water Scarcity, Risk and Vulnerability', in *Human Development Report 2006*, Published for United Nations Development Programme (UNDP), New York. Palgrave Macmilan.

Yadava, Promila. 2009. 'Adult Education', in *Yojana*, Vol. 53, September pp. 42-46.

Yedla, Sudhakar and Sojanya Peddy. 2007. Agriculture and Environment'. pp. 57-105, in Shovan Roy. *Handbook of Agriculture*, New Delhi, Oxford University Press.

Index